A Century of
Liverpool Lawyers

Published for Liverpool Law Society by The Bluecoat Press, Liverpool
Book design by March Design, Liverpool
Printed by GZ Printek SAL

Cover Photograph

The cover shows a group picture of 228 members of Liverpool Law Society assembled in St George's Hall in 1893. It includes the 1893 President, James Alsop, and many others whose firms or descendants are still prominent in Liverpool more than a century later, including WM Bartlett, GH Brabner, WS Holden, E Lloyd, GJ Lynskey, CH Rutherford, WA Weightman, and ES, JM & WM Quiggin

ISBN 1 904438 03 2

ACKNOWLEDGMENTS

A very large number of people have been kind enough to furnish us with oral reminiscences or given permission for the reproduction of material.

Many of the photographs have been reproduced with the kind permission of Liverpool Daily Post & Echo, Liverpool University, Liverpool Law Society and Universal Pictorial Press & Agency Limited. Numerous relatives of persons profiled have assisted as have many solicitors, barristers and judges.

Special thanks are due to His Honour Judge David Lynch for his advice and assistance throughout. His work in connection with Directory of the Northern Circuit 1876 to date, has been invaluable. Particular thanks are also due to Bill Lister, Chrissy Fagan and Veronica Wilkinson for their help in assembling and correcting material and to the very large number of other individuals who have given freely of their time. Their assistance is very much appreciated by Liverpool Law Society and its 2002 President, John Leith.

A Century of
Liverpool Lawyers

Fagan, Bryson & Elston

Liverpool Law Society

CONTENTS

INTRODUCTION

"Do as Lawyers do, strive mightily but eat and drink as friends." Shakespeare.

This book tells the stories of more than forty individual solicitors, barristers and judges from Liverpool over the last century or more. We have tried to preserve the individual styles not only of the lawyers portrayed but also of the storyteller and to steer clear of dry facts. Many of the lawyers portrayed were prominent but not all prominent lawyers, particularly in recent years, are portrayed individually.

We have not set out to make an objective assessment of each individual but rather to describe their lives and the lives of others at the time and, in so doing, to cast some light on legal life and Liverpool life during their times. We have tried to give those portrayed a human face and to provide information of interest to general readers, as well as lawyers. We hope in this way to celebrate the 175th anniversary of Liverpool Law Society.

For more than a century, Liverpool lawyers have been closely involved with Liverpool politics and the controversies of the day. Many of the early lawyers profiled are from the early 1900s when the principal political contests in Liverpool were between the Conservative (or Unionist) Party and the Liberal Party. It is a surprise to modern Liverpudlians to realise how many of those arguments revolved around religion and licensing of public houses.

During the times of such as FE Smith (later Lord Birkenhead) in the early 1900s, Liverpool was a Conservative and Unionist stronghold with normally the only non-Conservative MP being the Irish Nationalist MP, TP O'Connor, who represented the constituency around Scotland Road continuously from 1885 up to 1929. The disputes between the Liberal Party and the Conservative Party over alcohol created numerous opportunities for lawyers in the early part of the twentieth century. FE Smith built a large part of his early career and fortune on endless actions by the brewers to fight attempts to close public houses in Liverpool instigated very often by the Liberal Party and the Temperance Movement.

It is often forgotten that Liverpool was, for many years, the second city of the Empire with wealth and importance to match. The lawyers of Liverpool had an influence commensurate with the power of their commercial clients but their role in the life of the city went far beyond that.

Noel Fagan
Graeme Bryson
Charles Elston

FE Smith, Lord Birkenhead.
"Many people loved FE, most distrusted him, some despised him and he despised almost everybody." – one of FE's epitaphs.

Joshua Lace, first President of Liverpool Law Society in 1827.

LIVERPOOL LAW SOCIETY

by Tony Twemlow

Sir John McKaig, President, Roland (Rusty) Marshall, Hon. Secretary and George Richards, Librarian at the re-opening of the temporary Law Library following the destruction of Law Library in the Blitz of 1941.

On 25 August 1827, a few Liverpool men gathered in a dusty room in Clarendon Buildings, on the corner of North John Street and Lord Street to discuss a proposed Law Library for Liverpool. It had long been felt that Liverpool needed a Law Library due to the high prices of law books. According to the Annual Report of 1829, there were 52 members. Most of their names are now forgotten but some survived until very recently in the names of Liverpool firms. The first President was Joshua Lace whose name was reflected, until very recently, in the firm of Berrymans Lace Mawer. Samuel Brabner's name survives in Brabners Chaffe Street. The name of his contemporary founding member, John Holden, was reflected until 2001 in the firm of Brabner Holden.

Within six month, the fledgling library was sufficiently stocked with books either bought or donated by members. In 1834, the Society's name was changed from Liverpool Law Library Society to the Liverpool Law Society. By the time of the Annual Report of 1893, there were 348 members and the President was James Alsop whose name survived until recently in the name of the national firm Dibb Lupton Alsop, now DLA.

The main committee room of Liverpool Law Society before destruction in the Blitz 1941.

The membership fee in 1827 was £15. Expenditure on books in the first 12 months was £550 19s 3d – substantially greater than the equivalent expenditure in 'real' money today (and on behalf of a Society with a membership of 2,000 – not 52!). Our predecessors in 1828 clearly enjoyed a certain measure of affluence.

Unfortunately, the written records of the Society's affairs from 1827 to 1859 are lost. Those for 1859 – 1904 have been summarised thus:

"Each year the Society's accounts were printed, duly audited. Lists of the Officers for the year, and in early years when membership was small, a list of current members of both the Society as well as of all its Committees, followed. An erudite and sometimes tediously long presidential address would be printed, followed by a précis of recent legislation, reports of sub-committees which had deliberated on some controversial topic during the year, a list of the new books added to the library and, for many years, a further instalment in a constant running battle for national recognition of provincial law societies and respect for their views on professional matters at large by the legal bureaucracy in their London 'ivory towers'."

(*A Gentleman's Calling* by Peter Howell Williams (1980) p257 "plus ça change ...!")

Following the Companies Act 1867 the Society had, in 1869, been incorporated as a company limited by guarantee under the name 'The Incorporated Law Society of Liverpool'. In its Memorandum of Association the maintenance of the library became secondary to 'the protection of the character, status and interest of the Attorneys and Solicitors practising in Liverpool or within 20 miles thereof; the promotion of honourable practice; the settlement of disputed points of practice and the determination of all questions of professional usage or courtesy in conducting legal business of all kinds'.

In the early days of the Society, there clearly was a particular feeling that the national Law Society looked

The Liverpool Law Society library before the Blitz 1941.

after the interests of London solicitors to the detriment of the provinces. This led to the formation in 1848 of the 'Metropolitan and Provincial Law Association'. The Liverpool Law Society was active in promoting the idea of 'County Courts' and in seeking to persuade the 'powers that be' in London to provide continuous sittings of the High Court in Liverpool. It was not until 1872 that provincial members of the profession were permitted to be elected to the Council of the Law Society! The Liverpool Law Society was active in the negotiations to procure that long overdue right. Although the Metropolitan and Provincial Law Association has long since ceased to exist, this influential lobbying role has continued to this day. The officers of the Society still meet regularly with their counterparts from Manchester, Birmingham and Bristol.

In 1878 the first steps towards establishing a University in Liverpool were taken. The Society was active in ensuring that it would have a strong School of Law and its members raised substantial funds for that purpose. By 1886, the Board of Legal Studies had been constituted and three lecturers appointed. The Society's Committee urged all principals to make it compulsory for articled clerks to attend 'to encourage a love of learning'. The Board insisted that the Professor of Law kept chambers provided by, and at the expense of, the Society 'so that students may see him and consult him as to their studies'. The practice continued up to the Blitz of 1941 when, despite the outraged opposition of the then Professor of Commercial Law (Raleigh Batt), the University took the opportunity to move the Faculty of Law to Abercromby Square.

It appears that the first occasion upon which members of the Society dined together on a formal basis was on the occasion of its Jubilee in 1878 and that the practice of holding an Annual Dinner then began (although with some subsequent interruptions) in 1880. The most recent reincarnation of the annual dinner began on 30 October 1953 when the Society's tradition of top flight legal speakers recommenced with Lord Goddard

Liverpool Law Society's first post-World War 2 annual dinner, 30 October 1953. Hon. Mr Justice Arthian Davies, Alderman WJ Tristram (the Lord Mayor of Liverpool), Sir Percy Cowley, HR Pruddah (the President), Lord Goddard (Lord Chief Justice of England and Wales).

then the Lord Chief Justice. An example of the continuing connection with Irish affairs was the year of the Northern Ireland Peace Agreement in 1998 when the leading speakers were the Lord Chief Justice of Northern Ireland Sir Robert Carswell and Mr Justice Michael Moriarty, a High Court Judge from Southern Ireland.

The Society was prominent in promoting the introduction of scale fees for conveyancing. The first Remuneration Order and Scale introduced in 1881 was largely due to Enoch Harvey, the increase in charges to Sir Norman Hill, Sir Charles Morton and J L Williams and the practice of producing lump sum bills (rather than itemised bills) to Sir Norman Hill – all prominent members of the Society.

Bills were introduced by the Society in both Houses of Parliament. It is clear that then, as now (although perhaps more then than now!), the voice of Liverpool was listened to with respect.

The Society has had a number of City centre addresses. In view of the destruction of records, details are scanty but the Library was originally in Clarendon Buildings from May 1828 and by 1859 the Library was housed in Unity Buildings, Cable Street. Cable Street itself running from South John Street to Paradise Street, ceased to exist except as an entrance to a car park in the May Blitz of 1941.

In 1862 the Society's headquarters were located in Harrington Street and, for quite a long period certainly in 1881 and up to 1897, the Library was situated in 13 Union Court. From 1897, until the premises were destroyed by enemy action, the Society was at 10 Cook Street following which it established premises at 14 Cook Street.

1897 was also the year in which the Society was presented with a presidential jewel which remains the envy of all other office holders in the profession and outside and both locally and nationally. It was given

Mr Justice Robertson Crichton, Christopher Hewetson President of Liverpool Law Society in 1976 (prior to his becoming National President of the Law Society in 1983 and his Knighthood), John Bowron, Secretary General of the Law Society.

by one Joseph Gradwell. History does not record what might have been the reason for this extraordinary act of generosity. Its miraculous survival of the Blitz (locked in the Society's safe) gives the present day holders of the office of President an added incentive to wear it with pride and to ensure its safety!

In the twentieth century, the Society was active and pioneering in the promotion of arrangements to provide legal services to those who could not afford to pay for them. Between the Wars, a Poor Man's Lawyer scheme was supported by the Society, run by a Committee appointed by it and manned by volunteer solicitors and barristers. In 1973 the Society promoted, with financial help from Liverpool City Council, the Vauxhall Law Centre – the first of its kind – which uniquely catered for those who lived in a deprived area of the City.

The Society has been unlucky with fires in its premises. During the night of 3 – 4 May 1941, the Blitz devastated both the records and the offices of many firms, as well as those of the Society. The story goes that war time shortages meant that the Society's staff were more concerned to check the condition of some eggs (rare in war time) stored in the safe than the Presidential jewel! In January 1968, the Society's (then new) premises in Cook Street were broken into and set on fire. On both occasions, huge damage was caused to the Library (on the latter occasion more from the water putting the fire out than from the fire itself!).

The Liverpool Board of Legal Studies was incorporated as a company limited by guarantee in 1906. After providing education for solicitors and their clerks for many years, it eventually became moribund. In 1985 it was revived as a 'partnership' between the Society, the University of Liverpool and Liverpool Polytechnic (as it then was – now Liverpool John Moores University) to provide education for members of the Society. In more recent times the Society has continued and significantly increased the provision of education for its members to such an extent that it is now a 'core' part of the Society's business.

So, apart from shifts of emphasis, it would appear that the practical business of the Society has remained largely unchanged throughout its history: to lobby for the betterment of its members' practices and to provide services (mainly a library and education) to enable its members to provide a better service to their clients.

One of the strangest stories in the Society's annals is how it came to be the proud recipient, by bequest, of a grandfather clock which stands in the Society's Committee Room. It was left to the Society by a bachelor with no connection to the Society, the law or lawyers. The story goes that he told his solicitor that he wanted to leave the clock to a venerable Liverpool institution which would never die. His solicitor recommended the Society and the client accepted the recommendation. Let us hope that future generations of solicitors in Liverpool will share the pride in Liverpool Law Society held by its current members evinced by the publication of which this brief history is to be a part and that the faith in the future of the Society shown by that solicitor to his client will be demonstrated to have been well founded!

THE LIVERPOOL LAW STUDENTS ASSOCIATION

By Charles Elston

MOCK TRIAL (REX V AIRDELL) 1925
CGE Dingle, EW Elwell, C Phythian, JA Bush, L Coleman.
H Morgan, E Steel, EA Rowlands, HE Buxton, HW Stacey, HM Craig.
GR Hodnett, JP Wilson, SR Lynch, ET Furlong, RL Moon, JE Hadfield, LR Mullen, FE Pritchard, JH Bromfield, EC Arden.
S Dean, E Holland Hughes, Francis Weld, JR Howard Roberts, RW Bell, A Lawrence Kershaw.
J Lindsay, DH Brabner, WR Cafferata, T Holden, A Gleed, FB Creak, SH Brookfield.

All early records of the Liverpool Law Students Association (LLSA), like those of The Liverpool Law Society (LLS), were lost when the Society's premises in which the LLSA had its own room, were destroyed by enemy action in 1941. The Association is, however, known to have been in active existence as far back as the 1870s and in the last decade of the nineteenth century and the early years of the following century, it played an important role in establishing a School of Law at the University College which subsequently became the Faculty of Law when the University was granted its Charter. The LLSA had equal representation with the Bar and the LLS on the Board of Legal Studies, which was set up in 1886 to arrange and supervise the syllabus of the University College's legal studies. Faculty status for the School seems to have been generally regarded at the time as having arrived when the Queen Victoria Chair of Law was established in 1896 but was not in fact formally conferred until after the University College was granted its Charter as an independent University in 1903. The Board of Legal Studies was then reconstituted with provision for the LLSA to have 4 representatives on it – compared with 3 of the LLS and 1 of the Bar!

Possibly because practising members of the legal profession – and particularly of the solicitors' branch – were, in Liverpool, so much involved in starting legal education at the College and in the establishment of the Faculty of Law, the Faculty's premises were located at Cook Street in the midst of professional offices and chambers and quite remote from the rest of the University on Brownlow Hill. Most of the students were serving articles in those offices and it was natural for them to regard the LLSA as the organisation to provide them with extra-curricular activities rather for them to join other University students in the societies and associations which existed up Brownlow Hill.

In the pre-1914 period, the LLSA held debates, staged mock-trials, and from time to time published a magazine – frequently decorated by not very complimentary cartoons of prominent local solicitors. The Association was revived again after 1919 and resumed many of its previous activities. In 1925, it staged a mock-trial in the small concert hall at St George's Hall for which an admission fee was charged with all proceeds going to charity. Musical entertainment before and in the intervals of the performance was provided by the Band of the Liverpool City Police. A photograph of the cast of this performance appears in this book and it is noteworthy how many of the names of those taking part are still familiar and in most cases prominent in Liverpool's very different legal scene of to-day including Edward Steel (himself a Circuit Judge and father of Heather Steel J and of HHJ Elizabeth Steel – a former President of the LLS); EC Arden (father of Mary Arden J and of Roger); Denis Brabner (father of Michael); Trevor Holden (father of Lawrence); Cyril Dingle (one-time Mayor of Wallasey and father of John). Three members of the cast became Presidents of the Liverpool Law Society – Holland Hughes, JE (Jimmy) Hadfield and Rex Cafferata. The appearance on the photograph of FE Pritchard is something of a mystery as, apart from Francis Weld who was at the time President of the LLS and ex-officio of the LLSA, he is the only person not in fancy dress. Although membership of the Association was open to recently qualified solicitors and barristers, in practice the vast majority of active members were students and the proportion of them who intended to go to the Bar was small – although Edward Steel is another intending barrister on the photograph. By this date FE Pritchard had been called to the Bar and may well have been doing his pupillage and it seems quite likely that he had been called in to advise on Court procedure as he would be more conversant with such matters than the others.

When I became a member of the LLSA in 1934 it had ceased to organise anything as ambitious as the Mock Trial of 1925 but it did hold occasional debates and discussions and also football, cricket and rugby matches against the Liverpool Chartered Accountants Association (a much more numerous body) when we could raise a team. However, the main social function of the LLSA year had become the Annual Ball at the Adelphi – one of a series of such functions which took place on a Friday night during Winter months, when white tie and tails were de rigueur and dances were 'booked' and the procedure did not appear to differ greatly from that of Jane Austen's day although the proceedings became quite boisterous as the evening progressed. The organisation required for these affairs was considerable; there were costings to be worked out, tickets to be printed and distributed – and, much more important, ticket money to be collected in – and, greatest hazard of all, a Band to be booked and its arrival on time and adequately sober somehow ensured. All this I realised when I found myself Chairman of the Association in 1938/9 – when I was much occupied with preparing for my Law Society's finals in March 1939 (as were other officers). Having somehow survived the night of the Ball without disaster, when we subsequently found time to sort out the finances, it appeared that a sizeable loss had been made and that outstanding bills quite substantially exceeded the

Association's funds. Fortunately this dilemma came to the ears of the President of the LLS (and ex-officio of the LLSA) Vivian Heyne, then senior partner of Hill Dickinson, who sent a cheque for more than enough to keep the Association solvent accompanied by a note simply saying that when we went into practice we would find it desirable to make sure that income was sufficient to cover expenditure. There may have been more generous and understanding Presidents, but I doubt it.

After the 1939/45 War the LLSA was revived mainly as a result of strenuous efforts on the part of Brian Fraser Harrison and John Byrne (both now, sadly, deceased) and the Annual Ball was, for a time revived on a rather reduced scale, but the Association could not survive the removal of the Faculty of Law from the City Centre to the University campus and the steady drift towards an all-graduate entry into the Solicitors' profession and the end of 5-year articles so, like the smile on the face of the Cheshire Cat, it gradually faded away.

'A GENTLEMAN'S CLUB'

By Graeme Bryson

"Do as Lawyers do, strive mightily but eat and drink as friends"
Shakespeare.
Johnson observed that "he did not wish to speak ill of any man but he
believed that the gentleman was an attorney"
Boswell on Johnson.

In these days of equality it is almost impossible to realise that, in the first part of the twentieth century, a business or professional man's place was in one of a number of invisible but very real layers of acceptability. Ladies had yet to 'arrive'. The top layer in Liverpool consisted of the two noble Earls of Derby and Sefton followed by the traditional families of shipowners, importers and exporters, banking and insurance directors.

Lawyers as such were mostly in a slightly lower stratum, barristers included, because by the time they were of consequence, they had taken silk and moved to London. Some solicitors had achieved top acceptability but not all! Managers and clerks each had their place and no one ever questioned the general set-up. When the shipowners departed from the scene, everyone else moved up and the system gradually disintegrated.

All clubs were 'gentlemen only'. The city centre clubs – the Palatine (Union Court) in particular as I recall, and the Exchange (Fenwick Street) and Old Hall (Cotton Exchange Building) – were of the top grade. One entered a monastic palace of quiet gentility. As a young man, I was only ever a guest in those early days, but one realised that here was something special. In all clubs, surnames only were used, a follow through from public school days. I think that it was the Rotary Clubs with their American influence which brought in the use of Christian names. The Constitutional Club (now the Municipal Annexe in Dale Street) and Liberal Club (nearly opposite) were rather more 'liberal' but not much.

Each club had its own style and tradition. Charles Elston reminds me that the Old Hall Club, stationed in the Cotton Exchange Building, had widened its membership beyond the cotton brokers and traders. It was famed in Charles' recollection for the barman, a well known character, who mixed a unique Dry Martini. It was a very dangerous concoction for anyone obliged to work in the afternoon!

In the 'out of town' clubs, the Athenaeum (Church Alley), the Lyceum (Bold Street), the University (Mount Pleasant opposite the Adelphi), and the Racquet, there was an easier approach and less formality in the range of membership, but standards were still very high. Even today in my club, the Athenaeum, business talk and work-papers are frowned on.

The Racquet in Upper Parliament Street differed from the other clubs in that it was originally founded to provide, in addition to Dining, Reading, Smoking Rooms etc customary in such establishments, facilities for the games of racquets, squash, Eton fives, tennis under a covered court, and billiards. In the course of time, billiards gave way to snooker, while racquets and Eton fives were dropped. In its early days, and in my own boyhood too, many of the leading families still lived in the Parliament Street area, and in the south end of the city.

The Racquet Club also provided residential accommodation, and at least three Recorders of the city, Neville Laski, Rudolf Lyon and Sir Ernest Sanderson Temple ('Sandy') were regular residents, also silks such as Edward Wooll. Actually Sandy Temple was a resident at the time of the Toxteth riots, but he had gone home for the weekend. Not so fortunate was barrister Richard Murray who had to leave dressed only in his pyjamas to seek refuge in the nearby church of St Margaret's. Richard tells me that, in the morning, he telephoned the manager of Moss Bros, who sent a car to collect him, still in his pyjamas, and he was re-equipped in time to appear dressed 'de rigueur' before Her Majesty's Judges by 10.00am Richard himself was of course Liverpool's Deputy Assistant Coroner for many years, and is my near neighbour here in Hightown.

The Liverpool Chess Club, founded in 1834, and the Artists Club had an 'out of town' style in the city centre. My family arrived in Liverpool in 1919, and my father, a powerful chess player, joined the club which was then in the Temple in Dale Street. There was one large room divided by a curtain into chess and bridge areas. There was no dining table, meals being served on trays on stools, as one silently played or watched chess or bridge in action. A fair proportion of the members were lawyers, the leading family being the Rutherfords. Sir Watson Rutherford, featured elsewhere in this work, had been President in 1892. The club, he wrote, was famous as having no superior in the UK, or perhaps the world! In my time, his son Sir Hugo and nephew Laurence Rutherford were both Presidents and were daily attenders. They mostly played bridge but, as with many, they took part in the annual chess tournaments, divided into classes A, B, C and D. Guy Williams and Septimus Weightman favoured bridge but played chess from time to time

In those days the Assizes sat in St George's Hall, while the High Court Registry and the Liverpool County Court were in Victoria Street near the Chess Club. The lunch interval was usually about one hour which did not allow the court advocates much time to grab a sandwich and to watch one of the various games in progress. Conveyancers were a little more leisurely!

We had our annual important matches against the Leeds and Birmingham Clubs, and quite a few members played in the County team. The great Grandmasters would stay for a week or so, and sit quietly in the club all day willing to play any member for half a crown. On the Saturday they would play about two dozen members at the same time, rarely losing a game.

I had joined in 1929 on leaving school, and I became secretary some years later, working my way up from D to A rank, and like father, playing for Lancashire. One of our strongest players was local barrister Gerald Abrahams, while judge-to-be Frank Nance was as good and keen as most. A player of great ingenuity was Hector Munro, particularly so at our popular lunchtime game of kreigspeil chess where you were not told the opponent's moves and had to imagine them! There was always quite a little crowd of members to watch this exciting game. It sounds impossible, but Munro won as many as he lost against good opposition.

About 1937, the Rutherfords arranged for us to move the club to their new office block in North House, North John Street, the 'Cafe Nord' in the basement which had an Arabian decor. After the war, like other gentlemen's clubs, it faded away. The bridge players joined the Artists Club while the chess players used a cafe in London Road with Judge Frank Nance as the President. The various clubs did their best to survive by amalgamating, but one by one they disappeared leaving today only the Athenaeum, the Artists and the Racquet Club (now sadly with a doubtful future) out of a formidable list at the start of the century. And ladies have 'arrived' to join as members. Some diehards thought that it signified the end of the world, but happily this was not so.

Being retired myself, I do not know what part Liverpool's Clubs play in the workplace today. For years after the war, my own club the Athenaeum, like other clubs, was full at lunchtime, with tables having their regular members at the various tables – Chancery Registrar Bill Morris Jones's father and Nathan Silverbeck sat at my table. Those busy days seem to have long gone. Of course at the University Club they had one long dining table, and new arrivals just sat next to the previous person to arrive.

Circuit and District Judges now have dining facilities available at the QE2 building, and other facilities are available which practitioners may use. But what of the many other practising lawyers? Clubs today are different because they have adapted to the changing situation. Still, if practitioners are so hard at work that they cannot spare the time for a club lunch, I can only say that they are missing one of the happier aspects of professional life in Liverpool enjoyed many years ago, and still available.

THE LIVERPOOL LAW GOLF SOCIETY

By Charles Elston

The Liverpool Law Golf Society had its origin in the comparatively early days of golf in England having started less than 30 years after the foundation in 1869 of the Royal Liverpool Golf Club (RLGC), the oldest Club on Merseyside and one of the oldest in the country. The earliest document relating to the Society records the donation of a cup in 1895 by one Walter Cunliffe for the winner of 'The Liverpool Solicitors' Golf competition' – but this was not necessarily the first such competition. The original draw for the 1895 competition exists and shows that there were 47 entrants of whom one was a scratch player (EV Crooks, later Captain of the RLGC whom I remember in the mid-1930s as senior partner of Alsop Stevens & Collins Robinson as it then was) and two who were better than scratch – Finlay Dun (plus 1 and also a captain of RLGC) and T Dobell (plus 2). The competition was on knock-out lines with normal handicap allowances and this involved 6 rounds which were to be played at weekly intervals. The first winner was TB Blackburn (h'cap 8) and the runner-up FO Roberts, and these names figure frequently in the later stages for several years. Walter Cunliffe played in the Cup Competition for many years reaching the later stages several times but he never won his own cup.

In 1897, the names of three new players, all of whom I recall, appeared, namely H Christian Jones (of whom more anon), RD Cripps – later Registrar of the now defunct Liverpool Court of Passage and Walter Peel, later one of the Liverpool District High Court Registrars. For the first four years the competition was open only to solicitors practising in the area of The Liverpool Law Society but in 1899 it was decided to extend eligibility to all members of the Liverpool Bar. This provided what was unusual in those days – a social meeting for solicitors and barristers who were generally strongly discouraged from hob-nobbing with what the leaders of the Bar regarded as the junior branch of the profession, lest they might be thought to be seeking instructions. Another 1899 innovation was the addition of Formby to the 3 courses to which the competition had previously been limited – RLGC, West Lancs and Wallasey.

In 1900 revised rules for 'the Cup Competition' were adopted clarifying eligibility to take part, and this year also the name of Stuart Deacon appears as a competitor for the first time. Those who remember him only as the Liverpool Stipendiary Magistrate in the 1930s – a rather wizened and forbidding looking figure – may well be as surprised as I was to learn not only that he was a golfer but that he was a scratch player at Wallasey. He played regularly in the Cunliffe Cup until after the first World War. Other names which appear in the early 1900s include in 1900 CE Nield (father of Basil who became a High Court Judge – and CN- a County Court Registrar), in 1902 Percy Hughes, founder of Percy Hughes and Roberts, in 1907 S Brighouse – later Sir Samuel the very well-known Coroner for SW Lancashire who continued in that office until well into his nineties, and in 1908 HC Dowdall – later His Honour H Challoner Dowdall who figures elsewhere in this volume. Those who remember him only in his latter days may find it difficult to imagine him on a golf course, but he seems to have been a useful performer off a handicap of 15. Another surprise is to find the name of another, later County Court Judge, AT Crosthwaite, now remembered only in his latter days when he could not be relied on to remain awake after lunch if he did not finish his list in the morning.

In 1905 it was agreed that the name of the Society should become 'The Liverpool Law Golf Society' there having been some lack of consistency regarding the name used up to that time. In the course of time this has become the present title – and long may it continue. In 1906, it was agreed to add Birkdale – not then Royal – 'as soon as the extension to 18 holes is complete' to the list of courses where the Cunliffe Cup would be played. In 1906, it was recorded that there were 106 members of the Society of whom 66 played in the Cup competition. This must have been quite a sizeable proportion of the members of the profession at the time and seems to be the maximum size attained by the Society.

In 1914, Harold Christian Jones, previously mentioned, presented a cup for the Annual Bogey Competition which had been added to the Society's playing activities 4 years previously. This form of competition may require explanation even to present day golfers of some experience as it dates back to the days when in the British Isles the term 'bogey' represented what is now universally known as 'par' and not one stroke more than par as it always did in the USA. For British players there was the mythical but powerful figure of Colonel Bogey hovering behind them and he never missed a putt and did every hole in regulation figures. In a Bogey competition you played against this paragon and if you bettered his score at any hole you won it, if you equalled his score you halved it but if you failed to do so you lost. It was a cruel form of competition but it had the merit of speeding up the game; if, for instance, on the first hole at Hoylake you had played four shots into a strong south westerly without holing out – or even reaching the green – you could not win or halve the hole and so, unless your marker was still in with a chance you could proceed straight to the next tee. It appears that HCJ himself was the first winner of his own cup as his name appears on it opposite the year 1914. However, the momentous events which took place in August that year led to the Society's activities being totally suspended and they were not revived for 8 years when the existence of the cup seems to have been forgotten by all, including the donor although he lived for many more years. In 1986 the four unmarried daughters of Harold Christian Jones (two of whom figured prominently in Cheshire golfing circles) moved from the large house where they had lived with their parents for many years and they came across the cup and returned it to the Society. Since then it has been awarded annually to the player in the Cunliffe Cup competition who returns the lowest gross score – the original cup remaining the award for the best net Stableford score.

In 1922, steps were taken to revive the Society and a competition for the Cunliffe Cup took place with 44 players entering, including NB Goldie – later Sir Noel Goldie KC, MP Recorder of Wigan and one of the best-known eccentrics of the Northern Circuit of all time. Among others were TJ Benjamin, later a District High Court Registrar (as well as a great supporter of the Society) for many years, and Roland ('Rusty') Marshall, Senior Partner of Bremner Sons and Corlett and father of Michael and grandfather of Tim, the only example on record of three generations of a family being members of the Society and all three have held the office of Captain of the RLGC and President of Liverpool Law Society. Rather surprisingly the Cunliffe Cup competition was resumed in 1922 in the same form as when it originally started ie on knock-out lines with 6 rounds played at weekly intervals, and a Bogey competition also took place at a later date in the year but without the award of a cup. By 1925, interest had waned considerably, probably because many solicitors had had to accept that they could not leave their offices indefinitely in the care of their hard-working and underpaid staff but must do more themselves. There were in that year only 25 entries for the Cunliffe Cup and it was decided that they would play a medal round with the leading 8 performers taking part in knock-out play, the winner that year being Rusty Marshall. The Bogey competition was discontinued and never revived.

Matters continued in much the same way until 1939 and the number of entrants for the annual competition varied between 30 and 40. In 1930 JSB Lloyd became Secretary of the Society and he remained in that office until the outbreak of World War 2. Later, of course, he progressed to rather higher things as The Rt. Hon. Selwyn Lloyd CBE, QC, MP the holder of three of the Highest Offices of State and subsequently Speaker of the House of Commons and finally Lord Selwyn-Lloyd. In 1933 those taking part in the Cup competition included FE (Freddy) Pritchard and JD Robertson Crichton, both of whom became High Court Judges.

Again, the Society went into abeyance during the 1939-45 War and it was revived – largely by the efforts of Mr Registrar Benjamin in 1948 when CJ (Chris) Cunliffe (later a Circuit Judge in the southern counties and not related to the Cup donor) became secretary and Roland Marshall was elected Captain. The form of competition on this resumption was as it had been up to 1939 with the 8 leading players subsequently taking part in match play to decide the winner and this continued until 1971 when, in contrast to earlier times when 6 rounds of match play had regularly been completed in 6 weeks, it had become difficult for the 8 players concerned to complete the necessary 3 rounds before the next annual competition became due to take place. It was then decided that the Stableford system of scoring should be adopted for the Cunliffe Cup competition and this has continued ever since. When the H Christian Jones Cup came back to the Society in 1986 another trophy was also presented, this being in memory of Jack Ryecroft a long-term supporter of the Society who carried out the secretarial duties with much charm and efficiency for a number of years. The Jack Ryecroft Tankard is awarded annually to the best Stableford score by a player with a handicap of 18 or more (as Jack was).

Since the revival of the Society in 1948 no member of the Society has become a High Court Judge and no High Court Judge has played in a Society meeting – although I can recall FA Sellers, very active in the affairs of the Society when he was at the Liverpool Bar but then a Lord Justice of Appeal, making an appearance but not actually playing at a meeting at his former home course (West Lancs) in the late 1950s. However, many Circuit Judges have been active in the affairs of the Society including Chris Cunliffe (previously mentioned), Melville Kennan, Tom Pigot, John Arthur, Ifor Morris Jones, Roy Ward, John Morgan, John Roberts and Alan Booth. The last-named deserves very special mention. He first played at an annual meeting in 1950 and his latest appearance was in 2001 when he not only returned the third best net score but looked perfectly capable of improving on that performance in many future years. He has won the Cunliffe Cup on two occasions and been thereabouts on numerous others. On one occasion when the Cunliffe Cup Competition was at Alan's home course (RLGC) and he was still at the Bar, he was detained in Court longer than he had expected and reached the course after 4.00pm the first tee having been reserved for the Society from 1.45 to 3.00pm. Realising that there would be no other Society member to accompany him he had had the foresight to bring his pupil with him to mark his card. Starting at about 4.30 with a clear course ahead he was able to catch up the main body by the 16th hole and to hand in the second best score of the day. There was some suggestion that a judicial enquiry might be necessary to rule on the question of disqualification for late starting but it was agreed that if the rules needed to be bent a bit they would be and he was allowed the second prize – a share of the very modest sweep. District Judges who have been active members since TJ Benjamin include Tegid Jones, PC Winter and Richard McCullagh.

In addition to distinguished lawyers, several golfers of considerably more than local distinction have been members of the Society and have taken part in its competitions, the most notable being Ronnie White, a Walker Cup player who, in the mid-1950s was considered by many critics to be the best amateur in the British Isles but who decided that his legal practice had to take precedence over further golfing glory. Michael Reece (son of Monty a former captain of the Society and of West Derby GC and a very useful player), who captained Cambridge University, won the President's Putter of the Oxford and Cambridge Golfing Society on more than one occasion and played for Lancashire many times and still, despite – or

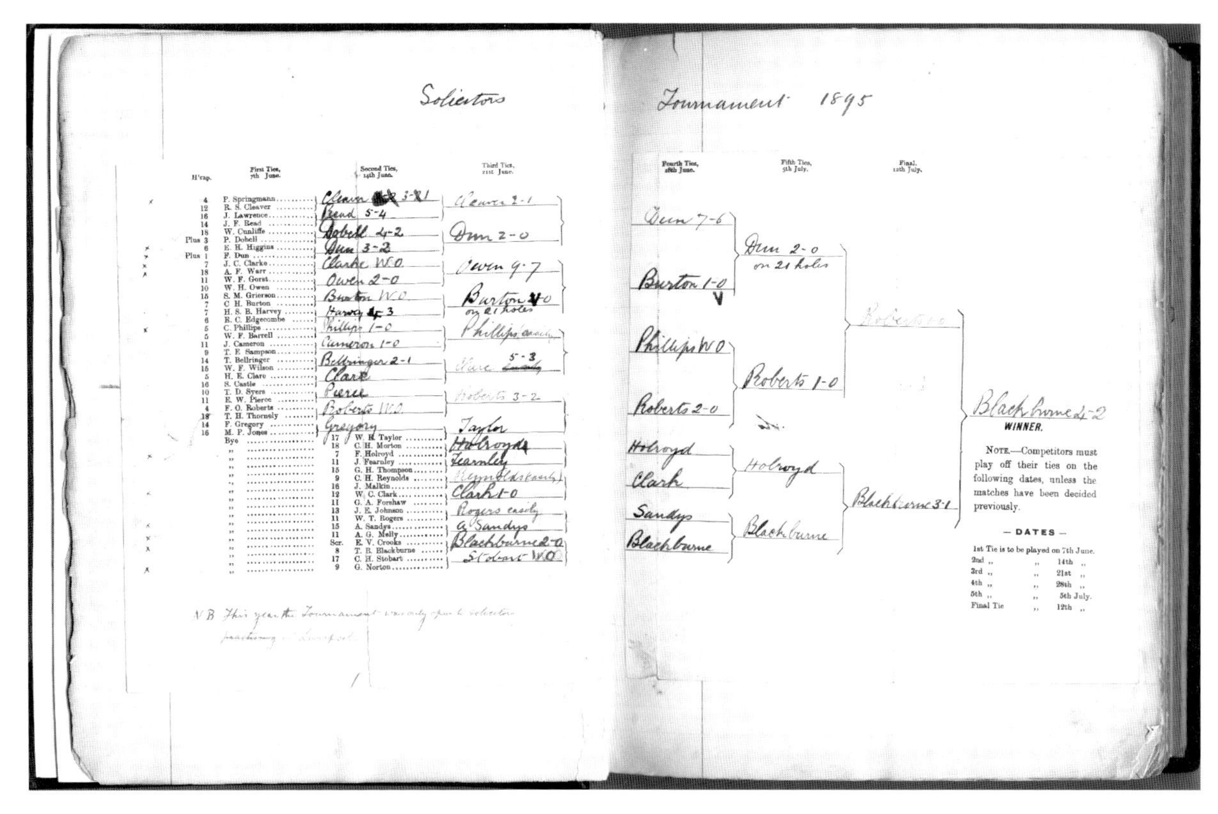

Solicitors Tournament 1895

H'cap.	First Ties, 7th June.
4	P. Springmann
12	R. S. Cleaver
16	J. Lawrence
14	J. F. Read
18	W. Cunliffe
Plus 3	P. Dobell
6	E. H. Higgins
Plus 1	F. Dun
7	J. C. Clarke
18	A. F. Warr
11	W. F. Gorst
10	W. H. Owen
15	S. M. Grierson
7	C. H. Burton
7	H. S. B. Harvey
6	R. C. Edgecombe
5	C. Phillips
5	W. F. Barrell
11	J. Cameron
9	T. E. Sampson
14	T. Bellringer
15	W. F. Wilson
5	H. E. Clare
16	S. Castle
10	T. D. Syers
11	E. W. Pierce
4	F. O. Roberts
18	T. H. Thornely
14	F. Gregory
16	M. P. Jones
	Bye

H'cap.	Second Ties, 14th June.
17	W. H. Taylor
18	C. H. Morton
7	F. Holroyd
11	J. Fearnley
15	G. H. Thompson
9	C. H. Reynolds
16	J. Malkin
12	W. C. Clark
11	G. A. Forshaw
13	J. E. Johnson
11	W. T. Rogers
15	A. Sandys
11	A. G. Melly
Scr.	E. V. Crooks
8	T. B. Blackburne
17	C. H. Stobart
9	G. Norton

Third Ties, 21st June. Fourth Ties, 28th June. Fifth Ties, 5th July. Final, 12th July.

WINNER.

NOTE.—Competitors must play off their ties on the following dates, unless the matches have been decided previously.

– DATES –

1st Tie is to be played on		7th June.
2nd ,,	,,	14th ,,
3rd ,,	,,	21st ,,
4th ,,	,,	28th ,,
5th ,,	,,	5th July.
Final Tie	,,	12th ,,

Scorecard from the first Liverpool Solicitors Golf Competition in 1895.

perhaps with the aid of – a hip replacement plays off a handicap of 4 and was in the team which represented the (English) Seniors' Golfing Society in their triangular tournament against the equivalent Societies of Canada and the USA in 2001. Also a member, Gordon Jeffrey has been Captain not only of the Royal Birkdale GC (where he was a scratch player) but also of The Royal and Ancient Golf Club of St Andrews, having previously been Chairman of the Championship Committee, which rules the world of golf.

In early times the Society used to play a similar Society from Manchester but this match fell into abeyance and was subsequently replaced by an annual match between teams from the Committees of the Law Societies of the two cities playing at alternating venues, with a dinner after the match and the visiting team staying overnight. During most of the last half-century the Society has played at least one – on occasion as many as five – matches against other professional bodies, the longest-established being against the Chartered Accountants which until recently has been played at RLGC and Formby alternately and like all the Society's meetings and matches is followed by a convivial meal.

Sadly, during the past two decades the participation of the Bench and Bar in the Society's activities has steadily decreased. Despite the best intentions and endeavours of their members to take part it has become more difficult for them to commit themselves to being on a golf course during normal working hours – a position which also affects solicitors but not to quite the same extent – and solicitors tend to retire or semi-retire at an earlier age. Despite all the problems there is every reason to hope that the 107 year old Society will continue in active operation for many more years.

THE LIVERPOOL COURT OF PASSAGE

by His Honour Frank Paterson

The last sitting of the Liverpool Court of Passage in 1970.
Judge Richard Forrest, Presiding Judge of the Liverpool Court of Passage, The Lord Mayor, Judge Rudolph Lyons QC, Recorder of Liverpool and Stan Kirkham (Clerk).

Hugh Gardner, at a meeting of the Liverpool Portmoot in 1624, was accused of disclosing secrets of the Jurors at the Court of Passage, he being one of the Jurors himself. This world has long forgotten Hugh Gardner and the secrets he is alleged to have revealed but it has not forgotten the Liverpool Court of Passage. Mr Gardner may not have been a trustworthy juror but he is entitled to some credit for prompting, by his conduct, one of the earliest uses of the name, Liverpool Court of Passage, to describe the Portmoot when sitting in a judicial capacity.

The Portmoot probably took the place of a Manorial Court. It would have been convened in Liverpool for hearing and determining causes relating to the port and particularly goods passing through it. In the closing years of its existence, the Liverpool Court of Passage was described as "one of the very few examples of the survival of a medieval borough court into modern times".

The Mayor and Bailiffs were originally the presiding judges. By an Act of 1834 provision was made for the appointment of a barrister at law, of not less than seven years standing, to be assistant to the Mayor. The Right Honourable the Lord Mayor of the City of Liverpool, as the Mayor became in 1893, always enjoyed by virtue of his office, the title 'Judge of the Court of Passage'. His duties became restricted to attendance at the Court on ceremonial occasions and to signing writs to be issued by the Court. The latter duty may have bewildered some litigants during the year the late Sir Harry Livermore held the office of Lord Mayor. The firm of Silverman & Livermore figures frequently in Court of Passage lists. A party might be forgiven, if startled, on being served with a writ signed by a senior partner in the firm he had instructed to look after his interests.

The judicial duties of the Court of Passage in modern times were fulfilled by a series of eminent Counsel selected from the Northern Circuit of the Bar. A person so selected held office for life or until voluntary retirement. Whilst holding office his title was 'The Presiding Judge of the Liverpool Court of Passage'. He was addressed in Court as 'My Lord'. Sittings were at the discretion of the judge. They were held in the Civil Court of St George's Hall. There were four or five a year, each of one week's duration. Judicial remuneration paid for by the Liverpool Corporation, was about £1,000 a year.

Pre-trial proceedings were the responsibility of a Registrar, including matters requiring detailed consideration of documents referred to him by the Presiding Judge for adjudication. The Town Clerk of Liverpool held the office of Deputy Registrar, a privilege and responsibility of which most Town Clerks were unaware.

A Registrar, discovering in a disputed matter referred to him, a solicitor from the firm of which he, the Registrar, had once been a member, directed his deputy the Town Clerk of Liverpool, to take his place. The Town Clerk promptly escaped this unwelcome duty by selecting a young barrister to perform it for him on the promise of payment of an appropriate fee.

The Registrar was supported by a staff in the charge of an official with the imposing title of 'Sargeant at Mace and Marshall'. He enjoyed a position and authority similar to that of the Chief Clerk of a County Court. The more colourful duties of the Sargeant at Mace have been described by Howard Channon in his 'Portrait of Liverpool' at page 11, as follows:

"Through the centuries he has had the authority to arrest a ship, nailing a writ to the mast (in these day of steel masts he ties the writ with string). He also has the power to arrest aircraft and has done so. Normally such action is taken when the owner is allegedly in debt. The emblem of the Sargeant at Mace has, for as long as is known, been a silver oar and it seems strictly he should still carry it when arresting a ship. In the early nineteenth century there was an occasion when, having crossed the Mersey to make an arrest on the Birkenhead shore, the Sargeant was obliged to return to his office to fetch the oar because the sight of it was insisted upon".

Surviving legal practitioners from the period immediately prior to the second Word War will remember the Liverpool Court of Passage as a convenient and expeditious tribunal. It was particularly suitable for those matters, in scale of importance and value, which fell between those appropriate for the County Court at the lower end and the High Court at the upper end of such scales.

The procedure was similar to that of the High Court. There was no restriction on the amount of damages that could be awarded.

The Court was swept away in 1970 following a report by Lord Beeching as though it was of no more importance than one of the many railway lines his Lordship had caused to be removed by an earlier report.

Charles Elston writes of this period as follows:

"Many aspects of the Court were distinctly Dickensian including the premises which the Registry occupied in the corporation building in Sir Thomas Street – where you quite expected to find quill pens in use. The Chief Clerk, appropriately named 'Sparrow', was dark, thin and gloomy but approachable and helpful. I recall Darrell Mace, a prominent solicitor advocate, telling me that when he entered the Court offices he always doffed his hat and said, "Good morning Sargeant – I'm Mace". The last holder of the office of Sargeant at Mace and Chief Clerk was Mr Elliot. He readily gave his opinion on the most intricate details of the Court of Passage procedure and was never challenged. He had, and for the most part stayed in, a cubby-hole within the General Office".

The Liverpool Court of Passage was held in high regard by litigants and legal practitioners particularly in recent years, largely as a result of the high standards of advocacy required and the quality of justice provided by Sir Francis Kyffin Taylor KC, appointed Presiding Judge in 1904. His retirement in 1948 at the age of 94 years was deemed premature. The Counsel appearing in his last case were Edward Youds, later His Honour Judge Youds, and Robertson Crichton, later the Honourable Mr Justice Crichton. At the conclusion of the proceedings the Judge autographed the respective back sheets of each Counsel beneath a message of good will. The back sheets were later to be seen, framed and proudly exhibited on the walls of the Counsels' Chambers.

The successors to Sir Francis Kyffin Taylor included Harry Nelson QC later a National Insurance Commissioner, Glynn Blackledge QC who died in office and, finally, Richard Forrest QC who had the distinction of being the last Presiding Judge when the Court was closed in 1970. He thereafter became a Circuit Judge.

Notable Registrars were Mr Cripps, followed by Mr Roland Marshall, senior partner of Bremner Sons & Corlett and, finally, Colonel Charles John Cocks, referred to by Howard Channon as "every inch a retired officer his bearing and his manner military ... an accomplished cook and a gifted pianist". He had been senior partner of the old established firm of Bartley Cocks & Bird. He was a life long bachelor and employed his former batman as his "manservant".

Many tales of the Court's cases have been told but few have been recorded in writing.

Hartley Shawcross, in his memoirs entitled "Life Sentence" at p26 writes of his first Liverpool case, an affair before Mr Registrar Cripps in the Court of Passage as follows:

"This case was a trivial enough affair, although I spoke of it later as an important commercial case. It concerned a parrot that my Chinese client had sold but had not been paid for, the defence being that the parrot did not talk as it had been warranted to do. In Court, however, the parrot did give voice and the Registrar gave judgment for my client, remarking that he liked the parrot's way of loyally repeating the name of his previous owner, 'Ah Fook'."

Betty Behn, a solicitor of vast experience, particularly in litigation, writes of a memorable case she brought on behalf of a client in the Liverpool Court of Passage:

"During the hours of darkness my client, a lady, was visiting a friend who lived in a Corporation block of flats. Unknown to my client and the Corporation, one of the grids on the property of the Corporation had jammed with leaves and rubble to such an extent that the lid would not close properly. My client tripped over it in the dark and sustained injury. The hearing to the case lasted for the whole of the morning. The Corporation contended that the grids of the property were cleaned out meticulously well by the caretaker. The judge asked if the caretaker was to be called. The answer was, 'No'. The judge directed the caretaker be called. After the luncheon adjournment the caretaker entered the witness box. The judge asked the crucial question, "Can you tell me whose job it was to clean out the grids in the courtyard at this block of flats?" Without hesitation the reply came, "I have been employed there for six months and I have been trying to find out whose job it was to clean out the grids in the courtyard of this block of flats." That was the end of the Defendants' case."

The issue as to the precise limits of the Court of Passage jurisdiction has figured twice in cases recalled by Betty Behn.

"The judge ruled in one case that the Court's jurisdiction extended to any point below the high watermark on the Birkenhead side of the River Mersey."

The second case was one in which a defendant company had a factory on the East Lancashire Road beyond the east boundary of the City. It was discovered the defendant company either owned or rented a large warehouse on the Dock Road within the City boundary. The warehouse was used for placing stock to await despatch to clients as and when needed. The judge asked to be supplied with the amount and value of the commodities in pounds sterling passing through the warehouse. It was in the light of answers to these questions the judge found that the defendant company, although having a factory beyond the Liverpool boundary, was carrying on a considerable business within the City of Liverpool and, accordingly, could be sued in the Liverpool Court of Passage.

It was in the late twenties of the twentieth century that a Liverpool householder did what Hugh Gardner is alleged to have done in 1624, namely disclose secrets of the jurors at the Court of Passage he being one of the jurors himself.

The householder in question was happy to enjoy the novel privilege of being directed to serve as a Court of Passage juror, thereby escaping temporarily the dreary monotony of his employment as a cotton broker's clerk.

He returned home after a day of what was, to him, a unique experience, listening to a claim for damages by a lady knocked down on a Liverpool street by a motor car. The members of his household followed his detailed account of all that had happened with close and admiring attention. The younger children of the family occupied themselves excitedly following the details of the collision on large plans and photographs of the scene supplied to the jury to assist in their deliberations. The discussion in the jury room was given almost word for word. All the jurors were sympathetic towards the Plaintiff. They were anxious to find a way to compensate her for the unpleasant injuries she had suffered. Unfortunately, an overwhelming majority thought the driver of the vehicle blameless.

It will be appreciated the case was heard at a time before it was compulsory for a driver to be insured against third party claims. One juror was inspired to suggest they should all return to the Court and inquire from the judge if the Defendant was insured. If the answer was, 'Yes' they might then make a small award to the Plaintiff which would probably satisfy both parties and only the Defendant's insurers would be out of pocket, which they could probably easily afford. This was thought to be an excellent idea until it was found that no juror was prepared to stand up in Court and ask the question, each one rightly fearing that it might provoke a rebuke from the judge, kind though he appeared to be. Eventually, with reluctance, it was agreed that they would have to dismiss the claim.

Before leaving the Court premises, each juror received one shilling towards expenses. This, according to one of their number with previous jury experience was, by Court convention, to be handed to the jury bailiff as a gratuity.

JUDGE KYFFIN TAYLOR, LORD MAENAN

By Graeme Bryson

When one considers the general size of buildings in 1850 it was a very brave effort for the Town Council even to contemplate such a magnificent classic edifice as St George's Hall but Liverpool wished to add to her status by having proper accommodation for her own assizes; the Queen's Judges must be received in style, in keeping with the growing pretensions of the town.

Inside its walls have taken place the trials which have had the whole population of the city tingling with involvement in the fate of some wretched creature who had failed to escape the law, and whose very life depended upon the result. The black cap, the horrible words of the death sentence, struck a very chilling note.

The whole city followed the latest developments of, say, the trial of Mrs Maybrick. Famous barristers battled for days or even weeks on the one side to vindicate the law and on the other side to save a life.

The assizes would last for a month or more three or four times a year. At the end of each assize, peace would descend upon St George's Hall. Liverpool Citizens would get on with their business. Their own traditional court, the Liverpool Court of Passage would move into the same court rooms which had lately been occupied by the assize judges.

No criminals, no policemen, no red judges, but a local court quietly trying civil disputes. The Court had functioned since the days of King John, for most of its history, with the Mayor and Aldermen as the Judges. It was originally a market court, passage perhaps being the fee for entering the Liverpool Market.

The Lord Mayor was technically the judge of the court but for many years a distinguished barrister sat as the 'Presiding Judge.'

In 1903, Mr Kyffin Taylor KC was already in his fiftieth year when he was appointed Presiding Judge of the Liverpool Court of Passage.

Who could then have guessed that he would continue to sit as judge there for the next 45 years to become almost certainly the oldest judge anywhere in world history? Who would have guessed that Lord Birkenhead who was Lord Chancellor and judge maker when Kyffin Taylor was aged nearly 70, would say years later, "The only mistake I made as Lord Chancellor was not appointing Taylor a High Court Judge, but I made the not unnatural error of thinking he was too old?" Taylor died in 1951, being then in his 98th year, three years after his retirement as Judge. As you will hear, there was a great deal more to his reputation than mere time serving, record breaking though that was.

William Francis Kyffin Taylor came of a distinguished and long lived local stock. His father was Archdeacon of Liverpool, tall in stature, powerful in frame with white flowing hair, Liverpool's most impressive figure of his day and probably its most intellectual in that he held three doctorates of Divinity, Law, and Civil Law. He was an uncompromising ultra Protestant in a tradition which remained popular here for many years. Not for him the ecumenical overtones which today bring the churches so much closer.

But life at home was happy indeed for the Archdeacon, his wife and eight children. Judge Taylor was the eldest son but there were two other sons, both local Members of Parliament, shipowner Austin for East Toxteth and solicitor Brigadier Gerald Kyffin Taylor for Kirkdale. The boys were educated at Liverpool College which has supplied so many eminent sons to the City and to the nation. The future judge entered Exeter College, Oxford, took his degree, joined the Middle Temple and was called to the bar in 1879, setting up Chambers in 8 Harrington Street, Liverpool from which he was to practise in the very court where later he was to be judge.

Tall, handsome and athletic like his father but rather fuller in the face and with light curly hair as opposed to his father's finely drawn features and biblical white flowing locks, Taylor gave the appearance of a typical clean living English public school product. Like many elder sons, he was more serious than his younger brothers, though he was later to develop a very delightful sense of humour, as indeed most judges appear to do, one sided though it often is.

Like his brothers he had political pretensions and was for a time Secretary of the Liverpool Constitutional Association, though I cannot find that he ever offered himself for election either locally or nationally, but it certainly made it possible for licensing briefs to come his way as you will hear in a moment.

After only four years at the bar, he felt able to marry and was very fortunate in his choice of Mary Fleming, daughter of Robert Crooks of Rosemont, Liverpool. They settled down in 28 Devonshire Road, Princes Park, from which address he was to be seen every morning striding down to his Chambers in Harrington Street. Annual holidays were usually in Abergele where his father had a house. He was to have no son who would carry on the title he was to receive so many years later but his daughter was a delight and continued to be a great help to him all his life.

By 1894 it was recorded that he was generally looked upon as the leader of the local bar. For fifteen years he had been busy in daily attendance at his Chambers when in 1895 he was one of the first specifically Liverpool barristers to take silk and become a Queen's Counsel.

Probably his most famous case was the prosecution for criminal libel of Sir Edward Russell then Editor of the Liverpool Daily Post.

Sir Edward Russell had published an article in the Liverpool Post & Mercury, which referred to a speech by Prime Minister Balfour that the new Licensing Bill would be the greatest contribution ever made to the cause of temperance.

"Brave words these," said the Liverpool Daily Post, "but now let us see how this greatest contribution ever made to the cause of temperance is operating in Liverpool to diminish the number of licences."

The article went on to congratulate the wine trade on the ability and courage of their friends the Liverpool Licensing Justices, suggesting in effect that the justices did not desire to diminish the number of licences but to hamper those who were striving to effect a sorely needed reduction.

Part of the trouble was that the fifteen licensing justices included the most distinguished citizens of the day, the majority of nine being in the Conservative party.

Six days later FE Smith, later Lord Birkenhead, moved the Lord Chief Justice and Mr Justice Ridley in London for an order of criminal libel against Sir Edward Russell, editor, and Alex Jeans, publisher of the Liverpool Daily Post.

The judges found that there was a 'prima facie' case against Sir Edward Russell only and the trial was directed to take place in Liverpool. Sir Edward Russell was a reforming influence of his day and took no steps to avoid the issue. His defence was that the libel was true and further that it was for the public benefit that it should be published. The trial took a week in December 1905 at Liverpool Assizes. Kyffin Taylor KC and FE Smith seemed an excellent team for the licensing justices but there was to be an even stronger team against them, in Rufus Isaacs KC (later Lord Reading), Horridge KC (later a High Court Judge) and Hemmerde, (later Recorder of Liverpool). What a galaxy of talent! Kyffin Taylor opened like this:

"When Magistrates are charged publicly in such language as this in the press with having violated their duty, they must do something. They want no damages. They ask for no damages. They only wish," he said, "to be cleared of such false charges."

When the Deputy Chairman of the Licensing Committee gave evidence it was Rufus Isaacs who scored the points and got the laughs:

"Sir Edward Russell is well respected?" he asked.

"Yes."

"These criminal proceedings were instituted without any communication to him?"

"Yes."

"No letter?"

"No."

"No call?"

"No."

"No request?"

"No."

"Why not?"

"It did occur to me but my solicitor Mr Frodsham advised against it."

"Is he one of the licensing Justices?"

"Yes."

"One of the faithful body of nine."

"Yes." (laughter)

As each day of the trial went by, the Daily Post gave the case full coverage with splendid pictures of the contestants and their counsel.

Every day, the public galleries were filled with the elite of Liverpool. Leading public figures gave evidence, including former Lord Mayors. Sir Edward Russell never faltered. Even when Mr Justice Bray said to him, "You don't deny of course that this was a grave reflection on the Licensing Committee." Russell answered, "Yes, a grave reflection."

Try as they could Taylor and FE Smith could not hold the great gifts of Rufus Isaacs and they saw the case gradually slipping away.

Taylor's final speech to the jury realised this. It was merely going through the motions. He started:

"In this case Sir Edward Russell has had the supreme advantage of being defended by Mr Rufus Isaacs. I cannot help expressing admiration of the two magnificent speeches he has made, brilliant in their language, telling in their appeal to you. I agree that the case should be dealt with in a broad spirit. The gentlemen whom I represent want it dealt with in no other way. They have no desire to press the case, but what is the real meaning of the words in the Daily Post? If it is defamatory I am not to be told that a Lancashire jury are to be swayed from the path of right by fear or favour. Sir Edward Russell has the respect of all but if it is a libel, there is no escape."

After only 18 minutes, the jury returned a verdict of 'Not guilty'.

The Daily Post reported that from every section of the court there came loud cheers. The Daily Post editorial went on to comment:

"Great Dagon, God of the Philistines has fallen. He has fallen on his face to the earth." That is now called 'rubbing it in'.

The result was a rebuff for the Conservative party and for FE Smith.

It was also a set back for Taylor, but he continued to be a powerful advocate, particularly in civil cases. He had already commenced his judicial career as Recorder of Bolton in 1901. Then in 1903, he was appointed Judge of the Court of Passage holding the office for such a long period of time that, as the old legal expression goes, "the memory of man runneth not to the contrary".

He gradually asserted an authority which raised the standing of the court to the unique position which it held in its day.

Maxwell Fyfe, when Lord Chancellor, was able to look back on his years in Liverpool and say that the standard of advocacy was high here. He went on to say:

"One of the reasons why the standard was high in Liverpool was the existence of the Court of Passage. This is a court with unlimited jurisdiction in amount, but with a geographical limit of the City and Port of Liverpool. We had the immense advantage in my generation of being trained by Sir Francis Kyffin Taylor. What a wonderful judge he was! No slipshod argument, no careless word, no irrelevant cross examination got away without either a word from him – which we all feared, not so much because it was a reprimand, but because we loved him so much – or else the arching of his mouth, which was quite enough to pull someone back into the proper line of the case."

Maxwell Fyfe was not the only barrister to speak in glowing terms of Kyffin Taylor. As early as 1905 he had been made a Bencher of the Inner Temple, while in 1926 he became Treasurer, probably the most prized position barristers can hold.

When, in 1929, the year I myself entered the Law, he completed his fifty years at the bar he was dined at the Inner Temple and given his portrait painted by Sir William Llewellyn.

Still he sat on at the Court of Passage, never seeming to get any older not even wearing glasses, occasionally quoting the classics upon which he was a great authority. He was also a great believer in brevity. On one occasion he startled the legal world by what is said to be the shortest summing up to the jury ever. It had been a dull, hopeless case and he merely turned to the jury, cocked an eyebrow and said with a world of significance in his quiet voice, "Well, gentlemen?"

It is frequently said that he was never overruled on appeal, but there was one occasion when his sympathetic approach resulted in an unexpected windfall to a plaintiff. The plaintiff had received severe injuries but had a poor case and should really have lost, but Kyffin Taylor, probably in an endeavour to save some costs, awarded the Plaintiff £10 which involved him finding the Defendant was negligent. The Plaintiff appealed to the Court of Appeal who in view of the finding of negligence found themselves reluctantly compelled to increase the damages very considerably.

Usually however, the Court of Appeal found no cause to complain, even of Taylor's method of deciding cases with the words, "On the whole I prefer the evidence of the Plaintiff".

In 1937, he made legal history and helped to establish new law when he awarded damages to two young Liverpool window cleaners Joseph Ledwith and Christopher Crothers for false imprisonment by Liverpool police. They had been detained on suspicion of taking coins from the public telephone in King Street, Liverpool. Basil Neild (later a High Court Judge) appeared for the boys while Hartley Shawcross appeared for the police. After a few minutes' general argument, Taylor told Shawcross that his line of defence was not valid.

Without further ado, and without any evidence being called at all, he awarded damages to the boys.

The Police appealed and were represented by Maxwell Fyfe KC and RS Trotter (later a Senior County Court Judge at Liverpool), while the boys were represented by Noel Goldie KC, and Basil Neild.

The appeal lasted for four days and included the most detailed history of the law over four centuries. In a reserved judgment, which took four months to prepare and a whole day to deliver, the three Lords Justices of Appeal gave lengthy reasons to agree with what Judge Kyffin Taylor had taken only a few minutes to decide 'off the cuff'.

Taylor certainly had a tremendous ability to see right through to the kernel of the particular problem before him.

He was kind-hearted to the end. His very last case involved a claim against the Corporation. Not wishing to cause hard feelings to either side, he called counsel to his room, suggested a proper compromise which was readily agreed to by all, and then autographed papers for each side to keep as a memento. Unusual perhaps, but very human. It was said that all his deputies became County Court Judges. This was true of Rice Jones, Hamilton and Fraser Harrison and there were probably others.

Then came the great climax. In the Birthday Honours List of 1948, Sir William Kyffin Taylor, Presiding Judge of the Liverpool Court of Passage, was raised to the Peerage with the title of Baron Maenan of Ellesmere, the oldest man ever to be elevated to the House of Lords.

As District Registrar of the High Court, I was honoured to be present on the 17th July 1948 when the 94 year old Judge, still in office, was entertained by the Lord Mayor and a great gathering of lawyers.

The oldest practitioner in the Court of Passage, Lord Justice Scott who presided, called it a "unique occasion of English Law. There is no one who does not admire and love him," he said. "I always call him "old bird" and he calls me "my boy".

Sir Hartley Shawcross, then Attorney General, made the principal speech saying:

"We always look on Taylor as our master. He is our guide, philosopher and friend. How gently he taught us to do our work, never angry, never ruffled, never showing signs of impatience; he was the perfect trial judge." May I finish with Lord Maenan's own words in reply, "I am not a great man in any sense of that word, but I have a kind and warm heart. I have also what I call accidental oddities, to which I think there is no parallel. What other occupant of a judicial office has held it for forty five years?"

FOUR GENERATIONS OF HOLDEN SOLICITORS

By Lawrence Holden

Richard Holden,
Great Grandfather of Lawrence Holden.

Four successive generations of the Holden family have practised law in Liverpool for a period of over 150 years. It is likely that there has been more change during this period than at any other time. The City of Liverpool has been at the cutting edge of change and experienced changes of fortune. We are now at a positive time of renaissance and it is instructive to look back.

In this light, it is interesting to explore the origins of one family and how they might have had a part to play in its endurance on the legal scene in Liverpool for a relatively long period of dynamic change. In the 1850s, the family and the extended family, was probably the dominant unit in society. This has largely passed but effects continue.

One of the cornerstones of the professionalism of lawyers is our independence. The Holdens came from a part of England which might have been designed as a breeding ground for a culture of independence.

It is likely that the Holden ancestors lived within a fairly tightly-knit community in and around the parish of Austwick in the West Riding of Yorkshire for over 800 years. Inglebrough and Pen y Ghent (two of the three peaks of the Yorkshire Dales) are within sight. A beautiful and fertile vale is dominated by awesome

William Stackhouse Holden,
Grandfather of Lawrence Holden.

and spacious limestone landscapes and the area is blessed by being distant from any centre of authority. Until recent times, staunchly independent yeoman farmers dominated the life of the area and the role of any single major landowner was small. The Austwick Manor Court records demonstrate how these independent yeoman regulated the life of their community. It is from this stock that the Holden legal practitioners arose.

The family had many connections with Liverpool for about 100 years before my great-grandfather, Richard Holden, took out his practising certificate on 30 January 1851 and started the legal practice. Transport was then so crude that one ancestor recognised that it was not practicable for a Liverpool relative to be an executor to his Will. Many of the family had interesting connections with Liverpool. Three generations of Reverend George Holdens had been fine mathematicians and put their skills to useful effect by writing the Liverpool Tide Tables. Other relatives had been brewers and brass founders in Liverpool. Interestingly, Richard Holden's father, Robert Holden, forsook Liverpool to return to the life of the yeoman. My great-grandfather however, like so many ambitious able young men from rural areas at that time, was drawn to Liverpool.

Liverpool at that time was highly dynamic and ambitious. It saw itself as a second Rome. According to

Trevor Holden,
Father of Lawrence Holden.

the 1851 census, the population was over 400,000 having already grown from about 25,000 in 1760 to 100,000 in 1815. Many of the Liverpool families that have endured were drawn from hardy, hilly country during this period. The magnetic pull of Liverpool was great indeed. It is interesting to speculate what influenced the young Richard Holden and how he responded to the substantial differences of city life.

Possibly he was drawn by tales of his great uncle, Francis Holden, who had been a close friend of the renowned William Roscoe at the early crucial formative stage of their careers. In the period 1769 – 1773, William Roscoe and Francis Holden met before work at coffee houses in Castle Street discussing (reputedly in Italian) all the arts and planning for renaissance in culture in Liverpool.

Richard Holden's mother and his mother-in-law were sisters and members of the Clapham family brought up at Eldroth Hall. Marriages mainly took place amongst the local landowning families. The tough environment and remoteness of the area would have made strong qualities of independence, essential for survival. The need to be both enterprising and to care for others, would have been strong. The Claphams had lived in this environment for 800 years, escaping there in 1066 on the invasion of William the Conqueror. They were on the wrong side at that invasion as they owed their presence in England to the fact that King Edgar had granted their ancestor, the third son of the Duke of Lorraine, lands in south London and around Inglebrough in about 960 AD. The European factor is not new!

Imbued with these qualities, the young and enterprising Richard Holden set up as a sole practitioner. His practice flourished and he became Town Clerk of Bootle. The arrangement of combining a private practice with the office of Town Clerk was common at the time and, no doubt, profitable.

His independence of spirit would have equipped him well to be the 'guide, philosopher and friend' to his clients in the rapidly expanding Liverpool. There is no doubt that he had a caring side too. He was a lay

Lawrence Holden.

preacher and particularly active in the Temperance Movement as alcoholism was a severe problem at the time. Ironically, alcohol led to his early death as, when he suffered a serious injury by falling off his library steps, his doctor prescribed brandy, for which he developed a considerable taste. In 1867, he had taken a partner, Stewart Cleaver and the firm's name was changed from Holden & Co to R Holden and Cleaver. He had nine children and when he died in 1873 at the age of 51 at The Breck, Anfield, his estate was worth approximately £3,000, which was a not insignificant sum at that time.

His practice was taken over by his elder son, William Stackhouse Holden (my grandfather), who, at the age of 21, had only just qualified in the year of his father's death. My grandfather retained close connections with his relatives in the ancestral area and clearly inherited the family characteristics of independence of spirit, integrity and a caring nature. He was reputed to be an extremely good-natured man who, in addition to looking after his widowed mother, saw it as his duty to support two invalid sisters and one who became widowed.

He was, indeed, a workhorse and there was no stopping him. On top of his business commitments, he took the Treasurership of his old school, Liverpool College and served in that honorary capacity for more than 25 years. If he worked hard, he also played hard and for many years took part in river and sea canoeing with the Liverpool Canoeing Club, going with them to America, Norway and the Western Isles.

From the 1920s onwards, the offices of Holden & Cleaver were at 26 North John Street, Liverpool. It was a non-litigation practice, largely concerned with Wills and Trusts.

My grandfather died in 1935 aged 83. He found it very difficult to retire and, I think it could be said without malice, he went on far too long. Right to the end he was never happier than when reading a legal document. From his records, it is clear that he had many interesting clients, not only in Liverpool but all over the country with addresses for clients in other places, Manchester, Middlesex, London, Devon, Buckingham, Rhos on Sea, Northants and Malvern being notable from his list of clients.

I have a copy of the address read at his funeral service, which took place in Liverpool Cathedral on 9 November 1935 and one passage has always impressed me deeply:

"To his clients and friends – and his clients were his friends – he was a marvel of kindness. Was, in this case or that, a charitable line possible? You knew for certainty that Holden would take it. Were you yourself in trouble? Holden would be the first to call and ask 'Can I do anything?'"

My late father, Trevor Holden, who practised from 1927 to 1968 and who died in 1983, was also held in the highest esteem by his friends and clients. He cared deeply and passionately about the rightness of things and his career as a solicitor was a true vocation. He had the difficult task of coping with his father, who was practising in old age, and then building up the practice again. The practice merged with that of Duncan Oakshot Baxter & Chevalier and was predominantly what we would today call a 'Private Client' practice, his partner, Arthur Chevalier, being a man of the highest principles.

Just at the time when the practice should have been developing well, the Second World War occurred. It must have been quite devastating in its effect on daily life. Being too old for military service, my father joined the Fire Brigade. In many of the darkest moments of the War he kept the practice moving by day and fought fires at night. He was notable for his bravery and on one occasion, by exceptional courage, prevented a major explosion in an oil storage depot. Whenever life as a solicitor has been tough, I have been so grateful not to have endured experience of survival during those difficult days.

The 1950s were difficult times, but my father enjoyed a very close partnership and friendship with Morris Vernon Jones and preserved great integrity. He took a great interest in the affairs of Liverpool people and demonstrated deep concern for poorer sections of the community, particularly in the Florence Institute in Mill Street, Dingle. He served with distinction as a Magistrate and did some pioneering things about the treatment of young offenders while serving as Chairman of the Juvenile Bench. It has been a continuing inspiration to find how soundly his relationships with so many of his clients have been based.

I am sometimes asked what my ancestors would think of the practice in its present form of the regional firm, Brabners Chaffe Street. Undoubtedly their first reaction would be one of utter incredulity. The thought of over 125 lawyers in one firm would, during most of the 150 years have appeared quite impossible. The minds of my ancestors would have been highly challenged by the changes in the profession in the last 25 years. I suspect, however, they would have appreciated my professional involvement in responding to the challenges of new information and communication technology and practice management, even though this appeared somewhat eccentric to most lawyers at first. They would also have been pleased that the Brabner family is recognised so clearly in the firm name as that family had consistently commanded their respect and had commenced practice some forty years before the Holdens. Its fifth member, Michael, has assumed the mantle of leadership with great distinction.

They might have been pleased that the firm is among the largest one hundred firms in the country. I am certain, however, that they would be proud that the firm continues to value longer-term relationships and strives hard to operate its substantial business on the basis of sound ethics and professional values, notwithstanding the real threats that these concepts are under. The instinctive independence of the ancestors is a sound basis for endurance.

THE HILL FAMILY

By Roy Hill

Sir John Gray Hill.

WTJ Gunn in his *Studies in Heredity* published in 1928 wrote of the Hill family that from James and Sarah Hill descended one of the most intellectual families that has ever arisen in England. James and Sarah had a son Thomas Wright Hill (Tom) who, on leaving school in 1777 at the age of fourteen, wished to be apprenticed to an attorney. However, his mother was incredulous of a lawyer and an honest man being united in the same person. Instead, Tom was apprenticed to his uncle, a brass founder in Birmingham. His mother would have been even more incredulous to learn that she was to be the matriarch of a line of eminent lawyers continuing for more than two centuries; lawyers who were to play a substantial part in the great social changes that were to come and whom the Crown was to honour for their services to the nation.

Tom, without previous educational experience, went on to found a school that was famed for its then highly unconventional system of education forward-looking even by today's standards. Two of his sons read for the Bar and achieved legal eminence. A third son is the best remembered today as Sir Rowland Hill, for his invention and introduction of penny postage. Other sons played their part in the social changes of the day. The

Sir Norman Hill.

younger son, Arthur, devoted his life to the headmastership of the family school then transferred to Bruce Castle Tottenham.

As these earlier generations contributed much to law and social development so did Arthur's son, John Gray, and his grandson, Arthur Norman, especially to shipping and its major port of Liverpool. Both were educated at Bruce Castle.

John Gray (Gray) born in 1839 served his articles in London and, in 1863, aged 24, was awarded a certificate of merit in his Final Examination. Two years later he joined the Liverpool firm of Duncan Squarey and Duncan to specialise in marine law. Within three years the senior partner died. The same year, his successor suffered a breakdown in health and retired from the firm. Gray assumed the mantle of senior partner. He acquired a marine practice that included the secretariat of the recently formed Liverpool Steam Ship Owners Association with its valuable connections.

John Gray Hill was a remarkable man. He was hardworking and of great intellectual ability with much business sense. As later described by the shipping historian Sir Clement Jones, he was a man who carried about with him, concealed but always on his person, the mysterious weapon called prestige, commanding respect always. A man fair and formidable when it came to an argument and who, in committee, ruled by a pleasant mixture of love and fear of which "we were all in rather a funk of him".

Under Gray, the practice expanded rapidly in its representation of growing North Atlantic shipping that included the two pioneers of steam, namely the Cunard partnership and the Inman Steamship Company. In 1874, Gray Hill moved the practice to 10 Water Street thus putting the practice in the centre of a thriving shipping and commercial Liverpool. He invited John Dickinson to join him as a partner and renamed the firm Hill Dickinson and Company.

In these earlier years, Gray Hill with his wife Caroline had resided at Apsley House, Oxton. However, in the early 1880s, with the growth in his practice, reputation and earnings, Gray Hill built a mansion, Mere Hall Oxton, with grounds ultimately comprising in excess of nine acres with magnificent views across the River

Martin Hill.

Dee to the Welsh Hills beyond. There, he employed a staff of seventeen including domestics, coachmen and gardeners. He was in every way prestigious amongst those who valued prestige.

A most surprising aspect of Gray Hill and his wife, Caroline, was their love of travel and the abandonment of their luxurious home for remote and perilous places, especially Syria that then comprised what is now Israel, Palestine and Lebanon under Turkish domination. In his *With the Beduins* Gray describes three of "Our annual flight from the east winds and leaden skies of England". Each was throughout fraught with risk of sudden death from illness, attack, murder and kidnap. Indeed, it is miraculous how they survived these perils.

Gray Hill and Caroline had no children of their own but gave assistance in their legal studies to Gray's nephews, Arthur Norman and Maurice. They were the children of Gray's brother, George Birkbeck Hill. The latter had assumed the headmastership of Bruce Castle but, for reasons of health, had been unable to continue, and the school had passed out of the Hill family. He and his wife planned professional careers for their three elder boys. Maurice was to go to the bar. Arthur was to be a solicitor. Leonard was to practise medicine. Each achieved eminence in his chosen profession and was knighted for his services to that profession.

Maurice qualified as a barrister in 1888 and practised first in Liverpool where he established himself at the Liverpool bar. Later, he was appointed Queens Counsel and subsequently the Admiralty Judge. In that capacity, his judgements came to be highly regarded by the legal profession.

Arthur Norman Hill (or Norman Hill as he preferred) was born in 1863 at Tottenham and educated at Bruce Castle. He served articles in London with solicitors, Gregories, and qualified Michaelmas 1885. The following year, he joined Gray Hill.

Norman married Mary Danson, the daughter of a well-known marine average adjuster. The marriage would appear an ideal one. Unfortunately, Mary's father was exceedingly possessive of his two daughters, Mary and Polly, to the point of downright cruelty. Much in the courtship resembled that of the poet Browning and Miss Barratt of Wimpole Street. Indeed, Norman at one stage despaired of ever achieving the marriage.

The ending of the 19th century and entry into the 20th century was a period of continuing expansion and

Roy Hill with his Partners in Hill Dickinson in 1964. William Goffey (then 79 and still a Partner), Leslie Adam, Roy Hill, Vernon Gwyther, Peter Watson, Peter Cawson and David Gregson.

prosperity for the United Kingdom and especially for Liverpool. The mercantile community were creating new businesses and forming new companies to carry on trade of every kind. Great Britain headed the greatest Empire of all times occupying one quarter of the world's surface. An Empire on which its peoples proudly proclaimed the sun never set.

The steamship was the arterial system serving that Empire. Steel was replacing iron in its construction. Propelling machinery was reliable and auxiliary sail discarded. Passenger ships were becoming larger and more luxurious.

Gray Hill was becoming ever more involved in the commercial and political activities of the day. He was engaged in the flotation of companies and taking founders' shares highly prized by the business community. Companies offered him numerous directorships. Many of these he had to refuse because of his already heavy commitments. One he accepted was that of the Law Guarantee & Trust Society Limited, a company established by Lincoln's Inn solicitors to provide guarantees of various kinds including for ships bail.

At the same time, Gray Hill was looking to spend more time in Syria and at his second home on the Mount of Olives. Thus, he sought a lessening of his workload. In 1893, he proposed Norman as his successor as secretary of The Liverpool Steam Ship Owners' Association. In that capacity, Norman became much involved in the shipping industry and questions of maritime safety.

In 1901, Gray Hill was elected a member of the Council of the Law Society especially to express the views of Liverpool. Two years later, he was elected President of the Society. The following year, 1904, King Edward VII conferred a knighthood upon him for services to his profession. He assumed the style Sir John Gray Hill.

From 1895, the Law Guarantee Trust and Accident Society was guaranteeing mortgages on licensed premises. In 1907, the then liberal Chancellor of the Exchequer imposed a new tax on beers and liquors resulting in a serious depreciation in the value of public houses. The Company faced a serious deficiency on its guarantees and in an attempt to remedy the situation made an issue of new shares.

As Vice-Chairman, Gray Hill felt under moral duty to substantially subscribe for the new shares.

Unfortunately, these measures proved inadequate to save the Company in circumstances of its increasing deficiencies. A winding up ensued in 1909 with substantial calls on shares and a total loss to Gray Hill on his investment of £57,400 then a fortune.

In 1914, then aged seventy-five, Gray Hill was planning to visit again his much loved Mount of Olive home when, on 14th June 1914, he died suddenly. So ended the life of a kind and distinguished gentleman of much wisdom who had lived his life to the full, yet in his closing years was entrapped by those very circumstances against which he had warned others.

Meanwhile, following his appointment as secretary of the Liverpool Steam Ship Owners Association, Norman Hill had become more and more involved in public work relating to shipping. In his early days, he was involved in the reform of light dues charged on shipping for maintaining lighthouses. That reform ended the practice of making a profit out of lighthouses.

Later, he was closely involved in two major Acts of Parliament of 1906 relating to shipping. The first, the Marine Insurance Act 1906, codified the law relating to marine insurance. It continues today as the primary source of that law. The second Act amended the Merchant Shipping Act 1894 that had codified and extended earlier legislation relating to construction and equipment of British vessels and their stowage and load lines.

In 1911, Norman Hill received a knighthood for services to Government concerning shipping. His style was Sir Norman Hill. The following year, the White Star Company invited him and his wife as first class guests on the return maiden voyage of the Titanic to New York. Sir Norman declined the invitation. Had he gone, then like many friends and colleagues, he probably would not have returned.

Sir Norman and his firm acted for the White Star Line in relation to the sinking of the Titanic. His brother Maurice Hill QC represented White Star in the Board of Trade Investigation into the sinking. Sir Norman himself, in his capacity as chairman of the Merchant Shipping Advisory Committee, gave evidence on studies of the Committee into numbers of lifeboats; sub-division of larger passenger vessels into watertight compartments; and statistical evidence with regard to loss of life at sea.

Prior to the Great War (1914-1918), Sir Norman served on a sub-committee of the Imperial Defence Committee. That sub-committee, at his instigation, recommended a mutual scheme of war risk insurance of ships with 80% re-insurance by the Government. That scheme was brought into immediate effect on the outbreak of war.

An early loss was the luxury passenger liner, the Lusitania, owned by the Cunard Company sunk by torpedo with the loss of 1198 lives. The Germans subsequently introduced unrestricted submarine warfare coupled with the command 'Sink without trace'. Their intention was to starve Britain into submission. Sir Norman was advocating his ideas for a convoy system whereby vessels would be classified according to speed and cargo capacity and grouped so as to maintain speed and position voyage after voyage. Ultimately the Admiralty agreed to adopt the system that proved so successful.

Sir Norman was chairman of the Port & Transit Executive Committee charged with wide powers relating to the flow of traffic through the ports of the country. In 1917, he reported a probable deficiency in available shipping for the year. The government was so alarmed by the report that it immediately prohibited import of all non-essential goods into the country. Sir Norman had been advocating this since 1915 as the most effective means of maintaining essential supplies into the country.

Following the ending of the war in 1919, King George V conferred a baronetcy upon Sir Norman Hill for services to his country and, especially, to shipping before and during the 1914-18 war.

Sir Norman Hill, as an acknowledged expert in maritime law, played a leading part in the formulation of the Hague Rules, namely, rules adopted by international convention at The Hague in 1923 to regulate the contractual terms of international carriage of goods by sea. The Rules replaced many differing terms of contract largely aimed at absolving the ship owner from responsibility.

Sir Norman was then sixty years of age. The war years had taken their toll. In 1923, after thirty years as Secretary of the Liverpool Steam Ship Owners' Association, he retired. He continued as the senior partner of his firm but acting principally in a consultancy capacity. His advice and help remained freely available to the Association who frequently called upon it. His nephew, Martin Spencer Hill, succeeded him as secretary of the Liverpool Steam Ship Owners' Association.

Martin was the eldest son of Leonard Hill (Norman's medical brother) who had articled him before the war to marine solicitors, Thomas Cooper & Co, in London. Following his return from the trenches, Martin had achieved honours in his Solicitors Final Examination and had joined his Uncle Norman as an assistant solicitor in December 1919.

In 1929, recognising the growing importance of London as the centre of British shipping, Martin Hill and another partner moved into London and opened offices there of Hill Dickinson & Co representative of the Liverpool Steam Ship Owners' Association.

These were hard times. The general strike of 1926 involving the mines, railway and transport was followed by the great depression of the 1930s that continued over the first five years of the decade. This all had appalling repercussions on the United Kingdom shipping industry with six hundred and fifty-nine ships laid up and those still at sea operating at about half capacity. Many loyal officers and seamen were unemployed with little prospect of finding alternative employment and little assistance available other than dole at twenty-six shillings (£1.30) weekly, plus two shillings (10p) for each child during the first six months of unemployment. A national retirement pension of ten shillings (50p) weekly was payable on attaining sixty-five years of age. That was often the only reward of masters and officers in a great British Merchant Marine who had served the nation so bravely during four years of a devastating war.

Some more enlightened employers had established company pension schemes following the 1921 Finance Act. That allowed contributions to rank for full tax relief and were the forerunner of today's provisions. Martin Hill and his firm were among the first solicitors to obtain such approval for its many commercial and shipping clients.

One such scheme was the Merchant Navy Officers Pension Fund in which Martin Hill took a great personal interest and for which he acted gratuitously or for nominal fees over many years.

Like his Uncle Norman before him, Martin Hill had a profound knowledge of maritime law. He was a member of the British Maritime Law Association made up of ship owning and cargo underwriting interests. That Association played a large part in bringing about a sensible interpretation of the Hague Rules.

During 1937, Lloyds' Recoveries Department asked Martin Hill whether he would take on the legal work of recovering marine claims paid by Lloyds Underwriters. He declined by reason of conflict of interest. He recommended, instead, his young brother, Maurice Hill who had taken part in establishing the marine practice of Clyde & Co in London. Lloyd's Recoveries accepted the recommendation so giving to Maurice Hill and this then young and thrusting firm a valuable connection into marine insurance.

In the days leading up to the Second World War, Martin Hill took a leading part in negotiating terms for the requisition of British shipping in the event of war. He was instrumental in drafting the relevant and complex form of charter known as T99A. In 1940, he was awarded the Order of the British Empire for his services to shipping.

On the outbreak of war, the Liverpool Steam Owners Association again set up its convoy committee to liaise with the Shipping Defence Advisory Committee. Liverpool became the shore headquarters of the Western

Approaches. The Government War Risks Insurance Scheme was already in place modelled on that of the 1914-18 war with the Government reinsuring 80% of losses later increased to 96%. The participating associations included the Liverpool and London War Risks Association managed by Martin Hill.

From the outset of the war, the enemy attempted to cripple the country's overseas supply lines with sinking again on sight by submarine and aircraft. That began on the first day of war with the sinking of the liner Athenia. It mattered not whether the ship was carrying passengers or cargo or of what nationality.

As the war progressed, losses inflicted upon the nation's merchant ships and their crews by enemy submarines were becoming unbearable. They threatened supply lines and very survival. Martin Hill feared that, despite all convoy and naval protection, the submarine menace would starve the nation into defeat. However, new developments in airborne radar enabled coastal command aircraft to find and attack the enemy submarines often at night when they surfaced to charge their batteries. Tables were turned and the enemy was losing submarines faster than they could replace them.

Sir Norman Hill died on the 7th January 1944, three months after the death of his wife. The shipping industry paid many tributes to his lifetime service to shipping. Sadly, a few days later, his only son, Norman Gray Hill, a Lieutenant Colonel in the Royal Army Medical Corps (Airborne Division), was shot down over Catania. The baronetcy died with him.

Following the war, the new Labour administration failed to appreciate the effect of indiscriminate penal taxation, nationalisation and bureaucratic control. Martin Hill repeatedly warned against taxing shipping in a manner that did not allow for its replacement. Ship owners did not earn a true profit until they had put aside sufficient monies to replace their ships at inflated prices. He pointed to the insidious effects of the flag of convenience that virtually paid no tax, whilst UK ship owners paid half their taxable profits to the Inland Revenue. He said and repeatedly said, "the British mercantile marine will gradually but surely decline if the earnings needed for replacement and expansion are continually taken away in taxation".

Martin Hill was repeating these warnings throughout the 1950s but to little avail, regardless of the political party in power. Yet how right were those repeated warnings and what little attention was paid to them by successive governments. Within half-a-century, their policies have seen the greatest merchant fleet comprising one-quarter world tonnage reduced to a meagre half per cent.

Martin Hill was a member of the British Maritime Law Association and the Committee Maritime International (CMI) and an adviser to the UK Government on matters of marine law. As such, he took part in several governmental conferences considering shipping conventions. These included arrest of ships; ship owners' limitation of liability; liability as a passenger carrier and the liability of operators of nuclear ships. All resulted in international conventions and legislation. Especially he was interested in nuclear power and led the UK delegation at the CMI conference. He believed that nuclear power offered the same golden prospects to the British Merchant Marine as steam had offered a century earlier.

Martin Hill participated within the International Chamber of Commerce in maritime legal discussions that included bills of lading and The Hague Rules. In May 1957, at the Naples biennial conference, the vice-president of KLM was forecasting rapid development of air transport and that within five years at least a million people would cross the Atlantic at increased speed and at considerably reduced fares. Martin Hill feared the effect that this would have on the great passenger liners of the day.

In October 1963, the Liverpool Steamship Owners' Association became merged into the Chamber of Shipping ending the Association as a national organisation. Martin Hill retired.

Roy Gray Hill, Martin's son, was born in 1922 into a world totally different from that of today. He completed his schooling in July 1939 and entered into solicitors' articles. After passing the Solicitors

Intermediate Examination, he joined the RAF aged 19 years. Prior to demobilisation, he passed the Solicitors Final Examination with distinction. In 1947, he joined the family firm of Hill Dickinson to complete his articles and to be admitted in 1949.

He looks back to the 1950s as good years filled with hope for the future and the continued prosperity of Liverpool and its shipping. People were generally courteous and kind one to another. He enjoyed living in a land of peace and unspoilt beauty where the air was still good to breathe. The River Mersey was full of ships, including the great passenger liners that were sailing to all parts of the world.

In contrast, Roy Hill looks back to the 1960s and the 1970s as horrendous times for Liverpool. As the city once led the nation in shipping and industrial development, it led the nation in its decline and collapse of traditional values. Conditions worsened as the decade progressed. Strikes were spreading from the dock shipbuilding and ship repairing industries and later the motor industry. Shipping companies were moving from Liverpool to London and many disappearing. Liverpool was losing its renown as a commercial and intellectual centre.

In November 1969, Hill Dickinson & Co. moved from Water Street to Castle Street. This was a move after 100 years from a building that had many maritime connotations, at a time when Liverpool was fast losing its maritime importance.

Roy Hill was fortunate in maintaining and expanding a wide practice. During the 1970s and 1980s, he was handling many marine problems including marine casualties in different parts of the world. The most newsworthy was the luxury liner Carmania that grounded on a reef off the Island of Salvador when navigating close into the Island to allow passengers a view. Academic work included that of examiner in the Solicitors' Final Examination.

Roy Hill continued the management of The Liverpool and London War Risks Association. In June 1967, hostilities broke out between Israel and Egypt. The latter blocked the Suez Canal entrapping the vessels Melampus and the Agapenor entered in the Association. The Association paid total losses in respect of both vessels that remained entrapped until 1974, when they realised mere scrap value.

On 1st April 1982, Argentina invaded the Falkland Islands requiring a task force of ships. Fortunately, sufficient British flag vessels still remained available ready to man the task force. The Government agreed to reinsure the War Risk Associations fully against war losses. Sadly, during operations, the Cunard vessel, Atlantic Conveyor, was the subject of air attack and sunk with the loss of her Master and five members of her crew. That was probably the last occasion on which Britain would possess sufficient merchant ships to support the nation in an emergency. The worst fears expressed by Martin Hill twenty-five years earlier were coming to ultimate fruition with the British fleet being decimated.

Roy Hill continued to act for the Merchant Navy Pension Fund, which then had large funds for investment including a valuable property portfolio. In 1983, he was asked by the three associations representing Merchant Navy officers to assist in their amalgamation, including the trusts and charitable estates at Mariner's Park Wallasey. These comprise residential property, widows' flats and an infirmary overlooking the River Mersey for retired seamen and their widows. They are a place of tranquillity in a sometimes selfish and violent time for the elderly. Roy Hill continues as chairman of the Trustee Company holding these assets following his retirement in 1994.

Roy Hill's son, Martin Gray, had joined his father as a partner in the firm. Following the breaking away of the London end of the firm and amalgamation in Liverpool, he decided that his best interests were served by joining the practice of Dibb Lupton Alsop (now DLA).

JAMES ALSOP

By John Gibson

Non-Conformist minister's son James was born in Birmingham. When he was seven, his family moved to Liverpool where his father transferred from being a Congregationalist to becoming a Unitarian pastor. After four years at the Hope Street Schools, James was enrolled at the Liverpool Institute where he excelled in academic work. His family was poor due to the disability of blindness afflicting his father and the hindrance that caused to his Ministry. James won numerous academic prizes and scholarships. With his scholarships, he virtually paid for his own education.

Phrenology was at the height of its vogue in Victorian England. James' head 'was read'. The phrenologist declared that the child was simply 'without fear'. He was to live up to this finding as evidenced in his adventurous life. He was known for being widely read as a young man. As a school boy, he suffered an accident when chopping wood on holiday. Despite the fact he had almost severed his foot he was determined to occupy his time with reading books and studying. He had no transport to the library. Undaunted, he hobbled to and from the library which was over one mile away.

His academic successes led him to think about studying at Oxford or Cambridge. His lack of family money and scholarships precluded this option. Thomas Avison of 18 Cook Street agreed to have James as an articled clerk. He excelled in this role and was admitted as a solicitor in 1869. In his finals, he was the

Tipron Martin & Atkinson Medal winner for the best Liverpool law student. He found time to study for the external examination of the University of London BA and was awarded a 'First'. He also was awarded a First in his LLB when he subsequently undertook studies for this University of London degree.

He became a managing clerk in another firm, but was soon asked to be a partner in what was to become Harvey & Alsop in 1872. The firm had started in 1821 and old Enoch Harvey was seen as one of the pre-eminent lawyers in Liverpool. He took James into a partnership without the usual premium as he could see that James was able, quick-witted and already a successful lawyer. James never left this firm. The firm became known as Alsop Stevens Crooks & Co by 1908. It grew and prospered and eventually James became senior partner. He worked hard and was seen as being one of the leading lawyers in Liverpool and a leading intellectual. In 1928, the firm moved to the India Buildings where it still has a large office in its new incarnation as Dibb Lupton Alsop – now known simply as DLA, a major international firm.

James was physically embraced by Garibaldi as a personal friend. He enjoyed friendship with many Members of Parliament. An active Liberal, he acted as agent in Parliamentary elections until he could no longer agree with the policy championed by Gladstone of 'Home Rule' for Ireland. He became a Unionist and was asked to stand for Parliament on several occasions. He declined the invitations. He preferred local public service in Liverpool. The City Council beckoned following his marriage in 1886! In 1899, he was elected to the City Council and, with brief interludes, was a Councillor and later an Alderman of the City until his death. He was particularly influential on the Education Committee, chairing it for many years. The Earl of Crawford even agreed to name a school after him following James' death in 1921. The 'Alsop High School for Boys' was said to be the most advanced school of its time, when built.

James served his time as President of the Incorporated Law Society of Liverpool in 1889. He represented the Society in opposing the Land Transfer Bill then going through Parliament as well as trying to reform the Liverpool Assize system. In 1897, he became a magistrate. In the Great War, he served on the War Tribunal which adjudicated over conscientious objectors, malingerers and all others who wished to avoid the War. For this he was awarded the OBE.

It is comforting for modern lawyers to know that our predecessors had problems and arguments with their clients also. The relevant portion of James's own statement given for the purpose of the Prosecution reads:

"On the 13 February 1908, about 5 o'clock in the afternoon, I was in my private office with my Partner, Mr Crooks, and another gentleman when I received a message that a gentleman wished to speak to me on the telephone, and that he was connected with the telephone in the telephone box in the outer office. I accordingly went out of my room into the general office and walked rapidly towards the box.

Just before I reached the box I heard an explosion, followed by another immediately afterwards, and I felt that I had been struck in the left arm. I turned round and saw the prisoner (Mr Vaughan) about two yards away. He had something in his hand, but he was not pointing it at me. I realised at once that I had been shot by the prisoner. I shouted "That's Vaughan, he has shot me in the arm; run after him!" I walked back into my room and found that my arm was bleeding profusely.

The bullet struck me at the back of the left arm, penetrating through the fleshy portion and was just projecting from the front part of the arm. I received first aid from PC Prince and was taken in an ambulance to the Northern Hospital, where the House Surgeon extracted the bullet and dressed the arm. I afterwards returned home in a cab."

Vaughan was a man of very weak intellect and a heavy drinker. He had developed an obsession about the proceeds of a property sold through James's firm. He was convicted and sentenced to five years and had to serve every day of it. After he was released from prison, he continued to pester James up to the time James died in 1921. It is believed that Vaughan died in or about 1925 in a lunatic asylum in Caterham, Surrey.

There is no truth in the oft-quoted story that when James was shot, one of his articled clerks at the time (reputed to be one of the Birchs of Birch Cullimore in Chester) chased after Vaughan down Castle Street shouting, "Come back, come back, you've missed."

James' biographers have illustrated that he was the leading light in the creation of the University of Liverpool. He certainly drafted its Charter and lobbied Parliament for a bill to create the University. He was awarded an LLD by Liverpool University and was President of its Council and Pro-Chancellor for nine years. In his speech following James' death the Pro-Vice Chancellor of the Liverpool University stated: "To no man living – perhaps to no man – does the University movement owe more ..." This was because he had been active in the creation of the University from its very inception.

The students of the University of Liverpool composed the following ballad in his honour upon his being made a Doctor of Laws:

"James Willcox Alsop you should know
As Chancellor he's quite a Pro
We'll have when he's beneath the sod,
A marble angel in the Quad.
Chorus
So here's to you and your degree
It's bonus gratis, nothing free,
We'll now without the slightest fuss
Admit you one of us."

Whether it was in ensuring adequate manpower in wartime for the battles such as the Somme, Ypres and Passchendale and so forth, or whether it was in ensuring justice was undertaken when he was a magistrate, James always saw his role as one of 'service'. His professional life as a lawyer allowed him to help people as well as allowing him to reap the fruits of his intellectual brilliance. His influence in educating the working masses of Liverpool was significant. However, his presence is still noted today by the existence of the institutions he founded or helped to continue in existence. His firm still has a number of the clients that he first brought to it, such as the University of Liverpool. Sydney Jones summed up James' educational work when he said that "Liverpool will gratefully record the pioneer work so ably performed in an earlier time, when Mr Alsop helped to lay the foundations of an enduring educational system."

ARTHUR WEIGHTMAN

By Charles Elston

William Arthur Weightman (always known as 'Arthur') can be regarded as the founding father of the present firm of Weightman Vizards, although fore-fathers can be traced a good deal further back through WAW's first partner named Field and also through the firm of Rutherfords which amalgamated with Weightmans in 1988, whose roots go back to the first half of the nineteenth century.

WAW was born on 27th November 1852 in the then leafy suburb of Seaforth, being the oldest of a family of eight – comprising seven sons and one daughter (who, perhaps not surprisingly never married having, no doubt, had her fill of masculine society in her youth, but instead busied herself with good works). The family was of some local distinction, WAW's grandfather, John Weightman, having been Architect and Surveyor for Liverpool from 1847 to 1865 and having had a rather tenuous connection with the Law in that he was responsible for the design and construction of the Magistrates' Courts in Dale Street, and also for some more popular public buildings including the Municipal Buildings on the opposite side of Dale Street and, as successor to Thomas Allom, the William Brown Library and Museum.

WAW served articles with the Mr Field mentioned above who practised in Fenwick Street and he was admitted in 1874 and joined Field in partnership the following year when the practice became Field & Weightman. This position continued until 1887 when Field was joined by his son Mark and by AM Hannay in the new practice of Field Son & Hannay; at the same time WAW took into partnership his brother Sep and John Pedder (both of whom had been articled to him) and the firm name of Weightman Pedder & Weightman was adopted. In 1908, Wilfrid Charles Cafferata, who had been associated with the firm for several years, became a partner. In 1913, when Albert Ernest Frankland (a nephew of John Pedder) became a partner the name became Weightman Pedder & Co until 1970 when the firm moved to Richmond House and the name of Weightmans was adopted.

The practice which WAW initiated in 1887 grew strongly and steadily throughout his long professional career and acquired an impressive list of clients both individual and corporate. Specialisation was not much practised in WAW's time and he was prepared – and competent – to take on most types of work other than Admiralty, which for many years figured substantially in the firm's workload and was dealt with by a large department under John Pedder and Wilfred Cafferata. However, as time went by, WAW dealt almost exclusively with wills, probate, trusts and Company matters and he attained – deservedly – a high reputation in these spheres. WAW served on the committee of the Liverpool Law Society for many years and was President in 1899/1900.

During WAW's childhood the family moved from Seaforth to Percy Street, Liverpool – at that time a very desirable address. Not long after he qualified, WAW married Miss Christiana Fernie, whose parents also came from Seaforth where they were near neighbours of the Gladstone and Muspratt families. Mr & Mrs WAW moved over the River to Bidston Road, Oxton where they brought up a family of four daughters and one son, John. In due course, John qualified as a solicitor but he had not reached the age when assistants were invited to join a partnership, when the 1914/18 War started. He joined up and was killed at Gallipoli in 1916. He was unmarried, and only one of his three sisters married.

Unlike a regrettably large number of principals in his day, WAW (and under his influence, the firm) was very considerate towards the staff and, for instance, an expedition for the whole staff – probably then numbering between 40 and 50 – to the Wembley Exhibition in 1925 was arranged. When Mr & Mrs WAW reached their Golden Wedding they entertained the whole staff to dinner and to a visit to the Empire Theatre where Gracie Fields was the star attraction. WAW was largely responsible for the firm becoming Honorary Solicitors to a large number of Charities and his own charitable activities were considerable, including being successively committee member, Hon. Secretary and then Chairman of the Birkenhead General Hospital for many years.

WAW was an active member of Trinity Presbyterian Church, Birkenhead, throughout his residence in Wirral. Unlike many of that persuasion he was not a teetotaller but was very moderate in his own consumption although tolerant of greater indulgence by others. He was, like most of his contemporaries, a member of a 'Gentleman's Club' – in his case the Exchange Club, then in Fenwick Street, where he lunched regularly but unlike some of his colleagues he was very seldom out of the office for more than an hour. In his younger days he apparently enjoyed a convivial masculine evening as there was in the office a reproduction of a cartoonist's depiction of a 'Glee Evening' at the Exchange Club with WAW, pipe in hand, conducting an invisible choir. He had a quiet but ready sense of humour with just a hint of sarcasm on occasion, as when a client en route to Aintree during the Grand National meeting called on him at his office wearing a loud check suit with field glasses over his shoulder. He was greeted by, "Not going anywhere special are you?"

WAW's room adjoined the board room which also housed most of the firm's library and there was a connecting door between the two rooms. On one occasion, two articled clerks – John Bromfield, nephew of Sep Weightman, and Rex Cafferata, son of Wilfred, were in the board room ostensibly doing some research but actually engaged in friendly (?) wrestling which had reached the stage of Rex being flat on his back on the floor with John kneeling on his chest when the door opened and WAW put his head round it. As the wrestlers looked up he simply said "When you are free Rex I've a little job I'd like you to do" and returned to his room. When the rather dishevelled Rex joined him there, no mention of the incident was made – nor was it on any subsequent occasion.

In the early 1920s, WAW prepared a will for a client who was known to be of very substantial wealth but liked to obtain full value for any money he paid out. The will was long and complex creating several trusts and life-interests, and after its execution WAW sent in the bill in the sum of 2 guineas (£2.10p.). A few days later, shortly after lunch, WAW was in his room dictating to his secretary Miss Berta Rodger (who told me this story) when the client entered unannounced and put the bill on the table together with a gold guinea and a gold half guinea. He said "I've never paid more than that for a will and I don't intend to do so now". WAW merely nodded and the client withdrew, whereupon he said "I dare say we will get the other ten and six in due course," and carried on dictating. He was quite correct – the client died a few years later leaving an estate valued at that date (about 1925) at more than £1.3m. and the administration of its various trusts provided a steady, if modest, income to the firm for well over 30 years.

WAW was short of stature and of wiry build. His normal method of going to the office in the 20s and 30s was to be driven by his chauffeur, Jenkins, from his house in Bidston Road to Birkenhead Park Station which took no more than 5 minutes in those days of little traffic. He caught an underground train to James Street station and then walked up the subway to Water Street – quite a climb but he did this every day until he retired at the age of 83. On his return, he would be met by Jenkins at Birkenhead, there being no difficulty in parking right outside the station in those pre-traffic warden days.

WAW was still quite active physically in his 80s and he retained a clear and concise mind throughout his life. He retired from the firm in March 1936 having then been a practising Solicitor for 62 years and head of the firm for 49 years. Although he reduced his workload considerably in preparation for his retirement, and never visited the office after his retirement, he remained a Trustee of a large number of Trusts and during the remainder of his life Berta Rodger visited him at his home from time to time with papers regarding these.

WAW died on the 13th January 1939. His funeral service at Trinity Presbyterian Church in Birkenhead was attended by principals of nearly all the legal, accountancy and stock broking firms in Liverpool.

WILLIAM GOFFEY

By Charles Elston

William Goffey must be a strong claimant for the title of 'the Liverpool lawyer who was actively engaged in practice for the longest period during the 20th Century'. Son of a Liverpool sailing ship owner, WG (as he became affectionately known) started his career in April 1901 at the offices of Hill Dickinson & Co at 10 Water Street where they had practised for the past 40 years and where they continued to do so for the next 68. Having become senior partner of the firm in I950, WG stepped down after they moved to Equity & Law House in Castle Street in 1969 remaining, however, in daily attendance at the office as a partner – and indeed eschewing the use of the lift to the fifth floor where he had his room – until shortly before his death in 1979 at the age of 94.

In his early days, his Admiralty work was almost exclusively concerned with fully rigged ships and he had encyclopaedic knowledge of their rigging and handling as he himself came from a ship owning family operating sailing barques out of Liverpool under the name Goffey & Co. For virtually the whole of his career WG dealt almost exclusively with Admiralty work, including not only proceedings of various types arising out of wrecks and collisions at sea, but the drawing up and advising on maritime documents such as charterparties and bills of lading and other matters affecting the shipping industry which was large and active in Liverpool until the latter part of the century.

One of the largest matters he dealt with arose quite early in his career out of a wreck, namely that of the 'Titanic'. Among the many important ship owners that Hill Dickinson acted for was Oceanic Steam Navigation Co. Ltd (alias The White Star Line), owners of the 'Titanic' and WG participated in the investigation into the loss of that vessel for the purpose of representing the owners at the inevitable Wreck Enquiry and in dealing with the resulting claims. He personally interviewed a large number of potential witnesses and took statements from them – all in his own hand – and in the course of the very lengthy proceedings he amassed a very substantial archive of great interest and value.

In another difficult case, which ended up in the House of Lords, WG acted for Cunard Steam Ship Co Ltd in relation to the collision in 1942 when the 'Queen Mary' ran down her escorting cruiser HMS 'Curacao' sinking her within minutes with great loss of life. The 'Queen Mary' was held one-third to blame – an outcome which WG had predicted from the start.

WG became accepted nationally and internationally as one of the leading experts on Maritime Law and practice. He was a man who had the humanities in full measure, and his learning and mastery of maritime law was unequalled; matters maritime were his life's blood. He was a great collector of shipping memorabilia and 10 Water Street contained many of his ships' models, pictures, etc – and even a ship's figurehead.

He also had a wide collection of chronometers, barometers, and grandfather clocks, all of which were auctioned after his death, selling for prices beyond his imagination. A special auction was arranged after his death which attracted collectors from all over the world. As a bachelor he eschewed social life, having a huge capacity for hard work and endless patience in teaching young members of the profession.

In addition to the memorabilia, WGs' room at 10 Water Street contained current and dead files, briefs etc. strewn – to the visitor, apparently at random – over the floor, on his desk, and on every other available flat surface. Despite the apparent disorder his remarkable memory enabled him to pick out the file or document he wanted, unerringly. It caused him a good deal of anticipatory distress when he realised that the whole contents of the room would have to be sorted and tidied up in preparation for the move from 10 Water Street in 1969.

WG was of a generation which used only surnames when speaking to colleagues or clerks who were addressed as 'Mr X or Miss Y' although his partners and assistant solicitors became 'X Esquire'. "Ah, X Esquire, a word with you if I may" presaged a lengthy session of memories before coming to the legal problem he wished to discuss.

Another indication of the generation gap was the marked difference between his invariable courtesy – indeed, affability – when you met him either by arrangement or by chance, and the correspondence received from him when you were engaged in a contentious matter with him, which could be distinctly curt. He and most of the contentious business practitioners of his generation would hold up their hands in disbelief at the thought of a 'cards on the table' approach.

And, yet another example, he was so thoroughly accustomed to an all male office that when in the course of time – and expedited by the shortage of males during World War I – female shorthand typists (now, of course, an almost extinct species) began to appear he could not accept this innovation and retained a male stenographer, Harry Lewis, to the end of his career.

Finally, an anecdote involving WG and Rigby Swift J, a profile of whom appears in this volume. This was told at a Liverpool Law Society dinner many years ago by the late Sir Fred Pritchard (Pritchard J for the all too short period from 1947 until 1952 when a severe stroke disabled him from continuing as a High Court Judge who also features in this book). Whether the story is wholly true or not, it certainly illustrates some of the characteristics of both those concerned. At a date before World War I, when both were rising young men in their different branches of the profession, WG worked very late at the office one day to finish his consideration of a case involving a difficult question of law, and having reached his own conclusions he wished to discuss them with the counsel he thought appropriate – Rigby Swift. In spite of the lateness of the hour, he summoned a cab and had himself driven to Swift's home, which he found in darkness except for one upstairs light. Ringing the bell brought no response and so he picked up some gravel from the drive and threw it up at the window showing light. This resulted in the window being raised and an irate Swift put his head out and said "Who's there and what do you want?" or perhaps stronger words to that effect. "It is I, Goffey," replied WG – grammatical at all times (another old-fashioned trait). "I have an important and difficult matter I want to discuss with you." "Go away, Goffey," replied Swift. "I'm a barrister, not a bloody midwife".

Even when confined to bed in his nineties after 1976 his mind was still sharp. His Hill Dickinson partners, Leslie Adam and Tony Huber, tried to persuade him that his house insurance needed to be updated. Reluctantly he agreed but insisted on vetting the Royal's Policy which he then proceeded to amend in detail. The Royal were reluctant to amend their standard National Householders Policy notwithstanding his scathing comments on its drafting.

FE SMITH, LORD BIRKENHEAD

By Noel Fagan

"Many people loved FE, most distrusted him, some despised him and he despised almost everybody." – *one of FE's epitaphs.*

Born on 12 July 1872 and brought up in Birkenhead and a pupil of the Birkenhead School, Frederick Edwin Smith, later Lord Birkenhead was known throughout his life as 'FE'. During his hugely successful legal and political career he looked to his background and his constituency of Walton in Liverpool as his base and inspiration.

His enemies described him as an adventurer which epithet FE accepted. He once said "The great Disraeli did not disdain the name of adventurer, and I am willing to be called one in the same sense. Life is an adventure. He who, started with nothing, fights hard while conceiving ambitiously, must be an adventurer." He placed great importance on the impression he created with his audience, whether legal or political. He took pride in his great successes appearing to be effortless, which was far from the truth.

He acquired the grand manner, for which he was later renowned, during his years as a student in Oxford. His maiden speech in the Oxford Union, whilst still a fresher, brought him immediate prominence. He was delighted that the laughter and applause from one quip alone was said to have lasted 5 minutes. In later life he remarked "The success of that evening marked an epoch in my life. I was therefore satisfied that I possessed a power of speech which, if sustained and developed, must lead me along one path or another, to some degree of eminence in the state."

He always claimed to have known poverty and, indeed, he was frequently in trouble with his creditors. However, his was not the poverty of the slums. It was simply that he had expensive tastes and however much he earned, he always spent up to the hilt.

In his early years he kept himself physically fit through extensive exercise, particularly rugby and tennis.

However, his lifetime of high living and heavy drinking took its toll and in his final years, his tall and previously impressive appearance, was marred by an impression of some dissipation.

By 1900, Liverpool was very prosperous with a population of 750,000. Like most seaports, the population was very mixed with large Irish and Welsh communities mingling with the native English.

The dominant political issue was the religious divide between the Roman Catholics (predominantly Irish) and Protestants. The divide was most bitter between the 'Green' areas of Scotland Road and the Docks, and the 'Orange' area near Netherfield Road, and less sharp elsewhere in the city. Liverpool was a Conservative stronghold until World War 2 and in 1900 the Conservative Party held 8 of the City's 9 parliamentary seats. The ninth seat (the Scotland division) was held from 1885 continuously until 1929 by the Irish Nationalist MP, TP O'Connor.

The Nonconformists were broadly represented by the Liberals who also represented some high Anglicans and non-Irish Catholics and the Liberals had a strong minority position on the City Council and also with the press where they were supported by the City's leading daily paper, the Liverpool Daily Post.

The formal influence of religion in Liverpool politics did not cease until March 1974 when there were 9 Councillors on Liverpool City Council representing the Protestant Party (yes that was its title).

Astonishing though it may be for modern readers, the litmus test for Unionist (ie Conservative) candidates in the early 1900s was their stance on the Church Discipline Bill. The Church Discipline Bill was a measure to control Papist influences in the Church of England and no Conservative candidate was adopted in Liverpool in those days if he was not a strong supporter of the Church Discipline Bill.

The democratic strength of Liverpool Toryism was reflected in the Liverpool Working Men's Conservative Association, a body with some 8,000 members in 26 separate branches throughout the City. The dominant cause of the Working Men's Association was the popular one of crude Protestantism. They were reinforced in their fervour by the Orange Lodges and the Layman's League. In 1900, Walter Long, a cabinet minister in Lord Salisbury's cabinet was forced to withdraw from his West Derby seat because he was suspected of being soft on the Church Discipline Bill. The cause of the established Church in those days was an issue of patriotism (Home Rule etc) rather than simply doctrinal.

Much of FE's early life is quite different to the legend and the stories which FE himself told in later life. Despite his stories of his childhood poverty in Birkenhead which FE liked to tell in middle age, the majority of his childhood was spend in comfort and possibly affluence. His father, Frederick, was the driving force behind a property firm, Smith & Sons, although his father resigned from Smith & Sons in 1883 to read for the Bar. FE was named Frederick after his father who appears to have been an indulgent parent and not at all the remote Victorian 'pater familias.' Indeed, his father declared his ambition "to be the friend of my children".

His early schools included a Dame School in Birkenhead run by a Mrs Kate Lewis but from the age of 10 he attended a preparatory school in Southport, a surprising distance away because at the time the Merseyrail tunnel had not been built. In 1886 he suffered the set back of failing the entrance scholarship to Harrow on the first day. He was in good company as a future Cabinet colleague, LS Amery also failed on the first day and FE and Amery were to meet later in Oxford and in government. This humiliating and rare failure in a generally successful academic career always rankled with FE In 1919, newly appointed Lord Chancellor, he met the unfortunate Harrow Headmaster (by then Dean of Durham) at dinner at Lady Londonderry's and attacked him about it across the table. The Dean had the grace to say "it was rather my failure".

FE entered Birkenhead School in January 1887 when the school was only twenty years old. FE carried off various prizes and showed a great talent for public speaking. He actually attended Birkenhead School for less than three years and left just after his seventeenth birthday in August 1889. He appears to have been attached to his old Birkenhead School and in 1924, when addressing the pupils of the School he said "You will never know the pleasant, easy life we knew in this country before the War, when there were hardly any taxes and we spent half our time complaining of the few there were."

The fact that FE spent two years at Liverpool University is not well known. It seems that FE himself, as well as his biographers, found it more convenient to forget those years. However, it seems likely that the two years he spent at University College, Liverpool, which had been founded only seven years earlier in 1882, may well have made his subsequent Oxford career possible. They appear to have enabled him to arrive at Oxford a good deal more mature and experienced than he otherwise would have been. The two year interlude at University College, Liverpool probably enabled FE to make the impact at Oxford which he made at the age of 19.

FE was determined to get to Oxford. There were very few scholarships in those days and even the fare to sit the examination, was almost beyond him. However, as so often in his life, his skill and luck did not fail him at this crucial moment. He travelled down in December 1890 and sat the joint scholarship examination for the two Colleges of Trinity and Wadham. Candidates were required to state their preference. FE chose Wadham on the ground that it was the only College he knew anything about (through John Thompson who was shortly to marry his sister, Clara).

After five days of examination papers, FE was the fourth name on the list of scholarships headed by his lifelong friend, CB Fry, perhaps the greatest all round athlete England has ever produced.

FE was extremely lucky in his choice of Wadham. Not only was it a beautiful College but it provided the ideal platform for him to built his later reputation and career. When he arrived there, Wadham was a small and previously disregarded College but his talents could shine more brightly than they might have done at Trinity, Balliol or Christ Church. CB Fry was the top scholar in FE's year but the year before had arrived AA Roche destined for the Bench and the following year these three were joined by John Simon another future Lord Chancellor (as well as Home Secretary, Foreign Secretary and Chancellor of the Exchequer) and by Francis Hirst who became a distinguished Liberal writer and editor for ten years of The Economist.

The quintet of Roche, Fry, Simon, Hirst and FE far surpassed their contemporaries of any other College and raised the reputation of Wadham to unheard of heights while laying the foundations of their own. As Hirst said at the Memorial Dinner held for FE at Wadham in 1930 following FE's death "He used to trace the beginning of his fortunes from the day on which ... he was elected as Scholar of Wadham College".

FE graduated after a huge effort in his final months with a First in 1895. His efforts over the final months were prodigious. The reason for the effort was financial – a First was not needed in order to go to the Bar.

FE had run up debts between £300 and £400 with the local tradesmen and needed a Fellowship. In his later years, he repaid the faith of the tradesmen by continuing to patronise the same tailor for the rest of this life. FE always said that his tailor made his career possible because the tailor induced his other creditors to be patient with him at a meeting of creditors in FE's room at Oxford.

Distracted by his sporting exploits, his close friend CB Fry achieved the still rarer distinction of a Fourth. Until his final months, FE's studies had been affected by his term as President of the Union. After a short gap following his First, FE took up a Fellowship at Merton for 3 years from 1896.

The secret of FE's immediate success when he went to the Bar was attributed by most contemporaries to his quiet three years of study at Merton as a Fellow. For those three years he had the leisure to read more deeply and widely than most barristers plunged straight into practice are able to do. He had a phenomenal memory and incorporated that knowledge permanently into his mental armoury.

Links between the Liverpool Bar and the Conservative Party were very close and there was a good deal of partisan work to be had. Most of the leading barristers had their eye on a seat in Parliament as a natural career move.

Throughout his life, FE always demonstrated that he could impress those who could help him ascend the next rung on the ladder of success. At this time around the turn of the century, it was notoriously difficult for a newly qualified barrister without any connections to get started at the Bar. However, FE spoke a few well chosen words of praise to the Liverpool barrister, Leslie Scott who shortly afterwards invited FE to share his Chambers in Cook Street, Liverpool. Leslie Scott later became Conservative MP for Liverpool Exchange and a Cabinet Minister but his Chambers included a veritable galaxy of talent, including future Judges in Mr Justice Swift, Mr Justice Greer, Judge Maxwell, Judge Thomas, Judge Tobin and future Silks in Leslie Scott himself, AG Steel and Collingwood Hope.

His opportunism but essential indifference to the passions of the religious zealots became clear early on. While building his practice from 1899 onward he sought alternative incomes and took on the job of local secretary of Lady Wimbourne's Protestant League at a salary of £300 per annum. He then thoughtlessly decorated the bare offices of the League with eight lithographs of the Virgin Mary. When Lady Wimbourne came to inspect she could not decide whether she was more upset by the Madonnas or the fact that he had managed to spell her name wrongly on the brass plate outside the offices, but she dismissed FE the following day.

Largely by luck, FE acquired an early instruction in a licensing matter from John Wall, a solicitor from Wigan who instructed FE while Leslie Scott was on holiday. He so impressed John Wall that other licensing work followed.

FE's early career was transformed by his licensing work. In March 1900 FE set up Chambers on his own in Cook Street. For the first few months FE's earnings dipped from their already modest level to 5 guineas in April, 20 guineas in May, 15 guineas in June but in September and October they rocketed to 135 guineas and 97 guineas. These were the months of the annual Licensing Sessions!

FE's breakthrough in the licensing sessions came through the firm of Edwin Berry through which most of the local licensing work was channelled. FE was recommended to Berry by the Conservative MP for Widnes, WH Walker (later Lord Wavertree).

The Temperance Movement was very influential with the Liberal Party and consequently the brewers gave large sums of money to finance the Conservative Party. Gladstone described his Government's defeat in 1874 as being "borne down in the torrent of gin and beer." The annual Licensing Sessions was a battleground between the Parties as the City magistrates tried to reduce the number of public houses but the brewers, backed by the Tories, fought vigorously for each licence, particularly after the Licensing Act 1904.

In his full first year in practice, FE earned £529 which was a huge sum for a first year. From this promising beginning he never faltered and his earnings from then on increased by approximately £1,000 each year. The dominant solicitor behind this phenomenal success was George Harley of Simpson North & Harley. Through Harley he acted in many cases for Robert Houston (ship owner known as 'the Robber Baron' and MP for 30 years for West Toxteth) and later for the soap manufacturer, W H Lever (future Lord Leverhulme). Houston and Lever were acquisitive and litigious local capitalists and through them FE made his fortune at the Liverpool Bar after his promising start in licensing.

FE soon moved his Chambers and growing entourage of pupils to larger Chambers at 25 Lord Street. His entourage included Harold Jager, Edward Wooll, Arthur Strong, William Dudley Ward, NB Goldie (most of whom became MPs) and Guy Rutledge (whom FE as Lord Chancellor later appointed Chief Justice of Burma).

FE used his 'devils' well and got the best out of them. He rarely corrected a pleading or even an opinion if he thought it would be in any way acceptable and they repaid his trust by doing their very best not to let him down. He rarely consulted an authority and would avoid studying a brief if he could. Harley knew him well enough not to provide him with a proper brief at all in many cases and simply sent a few statements and letters.

In one case, FE instructed Jager to look at a brief for him before a consultation at noon. FE arrived late and had no time to consult with Jager or look at any papers or the brief but when he arrived, introduced Jager to the solicitor as "my friend who has given me the greatest assistance in this case" and proceeded to ask the solicitor for his impressions. The solicitor obliged at some length, doubtless glad to air his legal acumen.

FE then turned to the client to seek his views and thus in a few minutes with great tact and skill FE elicited all he wanted to know. He then proceeded to give a masterly exposition of the law with delicate comments on the erudition of the solicitor. The client left delighted whereupon FE went for a lavish lunch at the Adelphi Hotel which he used to alternate with the Palatine Club for his lengthy lunches.

In 1901, FE married, and purchased a large house on the edge of Birkenhead Park – 2 Cavendish Road. The marriage was from the start an exceptionally successful one and Margaret Smith had enormous influence over her husband who was, from first to last, dependent upon her.

Immediately on his marriage, FE bought his first two horses and used to ride regularly with the Wirral Harriers and the Cheshire Hounds. After the birth of their first child, Eleanor, in 1902, FE moved from Cavendish Road to 'The Grove' in Thornton Hough which had stables for 18 horses.

At that time, Thornton Hough was a very powerful community. Lever lived there in Thornton Manor and George Harley in nearby Upton with Archibald Salvidge (Conservative Boss in Liverpool) living in Hoylake. All were within comfortable riding distance. Lever's habits were a bit spartan for FE but he was a frequent guest of Harley and Salvidge for Sunday lunch.

In the early 1900s Liverpool Solicitors did not employ London agents but themselves went to the capital bringing with them barristers briefed at the Liverpool Bar.

A good example of FE's tendency in his early years to become involved in high profile legal cases involving the contentious political issues of the day, was the leading case of Wise v Dunning on the Law of Riot. George Wise was the most controversial Liverpool Protestant Reformer of his day. His meetings frequently involved public disturbances to the extent that Mr Dunning, the Deputy Chief Constable, obtained an Order from the Stipendiary Magistrate that Wise keep the peace or go to prison after one of the his deliberately provocative anti-Catholic demonstrations ended in a riot.

FE did not defend his client's conduct but mounted an excellent legal defence based on Beatty-v-Gillbanks (1882) which held a man cannot be held responsible for causing, by his lawful action, the unlawful action of others. FE argued:

"The Appellant had not personally been guilty of a breach of the peace and conduct inducing to a breach on the part of other people was not enough It was admitted that the Appellant had used insulting language in regard to Roman Catholics but it was contended on his behalf that this was not sufficient grounds for making the Order."

The Lord Chief Justice congratulated FE on the quality of his arguments but nevertheless the Lord Chief Justice and two colleagues hearing the Appeal held Wise was responsible by the violence of his language and dismissed the Appeal. Despite their dismissal of his Appeal, FE won praise from all the Appeal Judges, including Lord Alverstone who wrote him a personal note of congratulation.

The Liverpool tobacco firm of Ogden attempted to win business from retailers by offering to distribute to the retailers Ogden's entire net profits and a bonus of £200,000 per annum for four years. Shortly afterward Ogden went into liquidation. Nearly 800 retailers sued Ogden over the next few years and FE was retained by the Liquidator to fight each claim individually and FE made the case into a goldmine.

The points of principle were whether the liquidation cancelled firstly the obligation for net profits and, secondly, the promise for £800,000 (£200,000 for each of four years). In 1904 the Court of Appeal and in 1905 the House of Lords confirmed the original ruling on the point of principle that liquidation cancelled the obligation to pay profits (because there would be none) but not each retailer's particular share of the promised £800,000.

From the Company's point of view the defeats in the higher courts merely reduced the amount of Company assets from which the trader's claims could be paid.

Eventually, 1,200 separate actions were being fought but the retailers then realised that all these actions were being fought at their own expense and only profited the lawyers. Eventually the retailers settled out of Court in September 1906 for what was left.

Over four years FE made approximately £20,000 out of Ogdens litigation. It was claimed at the time that his huge income from this litigation was not a matter of luck but that FE himself had discreetly manoeuvred to increase the number of claims on the Company. If so, his ingenuity not only created work and income for himself but was also a successful strategy for the Liquidator's defence because it was the very multiplicity of the retailer's actions which made them self-defeating and forced the retailers to compromise eventually.

By 1905 FE was earning £6,000 and had overtaken every other established junior on the Northern Circuit.

FE stories are numerous, but include:

- A Judge commented that having read FE's case he was no wiser than when he started. FE retorted, "Possibly not, my Lord, but far better informed."
- A Judge said "What do you suppose I am on the Bench for, Mr Smith?" – FE replied, "It is not for me, your Honour, to attempt to fathom the inscrutable workings of Providence."
- A Judge remarked he had read the pleadings and did not think much of FE's case to which FE replied, "I am sorry to hear that, my Lord, but your Lordship will find the more you hear of it the more it will grow on you."

By 1906 FE had an enormous income and reputation on the Northern Circuit. He was now ready to make his name in the House of Commons from 1906 onwards as the MP for Liverpool Walton and Cabinet Minister and Lord Chancellor.

On 16 February 1905, the Liverpool Daily Post reported that FE had been selected to stand for the Tories in the Walton Division of Liverpool. In order to secure the nomination in the Walton Division, FE was released by the Conservative Association in the Liverpool Scotland Division. FE was delighted with the change because the Liverpool Scotland Division was the stronghold of the Irish Nationalist MP T P O'Connor. Walton was now the largest constituency in Liverpool and predominantly working class. It extended some 4 miles from County Road, Anfield in the north to Smithdown Road, Wavertree in the south but was nowhere more than a mile across

The Liverpool Daily Post reported about FE, "The Tory Party have great hopes of him; they are warranted in having great hopes undoubtedly as a speaker and as an advocate he has genius. He has shown himself a ready, adroit and forcible politician, he is Ambition Incarnate."

The first necessity for FE was to satisfy the Orange Lodges and the Laymen's League of his allegiance to Protestantism and the Established Church. Accordingly at the beginning of March 1905 he devoted a speech to reminding his supporters of where he stood.

"... he would attach little importance to crosses, genuflections and such features of Ritualist Churches and services. They indicated a treasonable conspiracy directed at the very heart of the Church of England by men who were resolved, covertly, to approximate more closely to the Church of Rome (applause)…. he wishes to declare himself in the clearest manner a supporter of Protestantism as advocated by many prominent men in Liverpool during the past 10 years. His Protestantism, however, was not of recent growth. He had not, like the late Liberal Candidate for the Everton Division, for example, been seized with a virulent Protestantism on the eve of an Election (laughter). He would pledge himself to do his utmost to secure the successful passage through the House of Commons of the Church Discipline Bill (loud applause)."

The new system of an electric scoreboard attracted a gigantic crowd to watch the results. The huge Liberal tide was already clear before Election Day because Manchester and Salford, which voted three days before Liverpool in the heartland of Free Trade, resulted in a rout for the Tories who had espoused Tariff Reform.

The Liberals made two rare gains in Liverpool capturing Abercromby and Exchange narrowly. Watson Rutherford, the well known Liverpool solicitor, was returned with a reduced majority for West Derby. Finally, at 10.30pm, the Walton result was declared, giving FE a majority of 709 votes over the Liberal Jellicoe.

FE himself described the huge opportunity and change to his life.

"This election was incomparably the greatest milestone which I ever had passed – or ever was destined to pass – in my career. I was to be afforded the chance of measuring myself with whose who were to determine the fortunes of the country."

The door was open – it was now up to him.

Only a Tory rump of 157 MP's survived compared with nearly 400 Tories in the previous Parliament. The huge reduction in Tory numbers and the defeat of many senior Conservatives gave increased opportunities to FE.

One month after his arrival in the House of Commons FE made his maiden speech. Convention was, and still is, that maiden speeches should be short, polite, modest and unprovocative. FE scorned convention and set out to make his name resound in London as it did in Liverpool.

Although his hour long speech appeared spontaneous it was in fact carefully prepared. Amery heard a full dress rehearsal of the intended speech in Oxford a few days earlier and Joseph Chamberlain arranged for him to be given his opportunity at the prime time of 10.00pm.

The maiden speech dealt with the core issue of the Tory policy of Tariff Reform against the Liberal policy of Free Trade. Even the Liberal press had to concede …

"In sheer brilliance it was probably the most striking maiden speech delivered since Lord Randolph Churchill. It was excessively witty and it was impertinent beyond description. The delight of the front Opposition bench was pathetic. They rolled about with delight. You could have placed an apple in Mr Austen Chamberlain's laugh at any moment. Sir Edward Carson was so happy to look almost human. Mr Smith lashed Liberal members … one after the other …"

Immediately after his election as MP, FE sold his house 'The Grove' on the Wirral and moved his family, stables and Chambers to London. At first he rented a small flat near the House of Commons in appropriately enough – Smith Square (23 St Stephen's Mansions) and a few months later moved to 70 Eccleston Square, near Victoria Station where, in December 1907, his second child, their only son, was born.

FE established his new Chambers at 4 Elm Court in the Inner Temple, not in Gray's Inn though he resumed his dining rights there, and in 1908 became a Bencher. He brought from Liverpool his faithful Clerk, Peteil, but left his entourage of pupils, Jager and the rest, in Liverpool encouraging them to go into practice on their own. He still used his Liverpool pupils to devil for him politically and it was they who scanned the speeches of his opponents.

FE rapidly built up in London a practice which surpassed that which he enjoyed in Liverpool and was quickly in tremendous demand. His rapid Parliamentary success helped to spread his name in the Courts.

He also created enormous interest socially. Lady Violet Bonham Carter recalled his maiden speech "by a flutter of excitement in the Ladies Gallery above." From the moment he sat down after his maiden speech the doors of the highest society were open to him and he was sought out by all the great Tory hostesses, Lady Londonderry, Lady St Helier and Lady Desborough.

Lady Londonderry quickly became one of FE's most important Patrons. He repaid her fully by his unswerving advocacy for Ulster in the years to come.

The Press Baron, Lord Northcliffe, launched a savage attack on Lever Bros in 1906. Lever and other soap manufacturers were hit by a rise in the cost of raw materials. Rather than raise the price, Lever reduced the size of a 1 lb. bar of soap to 15 ounces and formed a soap trust with other soap manufacturers to prompt economies throughout the industry. The Northcliffe Press ran a campaign against Lever whom they accused of a greedy fraud on the British public. By November 1906 Lever sales were down 60%.

The first barrister consulted by George Harley of Simpson North Harley (Lever's solicitor) advised Lever against suing. Lever sought a second opinion from his young political opponent, FE.

Harley sent a telegram to FE at his weekend retreat urging him to return to London urgently. FE went to the Savoy to be greeted by a huge stack of papers, nearly 4 feet high and a request for his urgent opinion by 9.00am the following morning. FE ordered a bottle of champagne and two dozen oysters and worked throughout the night for eleven hours. At 8.30am next morning he gave one of the most robust and shortest opinions ever "There is no answer to the action for libel and the damages must be enormous. FE Smith."

FE himself played only a minor role in the Trial which vindicated his judgment at Liverpool Assizes in July 1907. FE was only the third out of four renowned Counsel retained by Lever including Carson KC and Horridge KC. After a succession of huge offers, Lever finally accepted an offer from Northcliffe of £50,000, more than four times the previous record for libel damages.

Lever conducted a number of more minor actions against Northcliffe over the next few years in which FE appeared. However FE wanted to secure the political advantage of Northcliffe's friendship. Because the Press Baron could be more useful to him than Lever, FE made it clear to Northcliffe that FE did not want Lever's money and "would much rather never have seen him".

FE prided himself on loyalty to friends but never regarded Lever as a friend but merely as a major client who had outlived his usefulness. As a renowned 'bon viveur' and hard drinker FE had come to dislike Lever's personal parsimony and self-righteous philanthropy.

In what was then the shortest period ever, FE took silk 8 years and 8 months after being called to the Bar.

By 1910 FE's earnings passed the £10,000 per annum mark for the first time. He was now rapidly expanding the property he had originally purchased in the village of Charlton in Oxfordshire.

His enormous income was rapidly spent to fuel his extravagant tastes. FE continuously extended Charlton and rapidly extended the stables and acquired a lavish fleet of motor cars.

His first love at the time was horse riding. He was not terribly interested in hunting but was passionate about riding and rode fearlessly and recklessly, jumping the highest gates, suffering frequent falls and trespassing cheerfully on all the wrong fields. He frequently scandalised the officials of the snobbish Bicester Hunt.

FE was very close to his younger brother, Harold. In 1907, Harold was still a partner in the family firm

Edward Carson QC and FE inspect the Ulster Volunteers in 1913 when Ulster was on the verge of Civil War over Home Rule in Ireland. The involvement of senior figures from the legal establishment with possible armed combatants was highly controversial at the time.

of Property Agents Smith & Sons in Birkenhead. However, he transferred his career and was called to the Bar in 1911 and took Silk in the enormously rapid time of 12 years in 1923.

Harold not only followed FE into the law but also into politics. He organised Birkenhead Toryism very successfully along the lines Archibald Salvidge pioneered in Liverpool. Harold became a Conservative MP for Warrington.

Harold shared Chambers for the last few years before the 1914 – 1918 War. In July 1914 Harold married Joan, the younger sister of FE's wife Margaret. Soon after the end of the War in 1918 Harold bought a country house near to Charlton. When Harold died in 1924, aged only 48, FE was distraught and lost much of his own zest for life.

By the time of his 40th birthday in July 1912, FE had an extraordinary reputation. The words "FE is up" was enough to empty the bars and fill the Chamber and the galleries in the House of Commons.

A Conservative and a lawyer from a landless and unmonied Birkenhead middle class background he had become the handsome and dashing hero of the Tory Party as no Tory had been since Lord Randolph Churchill. His insolence and swagger astounded the aristocratic leaders of society.

The Prime Minister's daughter, Cynthia Asquith, described him in her diary, "He is a magnificent bounder ... I can't help liking him".

By 1913 – 14 his annual income had risen to £14,195. This was a fantastic income for the time. However, FE's enormous income could never keep up with his huge extravagance. By 1913 FE had acquired a new property at 32 Grosvenor Gardens, just off Buckingham Palace Road. In addition to huge sums on his properties in London and Oxfordshire he was strengthening his very fine collection of books. His book selection was his pride and joy and he concentrated on the finest first editions of all the English classics, particularly the great novels.

32 Grosvenor Gardens remained FE's London home for the rest of his life. Once when he and Margaret were booking into a hotel FE noticed the guest who signed the book immediately before him happened to be the clan chief Cameron of Lochiel who had signed the Register simply 'Lochiel and Lady Cameron'. Not

to be out-done, FE promptly wrote on the next line '32 Grosvenor Gardens and Mrs Smith'.

Shortly after he became an MP in 1906 FE became close friends with Winston Churchill. Having recently crossed the floor in the House of Commons on the issue of Free Trade (after the Conservatives adopted a Tariff Reform policy in the early 1900s) Winston was intensely disliked by the Conservative Party. The friendship between FE and Winston did each of them considerable harm in their Parties.

Clementine Churchill never liked FE and disapproved of FE's influence on the impressionable Winston. FE's influence caused Winston to drink too much and gamble.

At that time, politics and the law were exclusively male pursuits and this suited FE. The communities he loved particularly strongly, Wadham College in Oxford, Gray's Inn, the legal circuits and the House of Commons were all male communities from which women were excluded. Although the great hostesses of the day had considerable powers of patronage, serious political discussion at their tables only began after the ladies had left the room.

FE's mother enforced the rules of male domination with vigour. When either FE or Harold came home in the evening as young men, the two daughters of the house were always ordered to immediately leave the armchairs so that the men could have the comfortable seats. Margaret's interests were artistic and musical, totally unlike those of FE, and Margaret was content to leave politics to him. By contrast Clementine Churchill was always trying to influence Winston's political conscience.

Although devoted to his wife, FE had a reputation as a 'ladies man' and very much enjoyed female company.

In 1910, FE defended Ethel le Neve, the mistress of Dr Crippen on a charge of being an accessory after the fact to the murder of Mrs Crippen. He was deeply hurt that his successful defence produced no word of thanks from his client.

In the years before 1914, the Home Rule issue became more important and divisive. On 28 September 1912, FE joined with Carson and others in signing the Ulster Covenant in Belfast whereby the men of Ulster pledged themselves to maintain the union with Britain.

On his return to Liverpool, FE and his wife were met by a crowd of over 100,000, the largest gathering ever seen in the City of Liverpool. However, while publicly supporting Carson's Ulster Volunteers, FE was negotiating behind the scenes with the Liberal Government and particularly Churchill and Lloyd George to avoid likely civil war in Ulster. His particular talent for oratory on a public platform was complemented by his skill at intimate negotiations and conciliation in private discussions.

For a period at the start of the War FE served at the Front. In 1914, FE was appointed Chief of the Press Bureau responsible for the censorship of war reporting. In this position he had the power to enforce the suppression of information but, in FE's own words, he preferred to 'give the benefit of the doubt' to battle reports. In practice, this meant that he allowed newspapers, particularly local newspapers, to publish letters from soldiers at the Front giving an extraordinary degree of information about the battles and the loss of life and the dreadful conditions at the Front. Thus, while the national policy of censorship prevented much sensitive military information from being published, particularly in the National Press, the population was able to understand the unfolding horror on the frontline, not only through private letters from members of their own families but through many of these being published in local newspapers. This had a considerable influence on the public's perception of the War. The Times circulation nationally was 150,000 and was dwarfed by the cumulative circulation of huge numbers of local newspapers, such as the Formby Times and the Southport Visitor, the Crosby Herald, as well as the Liverpool Daily Post and Mercury. In 1915, he was appointed to replace Carson as Attorney General on a reduced income of £5,000 per annum. It is often considered that his best public service was in this period. He was then at the height of his powers.

Sir Roger Casement had a distinguished career in the Civil and the Colonial Service for which he was knighted in 1911. He was, however, an ardent Irish nationalist and after the outbreak of war in 1914 went to Germany. In Germany, Casement tried to persuade Irish soldiers in prisoner of war camps to join an Irish brigade to land in Ireland and fight the British. He found it very difficult to get recruits.

He returned to England a year later for reasons which have never been clear and was indicted for high treason. The diaries of Casement were shown, perhaps improperly, to various persons connected with the Trial and in public life. Casement was a homosexual and the diaries included details of sexual perversion.

Considerable controversy was caused by FE and others showing copies of the diaries and also by doubts over whether the diaries were genuine. Casement was convicted and his appeal dismissed by the Court of Criminal Appeal. Casement was duly executed.

FE was returned in 1918 for the West Derby Division of Liverpool which, following boundary changes, contained most of the voters from his old constituency of Walton. Immediately on returning to London, Lloyd George offered him his old position of Attorney General outside the Cabinet, which FE refused. Lloyd George then replied "How about the Woolsack?" and required an answer by 10.00am the following morning.

As FE's family were away in the country he could not obtain Margaret's opinion. FE spent most of the night debating the matter in his mind and had not made a decision when he arrived at No. 10 Downing Street for the agreed breakfast meeting. It turned out Winston Churchill was breakfasting there also. By the time breakfast was finished, Winston and FE had both decided that he should accept the Woolsack.

The decision to become Lord Chancellor cut FE off from further political advancement and also from the chance of a return to the Bar. More seriously, it reduced his income substantially.

King George V wrote to Lloyd George asking for FE's appointment to be reconsidered on the ground that "His Majesty does not feel that Sir Frederick has established such a reputation in men's minds as to ensure that the country will welcome him."

The appointment was equally unpopular both with the Bench and the Bar. Nevertheless, FE received the Great Seal on 14 January 1919 and on 13 January 1919 as Sir Frederick Smith he presided over the hearing on his first appeal. On 3 February 1919, he was created a Peer under the title of Baron Birkenhead.

Very much against expectations, FE excelled in all three aspects of his work as Lord Chancellor, firstly in Cabinet, secondly as head of the judicial system and thirdly, as Speaker of the House of Lords.

It was particularly surprising that his judicial demeanour was above reproach. In later life he was proud of the fact that no observation of his made whilst sitting on the Bench was ever followed by the reporters' phrase 'laughter in court'.

His efforts as a law reformer were considerable. Although the great property legislation of 1925 was the product of others also, it was his parliamentary gifts which enabled the legislation to pass.

He attempted to reform the outdated Circuit and Assize systems but was defeated by the conservatism of local politicians who feared the loss of prestige which would follow the abolition of an Assize.

At least twice he resisted Lloyd George's attempts to influence judicial appointments. In Cabinet he seldom spoke and then only when he was certain he had something valuable to say.

In the House of Lords, Birkenhead successfully adapted the tone of his public oratory and Commons style to the totally different atmosphere of the Peers.

In the late summer of 1921, FE altered his stance from a policy of meeting force with force in Ireland to a conviction that settlement was necessary. In the delicate negotiations with the Irish Delegation in November and December 1921, FE quickly established a relationship of trust and confidence with Michael Collins.

Michael Collins recorded his admiration of FE's help and described him as a "lawyer but with a great difference. Concise, clearness of ideas, a great advantage, a good man." Quite a transformation from the period some 10 years earlier when FE supported Carson's Ulster Volunteers and their violent opposition to Home Rule.

On concluding the Treaty, FE remarked to Collins that by his signature he had probably signed his political death warrant to which Collins replied, "I may have signed my actual death warrant". This turned out to be true because not long afterwards Michael Collins was assassinated by the anti-Treaty force in the Civil War in Ireland.

When the Treaty was debated in the Lords, FE not only persuaded a reluctant House to agree a measure which struck at the fundamental principles of Unionism but also defended himself against the charge that he had deserted his own personal convictions in order to sign the Treaty. His recent friend and colleague, Lord Carson, attacked him with extraordinary venom as 'most loathsome'.

Following the famous Carlton Club meeting in October 1922 and the withdrawal of Conservatives from the Lloyd George coalition, the Government collapsed to be replaced by a Conservative Government led by Bonar Law and FE was replaced as Lord Chancellor. At the age of 50 he found himself "powerless, restless almost alone". He was disliked and distrusted by his own party, the Conservatives, both for his refusal to desert the Lloyd George coalition and for his support of the Irish Treaty.

The excesses of his behaviour prior to being Lord Chancellor and his personal extravagance seemed less attractive than when he was younger.

Intellectuals often despised FE's populism which pandered to some fairly crude emotions of the masses. Many intellectuals particularly hated his cynicism and hypocrisy. This contempt caused FE many problems throughout his career and particularly after his fall from power after the Carlton Club meeting in Autumn 1922.

Representative of the contempt of left wing intellectuals for FE was the Catholic poet, GK Chesterton. When FE criticised the Welsh Disestablishment Bill in 1912 as "a Bill which has shocked the conscience of every Christian community in Europe", GK Chesterton wrote a coruscating poem entitled *Antichrist, or the Reunion of Christendom: an Ode*, the last verse of which was:

It would greatly, I must own, soothe me, Smith!
If you left this theme alone, Holy Smith!
For your legal cause or civil
You fight well and get your fee;
For your God or dream or devil
You will answer, not to me,
Talk about the pews and steeples
And the Cash that goes therewith!
But the souls of Christian peoples Chuck it, Smith!

FE was able to overcome some of his difficulties with the Conservative Party and was appointed Secretary of State for India in November 1924 when Stanley Baldwin formed his second government. He was the first ex Lord Chancellor since 1754 to hold another Cabinet office.

His Indian policy was cautious. His knowledge of the gulf between Catholic and Protestant in Liverpool and throughout the British Isles helped him to appreciate the communal division between Hindu and Muslim.

He was active behind the scenes in trying to produce a conciliatory formula in the General Strike of 1926. His efforts were praised by Labour leaders of the time

Three close friends, Lloyd George, FE Smith and Churchill, 1922.

His extravagance had to be matched by embarrassing attempts to raise income in ways not thought suitable for an ex Lord Chancellor.

His financial problems in his latter years were caused, as usual, by his extravagance but, additionally, FE spent an anticipated inheritance from his old Client, the ship owner, Houston. Houston intended to leave FE a substantial fortune. His expectations were well known and were reported on Houston's death in 1926 by which time FE had spent much of the money in advance. Unfortunately it appears that he had offended either Houston himself or his newly acquired, fortune hunting, second wife, and in the end Houston's millions were diverted to his widow and his secretary and FE got nothing.

FE acquired various directorships in the City and a controversy arose over whether he was entitled to continue receiving a pension of £5,000 as an ex Lord Chancellor. However, he had entered the City too late to make an impression.

In the Spring of 1930, he fell seriously ill whilst on holiday in Biarritz. After an attack of pneumonia he died at 32 Grosvenor Gardens on 30 September 1930. After cremation, his ashes were taken to Charlton. His Will left everything to his wife. His gross estate was valued at £63,223 but this was wiped out by debts. Memorial services were held in Liverpool Cathedral, Birkenhead School and Westminster Abbey.

EDWARD GEORGE HEMMERDE KC

By William Lister

Spy cartoon of EG Hemmerde.

Edward George Hemmerde was born at Peckham in London on 13th November 1871, the third son of the manager of the Imperial Ottoman Bank. His life was destined to have all the elements of a Greek Tragedy.

He entered Winchester College in 1884, where he rowed, and was also a member of the Cricket XI in 1890. He went to University College, Oxford that year, ultimately gaining a First in Moderates and then stayed there gaining a succession of degrees until 1896, rowing and playing cricket among legends. He was also a creditable athlete.

As a member of the Standing Committee of the Oxford Union he daily associated with some of the brightest and best of his generation – people like John Simon, CB Fry, Hilaire Belloc and crucially FE Smith who became a close friend, and had a great influence on his life.

He was called to the bar as a member of The Inner Temple in 1897 and joined the Northern Circuit, his chambers being at 25 Lord Street, Liverpool, and he also had London Chambers at 1 Hare Court in the Temple. The Bar at Liverpool was regarded as a fashionable alternative to London, and its attractions included a group of 'Admirable Crichtons' whose ability was only equalled by the variety of their attainments, according to Sir David Maxwell Fyfe. The City of Liverpool was then at its zenith with its busy Atlantic Seaport, booming commercial activity (and litigation) and it was referred to as the second city of the Empire. It was no great distance from London, with train journeys taking just 4 hours. The midnight sleeper was popular. It was the heyday of Manchester men and Liverpool gentlemen, as the daily show of bowler hats in Liverpool city centre attested.

Ted Hemmerde, as he was always known, won the Diamond Sculls at Henley in 1900, which was probably then the most sought after and prestigious amateur single rowing title in the world. That year he also stood unsuccessfully as the Liberal candidate for Winchester.

The next 10 years of his life were to be a complex period of activity filled with an abundance of rich promise. He had already become a welcome member of Edwardian Society through his University acquaintances, his important manly amateur sporting reputation, together with the prospect of a seat in Parliament. This was the period of the long summer of Edwardian England. Weekend house parties and country house cricket were at their peak, in a social world that seemed destined to go on forever.

It is tempting to think that he was persuaded to practise at the Liverpool bar by his great friend FE Smith who was himself called to the Bar in 1889, and had entered chambers in his home city of Liverpool. Hemmerde was a guest at Smith's wedding in 1901.

They began to appear with and against each other in increasingly important litigation. At that stage great futures were predicted for both of them, and it was difficult to say who would go higher.

What Hemmerde was earning by way of fees at this period is unknown, but FE Smith's earnings are said to have topped the enormous sum of £6,000 in 1905, which he needed to support his extravagant lifestyle.

In 1906, Hemmerde fought 2 by-elections for the Liberals, winning at East Denbighshire after considerable personal constituency support from Lloyd George. FE Smith entered Parliament for a Liverpool constituency on behalf of the Conservatives that year, thus maintaining their parallel progress.

The big and fashionable cases continued. An example was when Lord Lever recovered enormous damages against Lord Northcliffe – indeed the damages were four times the previous largest libel award.

Smith and Hemmerde were appointed Kings Counsel together in 1908, and in 1909 Hemmerde was appointed Recorder of Liverpool by the Lord Chancellor of the then Liberal Government led by Asquith.

Hemmerde was an active speaker in the House of Commons, mainly on legal and financial matters and was clearly regarded by the Liberal Party of Asquith and Lloyd George as a coming man of the highest calibre, not only a potential Law Officer of the Crown but perhaps a future Lord Chancellor (an office that was to be filled in due time by his friends Smith and Simon). He was scrupulous in making his political speeches away from Liverpool.

Furthermore, his first play, *A Maid of Honour* was performed in that year under the pen name Edward Denby, at the Queens Theatre in London's West End. It had but modest success.

The 'Spy' caricature of the Edward Hemmerde of 1909, published in *Vanity Fair* on the occasion of his Recordership, shows a tall, slim, handsome and elegant young man with a carnation in the button-hole of his tail-coat; he is seen banging his fist into the palm of his hand, making a forceful point. The genius of 'Spy' was his ability to make a uniquely pointed observation of a man, and his caricatures chronicled their generation. (Smith's caricature had appeared 2 years earlier in 1907, and had been described as a devastating indictment of an ambitious and unpleasant person. It was also said that it might have ruined the career of a lesser man!).

It is necessary to pause here to consider the political situation in which Hemmerde now found himself, because it forms the basis for much of what happened to him in the ensuing 25 years. He had only been a member of the Liverpool Bar until his appointment. Politics were not an issue.

Feelings ran high politically and religiously, and the shadow of Home Rule lay more darkly over Liverpool than any other city save Belfast – just across the Irish Sea. It was a city dominated by the Conservative Party. Some would say that it was 'sewn up'.

The new Recorder stepped directly into this particularly Liverpool brew. It was said that his appointment 'took Liverpool by surprise'. It seems apparent that a Liberal Government had imposed a Liberal Recorder on a Conservative city, without the normal consultation. Liverpool was not just any Conservative city. The appointment may not have been an insult, but it was a provocation.

Hemmerde was a silk of just one year's standing at the time and aged only 38. It was a Crown appointment, like a High Court Judgeship, and was second only in importance (and remuneration) to the Recorder of the City of London. Liverpool City Council paid his salary. There must have been much consternation among the Conservative Leadership.

The outcome was that for the next 10 years, the City, in the person of the Town Clerk, sent him no briefs at all. This was an unheard of slight. Indeed it was studied insolence. Convention, courtesy and common sense dictated that a City brief its Recorder, if only to ensure that he did not appear against the City in important cases. Hemmerde did appear for the prosecution from time to time at the nomination of the Attorney General or the Director of Public Prosecutions, but they would be aware of the tensions such a nomination would entail.

Hemmerde endured the humiliation with stoicism closely akin to dignity, rightly putting it all down to party spite, but it must have galled him. However, his public dignity was not assailed, and he took his proper part in all the City's civic functions, and read the Address of Welcome to the King upon his visit to the City in 1913, which was to be his only moment of Civic dignity.

Up to the moment of his appointment as Recorder, Hemmerde's life had been one of irresistible and unbroken success – but there was a worm in the apple, that would prove well-nigh fatal to his career and reputation over the ensuing years.

The fact is that he was a gambler. People gamble for various reasons – desperation, excitement and greed being the ones that spring most readily to mind. Hemmerde's gambling was fuelled by greed. He had a brother who was a London stockbroker and Hemmerde became dazzled by the thought of the money he could make by speculating in shares on the Stock Exchange. He was making a lot of money, but he was the youngest son in an uncertain profession, and he wanted more money. No doubt he was given Stock Market tips at those House Party weekends and saw others making money from them.

In early 1910 he was already in financial trouble and having to borrow to meet his losses, and he borrowed £1000 from a friend named Joseph Benson. He wrote to Benson:

"It is extremely kind of you to assist me at this juncture by a transaction which is quite outside the ordinary rules of business security and which I recognise to be merely a generous and timely effort to help me over a very unpleasant financial crisis."

He agreed to repay the money in 2 months with interest at the high rate of 7% and he gave securities which he somehow recovered.

Around this time (perhaps before the losses were very great) Hemmerde had lunch with FE Smith and told him of his speculations. When Smith heard of the sums involved, he asked the waiter to get notepaper and an envelope. Putting these before Hemmerde, he ordered him to write to his broker to sell all the stock he had. Hemmerde scorned the idea. The amount involved must have been very large indeed to move Smith to such action, bearing in mind his own cavalier attitude to money. It could be said that this was a defining moment. If Hemmerde had yielded to his friend's strong advice, his life would probably have been quite different.

Not long afterwards, a close political friend received a telegram from Hemmerde saying that he must have £10,000 or he would be hammered on the Stock Exchange as a defaulter. The Liberal Whips raised the sum; four men in the party saved him. He then resigned his seat for East Denbigh in December 1910.

Thus in the year after his appointment as Recorder, and with various sources of income, namely high professional fees, his parliamentary pay, judicial salary and royalties from his play, he was in deep financial trouble that was destined to be his companion for the rest of his days, and in debt to those who had loaned him large amounts of money, which he had gambled and lost. It is also said that he borrowed to the limit from Liverpool money lenders, and on all occasions he utilised his privileged position to ward off his creditors.

His situation seemed to improve after 1910. He tried writing more plays, but they were not accepted. He had become friendly with Francis Neilson, a theatrical producer of experience, who had just won a Parliamentary seat for the Liberals, and it is said they decided to write a play jointly in order to repair their fortunes. The result was *Butterfly on the Wheel*, starring Madge Titheradge which ran for 119 performances at the Globe Theatre in London's West End in 1911. The plot was about a suffragette, a fashionable subject at the time. In fact, Neilson wrote all of it save for the ending of a Divorce Court scene, which could have been written by anyone in the Temple for a fiver, so Neilson was told. Hemmerde was not interested in helping further, but carefully organised the advertisement of it, which asserted that the play was by Hemmerde and Neilson. It also proved difficult to stop him appropriating all the royalties for himself. The play was adapted into a novel later that year.

Worse was yet to come: in 1912, Neilson wrote another play, *The Crucible*. Again, he allowed Hemmerde in, Henry Ainley starred, and the result was exactly the same. After that anything Neilson wrote was taken away from him, page by page, by his family. Hemmerde wrote two or three more plays on his own which were produced, but were not accounted successes. However, his reputation as a successful playwright was secured, and his name continued to be before the public in the high profile litigation in which he was so often briefed.

He returned to Parliament for North West Norfolk in 1912, and 1913 found his name associated with an unsavoury City scandal for which he was severely criticised in a section of the London press.

The war then came and no doubt the burdens of the Recordship of Liverpool were onerous during that period.

In 1915, his creditor Mr Benson had the temerity to approach him about repayment of the £1,000 loan made 5 years previously. He must have been surprised to receive a response in terms,

"I think it is a pity you write to me in such a tone. Have you the slightest idea what these times mean to professional men? I have not been to see you because I had absolutely nothing to tell you but what you must know already."

Mr Benson had creditors of his own, and persisted. He received another response:

"It is not that I won't pay you, but that I cannot do so. What I wrote was not that I saw no prospect at present of being able to repay the capital, but that I saw no prospect of being able to repay the capital at present."

Whether Mr Benson was able to understand the subtlety of Hemmerde's paradoxical distinction is doubtful, but he clearly retired baffled from the field of conflict.

Money continued to be a problem and so Hemmerde retired from Parliament at the 1918 General Election and concentrated on making his living at the Bar, becoming Leader of the Northern Circuit. His friend Smith had become Attorney General in 1915. In 1919, with the arrival of a new prosecuting solicitor in the Town Clerk's Department, briefs from the Corporation began to appear on Hemmerde's desk, but it proved to be a false dawn. Smith became Lord Chancellor in 1919.

The unfortunate Benson's financial problems had forced him into a Deed of Arrangement with his creditors, who were made of sterner stuff and they sued Hemmerde for the repayment of the loan. He simply did not have the money and could not even raise another loan, and so felt compelled to defend the action, pleading the Statute of Limitations 1623 as his defence. Quite simply, he said, the loan was 10 years old, and proceedings for its recovery had become statute-barred after 6 years. The creditors pleaded that the second 1915 letter was an acknowledgment of the debt, and that time had thereby started to run again.

The writ was issued in 1920. Once the case, at first instance, opened in March 1921, the genie was out of the bottle, and could not be put back in: Hemmerde lost his honour from that day. His arguments in law were strong, but the morality was dreadful. One will never know what went on behind the scenes, but it would seem to have been a case that was eminently settleable on compromise terms with reduced costs, even up to the moment that the trial started.

Hemmerde lost at first instance before Bailhache J, then won by a majority in the Court of Appeal in June 1921, and the creditors appealed to the House of Lords (whose judgments are reported in Law Reports (1922) 2 AC 507.) They found unanimously for the creditor in July 1921, saying that the 1915 letter was a sufficient acknowledgment of the debt to take the case out of the Statute. It is clear on reading the judgments that some of their Lordships were troubled by the merit in the arguments put forward on behalf of Hemmerde (who was never mentioned by name, but purely as 'the debtor') but it is clear that there was a very frosty atmosphere. In the event, therefore, Hemmerde had to find the cash to repay the debt, interest at 70% and the costs of both parties for 3 hearings.

The whole thing was an unsavoury spectacle. The Press had a field day. It was as if the Bishop of Liverpool had pleaded the Gaming Act. His friends, who had tried to dissuade him, despaired. It was an end of his professional hopes and he was a man dishonoured in public, but he did not see it that way.

It made a major difference to the attitude of Liverpool City Council, its leaders and Town Clerk. It must have caused consternation and loss of Civic pride. From that moment on they ceased to brief him once more. Liverpool Council would have loved to dismiss him as Recorder, but they could not as his was a Crown appointment. They decided to treat him as if he did not exist, but they under-estimated their man. Hemmerde later estimated that their professional boycott of him lost him £10,000 – £20,000.

There were other troubles, too, around this time that contributed to the deterioration of his relationship with Liverpool City Council. In 1920, there was a new Town Clerk, George Etherton (who stayed for 2 years) and Alderman Sir Archibald Salvidge took over as undisputed Conservative Leader of the City Council, becoming the 'uncrowned King of the City', and woe betide any Town Clerk who did not do Salvidge's bidding. At this moment Hemmerde joined the Labour Party.

If there was one thing that Salvidge disliked more than the Liberal Party, it was the Labour Party, and Hemmerde's membership of it, his debt case and subsequent divorce put him beyond the pale.

The Corporation ceased to invite him to Ceremonial junctions, even when Royalty was visiting the City. The Town Clerk ceased to brief him on behalf of the Corporation – even after consulting him in the early stages of cases. In effect, they not only shut the gates of the City against him, but pulled up the draw-bridge as well.

In 1921 there were Sinn Fein outbreaks in the City, and there was a prosecution at the Assizes. Hemmerde was not briefed for the prosecution and was offered the case for the Defence. He took it. His defence was vigorous and involved criticising Liverpool City Police for underhand methods. He was basically successful and even more successful in the Court of Appeal. His success was partially due to the effects of the Police Strike in Liverpool in 1919, when many potential senior officers were dismissed and the quality of the force deteriorated sharply.

The Watch Committee took strong exception to Hemmerde's conduct of the case in attacking the police evidence, which they thought not to be just, and to be unnecessary for the conduct of the defence, implying that as Recorder he should not make a strong defence and should not upset their policemen. The Town Clerk opined that he should never accept briefs for the Defence when there might be grounds for criticism of the Police and he said that the defence had created "a bad atmosphere not favourable to the Recorder." Hemmerde's rejoinder that the solution was in their own hands, and that they should brief him in such matters, was ignored. The sheer effrontery of the attitude of the Watch Committee was an insult to justice, but it shows how things were in Liverpool politics, and how low the Recorder had fallen in their esteem.

It is important to comment here that on no occasion was there any ground for criticising Hemmerde as an advocate, either in this case or any other. He did his work thoroughly and professionally in the highest traditions of the Bar and was popular among his Solicitor clients. As Recorder, he had the confidence of the Bar.

In September 1921, some well-known agitators seized the Walker Art Gallery in such numbers and in such manner on behalf of the unemployed of Liverpool as to constitute a riot, with a view to telephoning the Lord Mayor. They were tried before Hemmerde and convicted. Sentencing them was difficult, as prison would make martyrs of them. Furthermore, the circumstances of their arrest by Liverpool Police were profoundly disquieting to the Recorder, and the two main agitators had been badly injured. He did not send them to prison which was what had been expected, because the two concerned "had been cruelly and most improperly punished already by the police themselves."

He warned the Police about their violent conduct towards the citizens of Liverpool. He offered to bind over the prisoners. They refused, preferring to go to prison and become martyrs. He therefore sentenced them to one day's imprisonment, which meant immediate release. The following day the leading agitator asked to see Hemmerde, on behalf of all the defendants, to thank him for acting as he did. He said that they all felt that Hemmerde had put them on their honour, and that they would not let him down. They kept their word.

The Watch Committee was again upset, and held 'an independent enquiry' without any transcript of what had happened or been said, and without troubling to make enquiries of any sort from the Recorder. The enquiry's results do not seem to have been published. All this would have been more than enough for most men, but Hemmerde was undeterred.

Having joined the Labour Party, in 1922 he was elected Member of Parliament for Crewe, at a time when no party commanded a majority, and in 1924 Ramsay MacDonald formed the first Labour government, although it was a minority party.

Hemmerde anticipated that he would become Attorney General. There was no one of any stature to stand against him. MacDonald was conscious of the fragility of his Ministry and mindful of the scandal of the 1921 House of Lords decision; he could not afford the luxury of Hemmerde who did not get the appointment. He went public in the newspapers once again with his discontents which was typical of the man, but tactless in the extreme.

He also had to face the inevitable taunts of carpet bagging – that he had only joined the Labour party in the hope of office, and not because of any political conviction, but Professor W Lyon Blease, who was a practising barrister in Liverpool before he later became Dean of the Faculty of Law at Liverpool University, was to acquit him of that charge, writing at his death

"He was a man of considerable knowledge and whatever he was, he was not a time server and when he left the Liberal Party for the Labour Party, he did it from honest motives and not merely in search of office."

Hemmerde gave up his seat in Parliament later that year at the General Election, and retired finally from politics.

In 1926, he suffered the most grievous blow of all. His only son was killed in a factory accident on a coffee plantation in Kenya, where he was working as a trainee.

About this time, Mr Justice Rigby Swift invited the Town Clerk to lunch and told him bluntly that it was a scandal that Hemmerde was not briefed by the Corporation. The Town Clerk, Walter Moon, was taken by surprise and could only say that he would report the Judge's remarks in the proper quarter ie Sir Archibald Salvidge. Nothing happened.

In 1928 Salvidge died. He had been a great servant of the City of Liverpool, running it politically as a City-State, and making it more powerful even than Birmingham with its Chamberlain dynasty.

He was a nationally known figure in the Conservative party, was knighted in 1916, had the private ear of 3 successive Prime Ministers, and achieved that rarest of national accolades, the office of Privy Counsellor to his King, although a non-Parliamentarian. In his time Liverpool came to exercise greater influence in national affairs than any provincial city had done before or is ever likely to do again. It was due to his vision and drive that the Mersey Tunnel was built. But he did not like Hemmerde.

The next leader of the Council, Alderman (later Sir Thomas) White maintained the same attitude to Hemmerde.

In 1930 FE Smith, Lord Birkenhead, died at the age of 58.

On the face of the matter, the tide ostensibly turned on the briefing boycott, when Hemmerde was briefed in 1931 to lead for the Crown in the Wallace murder prosecution, the most important Liverpool murder case since the Maybrick trial 40 years before. It must be remembered however that this was a case being prosecuted by the Director of Public Prosecutions, who in fact made the nomination of Counsel, after consultation with the Attorney General. However, it was a chance for Hemmerde to shine in his own City, and perhaps change his circumstances.

Ironically, the head of Liverpool CID, who was in charge of the investigation, was the officer he had criticised so fiercely for underhand methods in the Sinn Fein case 10 years before.

The case against Wallace for battering his wife to death was not particularly strong, but the problem was that if it was not Wallace who else could it possibly be? The case was filled with double edged arguments.

"By this stage in his career, both through technical skill and sheer personal dominance, Hemmerde's impact on a jury was immense. He was a remarkably handsome and imposing looking man, to whom ripening age had lent an imposing authority. If he believed – and he usually did quite genuinely believe – that the side he represented was the side of right and truth, he threw into a case his very heart and soul. He conducted this prosecution with his customary fairness, but in a trial there are imponderables to take into account. In the Wallace case, one of them is the effect that would be produced by this able, forceful and convincing personality presenting a charge that he himself felt sure was true." (Edgar Lustgarten in *The Murder and the Trial*, 1960).

In the event, the jury convicted Wallace. The Court of Criminal Appeal took a contrary view, and for the first time ever reversed the verdict of a jury on the ground that it could not be supported having regard to the evidence.

Hemmerde's life returned to what had become its normality and his relationship (or lack of it) with Liverpool City Council irked him more and more until it came to a head, openly, publicly and in circumstances of scandal in 1934.

The Royal visit to open the Mersey Tunnel in 1934 had gone forward without any invitation to Hemmerde to attend. A few days later at the Quarter Sessions over which he was presiding he took the opportunity of "saying a few plain words upon the subject." It was, he said, "impossible for me to keep silence any longer, and in these few plain words I state quite clearly and categorically the real reasons underlying the Boycott." He also wrote a letter to the Liverpool Daily Post setting out the history of the Ceremonial Boycott, which was published.

There was no response from the Corporation, and he was ignored once again. He did not exist.

Letters of protest to Lord Mayors over his exclusion from both ceremonial and legal matters having produced no result at all, he wrote a formal letter of complaint to the Home Secretary on 1st September 1934, asking for his guidance and possible intervention. In the event the Town Clerk was compelled to report the matter to the City Council and a debate took place in public in May 1935.

The Town Clerk's report to the Council was brief and stonewalling. He said that up to 1913 the Recorder was invited to attend Civic Functions and that in that year he read the address of welcome to the King, but that he had not been asked to do so thereafter and that he had no right to claim to do so.

He said the Recorder had no right in law to claim to be briefed by the Corporation, and that finally he had no right to invitations to public functions, but that if he were, he would be entitled to his precedence. As a parting shot, he reminded the Councillors of the House of Lords case.

Liverpool had solved their problem of precedence by simply not inviting their Recorder. They had also solved the problem of briefing him by the simple stratagem of giving a general retainer to another silk, John Singleton KC who was considerably junior to Hemmerde.

The whips were on, and the council accepted the report. Game, set and match to the Town Clerk.

The publicity was immense, and damaged both sides. The following year the Leader of the Council, Sir Thomas White, retired, as did the Town Clerk and the new Leader of the Council, Alderman (later Sir Alfred) Shennan a Liverpool architect, moved swiftly to defuse the situation. As he was later to recall, writing in the Times on the occasion of Hemmerde's death.

"He had been an outstanding figure in the city for the greater part of this century, and won the admiration of all law-abiding citizens, for the way he maintained the highest traditions of his profession.

His zeal for upholding the law was only equalled by his insistence on correct etiquette, both inside the Courts and elsewhere, and many will recall the unfortunate controversy which was waged between him and my predecessor on the order of precedence on ceremonial civic occasions. With the latter's death, the dispute was closed, and following my election as leader of the City Council, he and I always walked alongside each other, and our relationship was most cordial and one of mutual respect ..."

So ended 14 years of invidious strife, and Hemmerde then settled down to repair his practice and reputation. He was Recorder throughout the second World War, with all its strains and he retained his popularity with Liverpool solicitors, as his practice began to grow again. The fashionable London practice of his younger days was but a distant memory.

He was still practising when he died on 24th May 1948. He had been at Manchester Assizes in a case, returned to London, where he was working on papers in his chambers when he was taken ill and died at home of a heart attack the following day at the age of 76, having been the Recorder of the City of Liverpool for 39 years.

Edgar Lustgarten, a practising barrister and a member and close observer of the Northern Circuit said of Hemmerde at this time in his book *The Murder and the Trial*, 1960:

"Hemmerde was something of a stormy petrel. At the fiercely competitive Liverpool Bar of the early nineteen hundreds he had established himself with such rapidity and brilliance that there were those who predicted an even greater future for him than for his dashing colleague FE Smith. He took silk early, entered politics, and for a while his youthful promise looked certain of fulfilment. Private transactions, ill-judged or unlucky, did him grave and permanent disservice; irrepressible combativeness and an outspoken tongue involved him in injurious dissensions; an honourable but unbending pride did nothing to win back those he had estranged. His practice suffered, and though he could always command a fair volume of work upon the Northern Circuit, there is not the faintest doubt that in the twenties and thirties his stature did not equal his professional capacity ..."

Professor Lyon Blease wrote:

"With all this incapacity to bear grievances with dignity, Hemmerde had something heroic about him ... He did his work thoroughly and well and at the end of his life he was busy. He kept his head high in more senses than one and had the figure and movement of an athlete, even in his old age."

Whilst we inevitably look at past events with the eyes of today, with a controversial man like Hemmerde, the only true judgments, to give the measure of a man in his own generation, are those of his contemporaries.

Hemmerde the man, apart from Law and Politics, is difficult to discern. He lost his only son, and after divorce from his wife his closest relative was his only daughter, who does not seem to have married. He named no Club in his formal biographies (perhaps he was excluded as a result of the 1921 case). Apart from politics, he gave golf and cricket as his interests in Who's Who. He lived in London at 13 Beaufort Gardens, South Kensington and earlier at 23 Cadogan Gardens SW1. He never had a house in Liverpool. Sir Hartley Shawcross, in his autobiography, says that he was the most cultured silk on the Northern Circuit. Finally, it must be said that in what is written of Hemmerde there are no affectionate anecdotes, nor is there any humour. To his Solicitors he was urbane, charming and helpful.

Hemmerde left no will. His daughter Cynthia was the Administratrix of his estate of £402.1.9d. He rated a short obituary in Wisden. What more could any Englishman want?

JUDGE CHALLONER DOWDALL

By Charles Elston

Although Harold Challoner Dowdall was one of the two Judges of the Liverpool County Court for nearly 20 years and achieved distinction in several other spheres, when he is remembered today it is likely to be for a rather farcical incident in his life. In 1908, when he was 40 years old and still at the Bar in Liverpool, he achieved the unusual distinction for a junior counsel of being appointed Lord Mayor of Liverpool, and in accordance with normal practice, arrangements were made for his portrait to he painted. He and his wife (of whom more anon) moved in artistic circles and were very friendly with Augustus John (then teaching at the Liverpool School of Art) and he was engaged to paint the portrait. When the finished article was produced it was found to give more prominence to the Lord Mayor's flunkey than to the Chief Citizen himself and the City Council refused to accept it for hanging at the Town Hall. The rejected article ultimately found a home in the Melbourne City Art Gallery where it may well still hang to this day.

Henry Challoner Dowdall was born in 1868 into a wealthy Liverpool family and after education at Rugby and Trinity College, Oxford, he was called to the Bar and entered chambers in Liverpool in 1893. During the pre – 1914 War period he was a part-time lecturer at the Faculty of Law of Liverpool University and even after he became a Judge he continued as an Honorary Lecturer on Ecclesiastical Law. Immediately after his period as Lord Mayor he became the first Chairman of the Liverpool Council of Social Service and continued in that office for 12 years ; then in 1913 he became Chancellor of the Diocese of Liverpool, which office he retained until 1948, adding the Chancellorship of Bristol Diocese in 1919. His successor at Liverpool was Basil Nield, later a High Court Judge and he records that he visited Dowdall at his home for advice as to the duties of the office. Dowdall, then over 80, willingly gave it, and added "I have granted very many faculties, but now I have very few left". He was also active in ecclesiastical affairs in another capacity, being the first chairman of the Legal Board of the National Assembly of the Church of England.

Dowdall took Silk in 1920, and in the following year was appointed to the County Court Bench, remaining in that office until his retirement in 1940. I can well recall him in the late 1930s sitting in Court with a rather resigned air dealing with run of the mill County Court cases and Workmens' Compensation Act hearings which, strictly, were Arbitrations and not Court actions but were hotly, not to say aggressively, contested by some of the powerful young advocates then cutting their teeth at the Liverpool Bar – such as Freddy Pritchard, Scholefield Allen and Dick Forrest. It was not easy at that time to imagine that the Judge had had a varied, interesting and by no means undistinguished career, and it was not until I was consulting reference books for the purposes of this article that I became aware of another facet of his legal career of some note. 'Who Was Who' records that he was 'Draftsman of the York/Antwerp Rules 1924'. These and the 'Hague Rules' represent a highly commendable achievement of co-operation among maritime nations towards establishing reasonable minimum standards of safety at sea and of liability for loss and damage. It seems likely that Dowdall was a member of the drafting team rather than sole author, but even so to have played a part is something he could well be proud of.

In 1897, Dowdall married Mary Frances, daughter of the 16th Lord Borthwick, and she was not only greatly interested in and a patron of the Arts contributing to a number of artistic journals, but also, apparently, a considerable beauty whom numerous painters (including Augustus John) chose to paint. A portrait of her by a well-known portraitist of the day, Charles H Shannon, is in the Walker Art Gallery, and another of her by Augustus John was exhibited at the Walker in 1900 but was retained by the family. Shannon also painted Dowdall's mother and this is also held by the Walker.

When Dowdall became a Judge (or possibly before) the family moved to Oxford and from then until his retirement he used to commute to Liverpool, by train, on a weekly basis. He normally dealt with Workmen's Compensation Act cases on a Friday and it was understood that any case which continued after the luncheon adjournment would get short shrift and would not be allowed to prevent him catching the 3.30 train from Woodside to Oxford. I was familiar with Dowdall's appearance because from Monday to Thursday he lived in lodgings in Hoylake not very far from where I lived and he was to be seen – a tall and rather distinguished figure – walking to and from the station. He regularly attended concerts organised by the Hoylake Chamber Concerts Society (of which my parents were founder members – and which is still going very strong after 75 years) and he rather displeased the (female) Hon. Secretary by remarking to her after a recital by the well-known pianist Dame Myra Hess, "Yes, Very nice – but Brahms, don't you know, it really needs a man". He was a man with more sides to his character than he was usually given credit for by those who appeared before him.

MR JUSTICE RIGBY SWIFT

By Judge David Lynch

Rigby Philip Watson Swift was born in St Helens on the 7th June 1874. His father, Thomas, had been admitted as a solicitor in 1862 and had a thriving practice in the town. Thomas had a brother, William, who was Clerk to the Liverpool County Justices. Three of Rigby's elder step brothers became solicitors and one, Ernest, was appointed Registrar of the St Helens and Widnes County Court.

In 1882, Thomas, then aged 50, took the bold step of giving up his practice as a solicitor and went to the Bar. It was a gamble which paid off. He set up chambers at 10 Orange Court, Liverpool and soon flourished. He moved his family from St Helens to 36 Linnet Lane, Sefton Park. With such a family background it is not surprising that Rigby saw his future in the law.

After 5 years at Parkfield School and aged 17, he decided he would become a barrister. He went into his father's chambers and, very much as an articled clerk, spent the next four years learning law and procedure, taking an external London LLB in his spare time. By this time his father had moved Chambers to 8 Harrington Street. There is no doubt that this very practical approach to study under the watchful eye of his father gave him an advantage over his competitors. The Liverpool Bar was extremely strong at this time. Tobin, Kyffin Taylor (Lord Maenan), Lawrence (later Lord Justice), William Pickford (Lord Sterndale, master of the Rolls), Greer (Lord Fairfield), Horridge (High Court) and FE Smith (Lord Birkenhead) held sway in the City.

Rigby Swift (centre) during the Whitehaven Colliery Disaster inquiry, 1910. On the right is Frederick Bodel (Swift's Junior during the inquiry) who was killed at Ypres in 1917.

On the 26th June 1895, Swift was called to the Bar at Lincoln's Inn and elected to the Northern Circuit on 30th July 1895, proposed by Pickford. It took time to make his mark. After two years he described himself as 'excessively impecunious'. It was a state of affairs which would not last!

The accounts which I have taken from Edgar Fay's excellent biography of Swift show the following gross receipts:

Age	Year	Guineas
21	1895	38
22	1896	52
23	1897	124
24	1898	240
25	1899	422

On the death of his father in 1899, Swift took over the Chambers. He was soon joined by young men of ability to help him pay the rent. Greaves-Lord (later a High Court Judge) was the first. In 1902, Swift married Martha Walmsley at All Hallows, Allerton.

In 1904, he earned over 3000 guineas which enabled him to move to larger chambers on the ground floor of 25 Lord Street immediately below FE Smith. By 1910 Leslie Scott, FE Smith, Tobin and Greer were in London. Swift became the leading Liverpool Junior – the solicitors' first choice. He was a superb jury advocate. He began to spend more time in the Court of Appeal and the House of Lords.

In October 1910 Swift decided to seek his fortune in London. Horridge had just gone to the High Court and Swift took over his Chambers at 1 Garden Court. His first application for Silk was unsuccessful but in 1912 he was one of 17 names in Lord Haldane's list. Another was a fellow Northern Circuiteer Gordon Hewart (later Lord Chief Justice).

Swift fought St Helens for the Conservatives in January 1910. He lost to the sitting Labour Member Thomas Glover by 795 votes. As with Silk he succeeded at his second attempt, this time only eleven months later in December. The Liberals introduced the Parliament Bill designed to prevent the House of Lords obstructing government legislation. The Government went to the Country as the issue was of supreme constitutional importance. This time Swift won by 264 votes and held the seat for 8 years until replaced by James Sexton.

Swift did not enjoy his time in Parliament. He found politics and the law a difficult mix. Rather than making a fuss in the chamber he sought to resolve the problems of his constituents by dealing directly with the Government department concerned. The Prime Minister commended him for the considerable time he gave to Government wartime Boards and Commissions.

Swift was a tremendous success in Silk. He had too much work. He decided to charge 100 guineas to take a case out of London. The following year he raised the figure to 200 guineas but it did not help. If anything solicitors were more anxious to brief him. In 1915, he was made a Bencher of his Inn.

FE Smith was appointed Lord Chancellor in January 1919. In June the House of Commons passed a motion increasing the number of Queen's Bench Division Judges from 15 to 17 (there are now over 70) in order to combat the ever increasing arrears of work. On the recommendation of the Lord Chancellor, the vacancies were filled by Swift and another Northern Circuiteer His Honour Judge Acton, who was the first County Court Judge to be promoted to the High Court. Swift was only 46. He was the youngest High Court Judge.

Although severe when it was necessary Mr Justice Swift was a merciful Judge. He was a frequent visitor to prisons and the conditions he saw resolved him to avoid prison sentences wherever possible. He said in 1930, "I have defended them, prosecuted them and for years I have tried them. I know that there is a very great deal of good in the very worst of them."

He was, however, as were most judges of his time, a forceful judge. He dominated his Court. He would not tolerate what he perceived to be a challenge to his authority or a lack of respect for his Office. Of the Bar he demanded the highest standards. No member of the Circuit went before him less than fully prepared.

If he saw a second rate performance, he would take the offender severely to task and he did not hold back. He developed the habit of tapping on the Bench three times with his pencil before intervening to reprove Counsel or the witness. Advocacy was so important to him. He said,

"Young Lawyers are taught about contracts, tort and real property. Yet I have never heard of anyone teaching the laws of advocacy. Law students should be taught how to stand up, how to speak up, how to dry up and how to shut up. My criticisms are not letting down the Bar, I am doing my best to make a better Bar."

Swift had a good sense of humour and enjoyed resourcefulness in the face of an apparently hostile Tribunal. Once he thought a barrister was too long on cross examination. Tap, Tap, Tap. "Where are we getting Mr Pritchard?" he enquired with feigned weariness. "About the middle of my cross examination, my Lord," was the reply. The judge always enjoyed telling that story.

Swift never forgot his roots and was delighted when in 1935 he received from Liverpool University an Honorary LLD. It much pleased him to receive it at St George's Hall where he had learned his craft.

He sat with distinction until his death on the 14th October 1937. He was 63 years old and had survived his wife by six months. Lord Hewart said of him, "He was an independent, humane, learned and direct judge. He never left anyone in doubt as to what his opinion was. All of us who knew him knew not only his acute mind, but his heart – his large heart and generous disposition."

FRANK WELD

By Brian Whitlock Blundell

Frank Weld. *Walter Weld (Frank's father).*

The coast road from Woodvale to Southport was laid on the track of the Cheshire Lines railway from Liverpool Central to Southport Lord Street. Francis Joseph Weld (known as 'Frank') travelled on the first train in 1884 and on the last in 1952. He was a man of the railway age and never owned a car. He had no need of one: there was always a porter from Birkdale Station (on the surviving line to Southport) to trundle his bags the short step to his house, 32 Weld Road, from and also to the train.

The Welds were major landowners with estates in a number of counties, the main one being at Lulworth in Dorset. Frank Weld's father, Walter, was a son of the Leagram Estate at Chipping in Lancashire which had been retained by the family when Thomas Weld gave Stonyhurst to the Jesuits in 1794. Walter built 32 Weld Road in Birkdale, then being developed on part of another Weld property, the Ince Blundell Estate. He practised as a Solicitor in Liverpool and was joined later by Frank who qualified in 1897.

Frank was President of the Liverpool Law Society in 1924. He was a brilliant conveyancer in the days when that meant something. He had a keen legal brain and when the Law of Property Act 1925 was passed he spotted a weakness in it which affected the two Weld-Blundell ladies who held the Ince Blundell Estate as tenants for life. It was he who secured a correction in the Law of Property (Amendment) Act 1926.

The firm moved from 15 Lord Street to 14 Castle Street, where Frank was joined by another member of the clan, Edric Weld. The firm flourished but the office nearly came to a halt once a year when Frank was arranging the annual meeting of the Fifteen Club of which he was secretary. This was a Catholic club of 15 peers and 15 commoners who dined once a year at Claridges.

Frank was a senior member of the Knights of Malta and the commuters on the Liverpool train sometimes enjoyed the sight of him going to a meeting in full fig, a truly magnificent full dress uniform with a cocked hat.

Frank never married, but he was the guardian of Lord Acton's children. He brought up that boisterous family – a boy and four girls – at 32 Weld Road. He entertained in some style, with a house party for the Grand National. At his dinner parties, if things were dragging, he would take his parrot out of its cage and pass it round the guests. On other occasions, if things were going well, the party would move off to the Fun Fair. The sight of Frank Weld, no longer young, in white tie and tails flying down the roller-coaster sticks in the memory.

He died in 1958 aged 84. The world was changing fast. 32 Weld Road was sold and demolished. The Ince Blundell Estate was broken up, but happily his father's family home at Leagram soon came into the hands of his nephew, Charles Weld-Blundell.

SIR WILLIAM WATSON RUTHERFORD BART ET AL

By Graeme Bryson

Sir William Watson Rutherford.

There were many worthy Liverpool lawyers in the Rutherford family over quite a long period but Sir William Watson Rutherford Bart was the 'fons et origo'. In my young days, the very name Rutherfords Solicitors breathed confidence. Sir Hugo Rutherford and his cousin Laurence Rutherford then stood at the helm. Hugo had married Isobel Smith sister of Bertie Smith, senior partner of my own firm, TJ Smith and Son. Hugo Rutherford, as President of the Liverpool Chess Club, signed my prize in 1929/30 for winning a Chess Tournament – Osborne's Law Dictionary! The Rutherfords for generations had daily lunch at the Liverpool Chess Club in the Temple in Dale Street. In due course, my father and I and many other Liverpool lawyers joined them. The Club moved in the thirties from The Temple to the basement of North House, with Rutherfords only a few storeys above in the same building! North House was a posh new building(1931) created and occupied jointly by the Rutherford family and architect Sir Ernest Shennan, leader of the City Council. Ernest Shennan called at my own firm at 8.00am every morning to discuss the profitable (I would think) development of the suburbs.

The Liverpool Chess Club was always divided into half bridge and half chess. After a distinguished

Laurence Rutherford.

century as a gentleman's club, the club did not survive the Wold War II. The bridge players, with quite a few lawyers including Hugo and Laurence Rutherford, moved across Dale Street to the Artist's Club.

But to go back a bit, the first of the legal Rutherfords in our present context was William Watson Rutherford, born in Liverpool in 1853, and like his Chancery barrister brother John (father of Laurence), schooled at Merchant Taylors, Crosby. On qualifying as a solicitor, he became in due course a partner with Alderman John Hughes, under the lengthy title of Miller, Peel, Hughes and Rutherford. Miller lived in the castellated 'Millers Castle' a folly which he had built in 1831 before the northern docks were extended. The firm's Brewery and Conservative party interests brought WW into local political life as Councillor for Netherfield. When Chairman of the Tramways Committee, he changed the city street trams from horse-drawn to electric.

Earlier, he had failed to enter Parliament, but another opportunity came when he was Lord Mayor in 1902/3. So he resigned as Lord Mayor, fought and won the election at West Derby, defeating Richard Durning Holt, and he was then re-elected Lord Mayor! The local press reported that he "finished his year with the brilliance of a meteor."

In 1892, he had been President of the Liverpool Chess Club, said at the time to "have no superior in the United Kingdom or elsewhere." He was made a baronet in 1923, but he enjoyed the honour for only another four years at his home Ingleside, Carnatic Road, Liverpool.

About this time (the twenties), there were four Rutherfords in the firm and the title was shortened to 'Rutherfords', which is how I first remember it. Charles Henry Rutherford was Lord Mayor in 1921, and in due course he succeeded his cousin, Sir Watson Rutherford, as senior partner. Being the eldest son, Hugo inherited the baronetcy, and moved up to be senior partner of Rutherfords. He had attended Rugby School and Liverpool University, and had served in the 1914/18 war with the 14th Battalion, the Kings Liverpool Regiment, becoming a Member of Parliament in 1931. He remained faithful to Liverpool, living at Woodlands, Wood Lane, Gateacre. On his death in 1941, his cousin Laurence became senior partner.

Laurence ('LER'), though a first class lawyer, had wider non-political interests, becoming a member of the Committee of the Liverpool Law Society, and President in 1951. He had also been Consul for Rumania (as it was then spelt), being awarded the Star of Rumania. On the Rumanian National Day, and on other relevant occasions, he would fly their national flag from his office window in North House. Consular life was not always dull. On one occasion in his consular office, two Rumanian aristocrats drew pistols and were about to settle their 'affaire d'honneur' with pistol shot. LER persuaded them to wait for a properly conducted duel which, happily, never took place! In the 1914/18 war, he had served with the 7th Battalion of the Kings Liverpool Regiment, being wounded in France. He also served as a Staff Officer at Western Command at Chester. He was a senior mason and Provincial Grand Master. On Hugo's death he was discharged from the army on compassionate grounds. He had 'done his bit' in the First World War.

In 1947, I left private practice to become District Registrar of the High Court, and I was able to realise, even more, how expert and professional were Rutherfords, and other firms too, of course. In particular, many firms had extremely capable managing clerks dealing with contentious business in Chambers, and with specialised work such as Chancery, Admiralty, and the Commercial List. They were very experienced, and stated their case in Chambers very simply and without passion. It was a pleasure to deal with them. Harold Edge of Rutherfords (not related to Michael Edge a later partner) was a typical managing clerk of that time. He, like them all, was loyal, knowledgeable and reliable. In military terms, they were the sergeants of the establishment and quite indispensable. Like their principals, they seemed to go on for ever, as pensions and early retirements were not much on offer in those underpaid days.

The Second World War ended with Laurence the sole remaining member of the family in 'Rutherfords'. He was very forward looking and was keen to embrace the new technology. I well remember the Lord Chancellor's Department insisting on me using a tape-recorder for letter writing instead of verbally dictating to a charming lady of the civil service. It seemed like the sad end of the world. But LER had actually welcomed and installed this new technology well ahead of its time, though I think that his long-serving typist must have had thoughts similar to my own.

LER used to claim that he was the last President of the Liverpool Law Society to pay out of his own pocket for the top table guests at the annual dinner. I well remember my own father, when President, having the same privilege. Happily, there was a 'whip round' of his partners to pay the bill. By the time I was President, things were easier, though the President's Committee Dinner was still a personal and expensive commitment.

LER opened all the mail every morning (as did my own senior partner), which he distributed to his partners at a daily gathering, so he was kept in touch with developments. He was usually last to leave the office at about 6.30pm which cannot have been all that popular with his colleagues and staff. He virtually died in office, as he was working as normal at his desk the day before he died. In 1967, he had a massive heart attack at the age of 75, when the city lost a leading citizen, and many people, including myself, lost a good friend.

I had not seen much of him in his later years. He had a great natural charm and likeableness, which were of a slightly different nature to that of Hugo, though I would not for a moment criticise Hugo.

There were no Rutherfords to follow, but the firm remained strong with names such as Patricia Ellis (Mrs Watmough), Geoffrey Watmough, Philip Crowe, Joseph Arthur Sykes, Tony Ensor, Patrick Kenney, Michael Edge, David Morgan, Michael Ball, Edward Naylor and Andrew Holt. So in 1988, after due consideration, most of the then partners and staff walked proudly into Weightmans. The Rutherford family as lawyers in Liverpool are now a memory, and not a bad memory either, though a little confusing at times as there were so many of them, and mostly very distinguished.

I have been extensively helped by Patrick Kenney who knew Laurence Rutherford from childhood, was articled to him, and was his partner in 'Rutherfords', right through to the merger with Weightmans and beyond!

For the benefit of post-Latin solicitors, 'et al' is short for 'et alios' ('and others' ie the other Rutherfords). In the early years of the twentieth century solicitors would use it in a heading when writing to their own clients, eg *Yourselves ats Smith et al.* I remember Judge Fraser Harrison asking me what 'et al' meant many years ago as barristers would not have had occasion to use the expression. Also, I had to tell him what 'ats' meant!

'Until some decades ago 'ats' (at the suit of) was used instead of '-v-' in a letter heading by a Defendant's solicitor writing to his own client, with the solicitor putting his own client's name first.

Just a final note on Latin which had been a major feature of English law for centuries. I was a joint editor with the Queen's Remembrancer, Master Jacob, of a section of the 4th Edition of Halsbury's Laws of England in 1976 under the general editorship of the Lord Chancellor, Lord Hailsham. He made two firm rules, first that every sentence had to show an authority and, secondly, that no Latin was to be used! I have just looked at my Osborne's Law Directory referred to above. A high proportion of all entries are Latin and, of course, to become a solicitor it was necessary to pass in Latin in matriculation. It must be very easy now to practise the law!'

THE CLASS OF 1932

By Graeme Bryson

Gilbert Farnum, Harry Fry, Norman Ward, Henry Howard-Watson, Alex Cooper, Archie Owen-Hughes, Albert Cohen, Harold Morris. Graeme Bryson, Hilda Boyars, George Routledge, Bill Caldwell, Said Ala-ud-Din. Tom Roberts and Hugh Lamberton are the only Graduates missing from the photograph.

This is the Class of the Faculty of Law at Liverpool University which commenced study in 1929 and graduated in 1932. Their lives and careers therefore span the middle and later part of the century and are representative of the legal profession at that time. Out of fifteen Graduates only one was a woman, no-one got a First Class Honours, there were five Class 2 and five Class 3 Honours and five Ordinary – quite different to the spread of Degrees in modern law Faculties.

In addition to myself the others are:

Tom Roberts and Harry Fry

They both came from Liverpool College, very muscular and self assured. They were typical Liverpool gentlemen of their time.

Harry Fry was a great, heavily-built rugby forward, playing for Liverpool and Lancashire and England. He was articled to Liverpool's Town Clerk, but after the war became a Masonic paid official. He had a 'good war' I believe, with the Royal Army Service Corps, and after the war he and I reformed our old regiments in Tramway Road/Aigburth Road. His wife was in a wheelchair for many years, and he was very caring.

Tom Roberts was equally burly though not quite so tall. He was a cricket wicket keeper, playing for Bootle for many years. His career is described in detail in Ted Birch's piece later in this Volume.

Tom and Harry always sat at the back of the class playing some form of shove-halfpenny and apparently ignoring the lecturer, which earned a rebuke from all the lecturers from time to time. In a class of a dozen it was rather obvious, perhaps intentionally so. Redbrick universities were only slowly admitted to the social scene, and I think that Tom and Harry both felt that they were letting their school down, by taking the degree course and not just being 'articled' and joining the Liverpool Law Students Association, where the better families were represented. This was then the Liverpool custom in business and professions if one did not go to Oxbridge. Sir John Brocklebank, the shipowner, left Oxford and was sent to do a stint as a platelayer in a Newcastle shipbuilding yard before joining the family firm.

Albert Cohen

Also a well known sportsman, a cricketer and a delightful slow bowler, pitching the ball well into the air in a most tantalising way. He came with a strong sporting reputation from Liverpool Institute, and was a first team regular for the University for the cricket and hockey teams. He played for me in my Hightown Club Presidential cricket game, and was very upset when Ken Cranston, previously the England Test Captain (my Captain) 'took him off'.

He had a cricket trial for Lancashire as a young man and he was a leading figure in the Liverpool Competition for Bootle, and later for Southport. He was a Major in the Second World War and apart from the War he practised with Phillip Binnes and later Alex Cooper and played a major role in the Liverpool Law Society, becoming President in 1973/4. He was a very fine after-dinner speaker and his speech at the 1974 Dinner entitled 'Cohen on Keys' was one of the finest ever. He was a delightful fellow student. However, his final years were very difficult for him and his wife, Nancy, as his mental faculties failed.

Said Ala-ud-Din

Ala-ud-Din came from Palestine, returned there immediately after graduation, and was never heard of again. In many ways we were close friends, and he often came to my family home. Nowadays, Palestine and the Holy Land are only a few hours away on a holiday or pilgrimage aeroplane, but in 1929/1932, they still seemed as far away as the moon.

Henry Howard-Watson

His father was a Dale Street defending solicitor of the John A Behn variety with a wonderful office full of ship models. Henry had been head boy at Merchant Taylor School, Crosby, but he was a very slow learner at law, and we were surprised that he did well in the finals. He joined his father in practice, but my recollection is that he died not many years afterwards.

Bill Caldwell

Bill Caldwell was a professional accountant in practice in Warrington, where he was also a Town Councillor and where he became Mayor shortly after. He seemed to be a model of professional propriety and much admired for it. A charming man by nature. Most of us were fresh out of school, while Bill Caldwell seemed to be middle aged. At that time the lectures were from 4.00pm to 6.00pm so that professional people could work in their practices all day, as was the case with all the professors and lecturers. In today's terms, it was almost like going to evening class.

Hilda Elsie Boyars
During the three years course, I do not remember her speaking to any of us. She was, I think, a clerk in the Midland Bank, and she never progressed towards the Bar or to be a solicitor. She came to the lectures and departed and that was it! I never met her again or heard of her. Lawyers at that time were virtually all masculine. The part she played seemed to fit in with the times.

Alexander James Bryce Cooper (often known as 'Mac' because of his Scottish roots)
Alex Cooper was a brilliant chap and got first class honours in his solicitor final examinations, together with various prizes. We were all surprised that his LLB was not with first class honours. He was articled with Simpson North Harley, just opposite the Town Hall. and was transferred to the London Office. He remained with Simpson North Harley until approximately 1970 when he joined his old friend, Albert Cohen, in partnership shortly after Albert's partnership with Phillip Binnes ended. His Scottish roots were evident in his clients such as the Scottish Provident Institution. He recorded everything he did twice, once in the file and again, separately in his diary.

A life long lover of Liverpool he was also a life long fan of Liverpool F C and was the proud possessor of a Season Ticket for a seat near the half-way line in the Main Stand for many years prior to his death. He found it difficult to adjust to change and died suddenly in 1976.

George Routledge
George Routledge seemed to be the same age as our fathers, and he was a father figure to us all. We all liked him. He had been a clerk in the Wallasey Ferries, but at the age of forty or more, he came into money, and decided to take up law as a profession. He made very heavy going of the course, and only just got his degree. To his great credit he went on to become articled and to pass the solicitor's final examination.

He then set up in practice in Birkenhead, and took Norman Ward into practice. I did not meet him again, but recently at a charity function, I proposed a vote of thanks to the actress Patricia Routledge. I was very surprised when she told me that George was her father and her brother was Graham Routledge who left the Bar to enter the Church of England and became a Canon of St Paul's Cathedral but died all too young.

Norman Ward
Norman was almost the typical Victorian fat schoolboy. He seemed very slow thinking and he joined George Routledge at the foot of the LLB exam table. They were always friendly, and he joined George in practice.

Archibald Owen-Hughes
Called Tubby and was a distinguished pupil at Bootle Secondary School. He went on to take his solicitors' final with me, staying at the same hotel in London. After the war, he transferred to the bar, and was in practice in Liverpool until a few years ago.

PROFESSOR LYON BLEASE

By His Honour James Scarlett

If Lyon Blease had been asked how he wished to be remembered, I think he would have replied, "As someone who cared for people with a sincerity which was infectious." To encounter him made you feel that you mattered as a person. Whether as a suffragette, whose cause he championed with speeches throughout the length and breadth of the land, or as a student whom he taught in the Faculty of Law of the University of Liverpool, whether as a member of the Liberal Party, in whose interest he stood for Parliament more than once but unsuccessfully, or simply as a friend in Liverpool, that importance of being accounted a person characterised the experience of meeting him. Had he been alive today, he would have welcomed the Internet with its vast opportunities for learning, but would have been fearful of its possibly restricting effects on personal encounters.

Walter Lyon Blease (known as 'Lyon') was born in 1884, the son of Walter and Mary Cecelia Blease. Walter Blease was a Chartered accountant and partner in the family firm of Blease & Sons, and a magistrate of the city of Liverpool. Mary Cecelia Blease came from a family in which the Liberal tradition was strong. Walter Blease carried into the 20th Century many of the virtues and pleasures of Victorian England. One of those pleasures was tobacco, but to his grandson he once said "Before entering Bold Street, I always knocked out my pipe, in case I met a lady whom I knew." Such was his respect for the greatest city of

England outside the Metropolis – a respect and love for the city which Lyon Blease inherited and shared. He demonstrated that by often walking from his house in Cressington Park to his chambers in Cook Street in the centre of the city, to experience both the grandeur and the poverty of its streets and to encounter its citizens. He wanted the interests of the North of England to be heard and debated in Government and, had he entered the House of Commons, he would have exulted in the cut and thrust of political life, and would have been a vigorous representative of those whom he longed to serve.

Lyon Blease was tall, gangly and very recognisable. Paddy Bryson tells the story of one occasion when Lyon Blease had the amateur role of Julius Caesar at the David Lewis Theatre. He had been duly stabbed and had declaimed 'et tu Brute' and fallen lifeless to the stage and was borne off stage shoulder high on a stretcher carried by two burly soldiers. However, he was so tall that he overlapped the stretcher at both ends by a subsantial margin and the audience was much amused.

If devotion to the city of Liverpool was a mark of Lyon Blease's life, it was almost matched by his love of European Civilisation, and the countries where it flourished. Foremost amongst those was Russia. Of his books perhaps the greatest is his biography of General Suvorov, published by Constable in 1920. He began to write it in 1917 while serving on the staff of a hospital in St Petersburg. On being sent to the Rumanian front in November 1917, his small library of the books which founded his research was placed in a box, later to be pillaged by participants in the Revolution. Subsequently recalled to Odessa, he left Russia eastwards to Vladivostock and later worked in Tokyo, editing an English newspaper.

In the years between the wars, he travelled regularly to Europe, almost always to Switzerland to walk in the Alps in the summer and to enjoy meeting visitors from other countries of Europe, and often to Czechoslovakia where he gave lectures. His house was a mirror of his love of European Civilisation, notably that of Italy. He was a skilled engraver and carved furniture and was a knowledgeable collector of fine books, notably the limited editions of works printed in the Golden Cockerel and Gregynog presses. He also collected pottery, and had a considerable collection of the works of Bernard Leach, whom he had met in Japan. For some years, he was Public Orator of the University of Liverpool and cherished the power of rhetoric; perhaps it comes as no surprise that he loved the stage and relished amateur acting. As a participant in the BBC's *Round Britain Quiz* he enjoyed the challenge of that contest and his encounters with Gilbert Harding. If this seems an unending catalogue of talents, he will be remembered for holding them modestly and with integrity.

Lyon Blease was rather Dickensian in character and manner, as was his Chancery contemporary, Bertram Benas and they were both called to the Bar in 1906 which gave rise to much mutual argument as to seniority. It was very appropriate that in 1921 Lyon Blease was appointed to be Queen Victoria Professor of Law at the University of Liverpool, a position which he held until 1949 when the returned warrior, Joe Turner, took over the professorial Chancery duties at the Law Faculty. He was a popular and good lecturer, despite the dryness of the subject. As with Bertram Benas, the (Birkenhead) property legislation of 1925 made his type of practice increasingly non-profitable and he gradually faded from the Liverpool professional scene,which was a shame after a life time of such worthwhile pursuits. He died in 1963 strongly and fondly remembered by most Liverpool legal practitioners.

MR JUSTICE PRITCHARD

By Charles Elston

When I was an articled Clerk (1934/1939) FEP was, until he took silk in 1937, probably the busiest and best-known of all Liverpool Juniors and he appeared regularly and frequently at the Assizes in both civil and criminal trials. At Assizes he usually appeared with a Leader, but I can recall being in Court on several occasions when he appeared alone, and his quiet, unemotional but authoritative advocacy was impressive and effective. He was never at any pains to disguise his rather low opinion of the judicial abilities of the local County Court Judges and Magistrates and in Lower Courts his manner could appear somewhat condescending. It was no surprise when he was appointed a KC at the then early age of 38. Thereupon, of course, he moved to London chambers and took up residence in the London area but he came regularly to Liverpool when the Assizes were in session and his services as a Leader were soon in demand. FEP's first name was simply Fred – as was his father's – but those who knew him, and most of those who did not but liked it to be thought that they did, always called and referred to him as Freddy.

Having been an Officer Cadet at the Royal Military Academy at the end of World War 1, on the outbreak of World War 2, FEP was commissioned in the Royal Artillery, but he was very soon transferred to the Judge Advocate's Department and from 1939 to 1942 he was a Deputy Judge Advocate with the rank of Major. He was then promoted to Lt. Col. and became an Assistant Judge Advocate General.

At the end of World War 2, FEP returned to the Bar and he also received the (very part-time) appointment as Judge of that historical relic, the Salford Hundred Court of Record but in less than 2 years he was appointed to the High Court bench (again at an age – 48 – which was early at that time). The appointment was announced, and took immediate effect, on the day before an appeal from a decision in favour of the Plaintiff given at Lancaster Assizes was to be heard in the Court of Appeal. I had the conduct of this case on behalf of the Defendants and in the Court below FEP had led RS (Bob) Nicklin (later a County Court Judge at Birmingham) and both were to appear on the appeal. The case did not involve any issue of principle or very large damages, but FEP had been surprised and affronted by the adverse decision at first instance and strongly urged the Defendants to appeal. I travelled down to London on the evening of the day before the appeal hearing and first became aware that we no longer had a Leader when reading the Times over breakfast the following morning. When I reached the Law Courts I found Bob Nicklin pacing the corridor and his first words were "How infuriating of Freddy – he gets us all to the Court of Appeal then goes and gets himself appointed a Judge, leaving me to carry the can when I can think of nothing to support the appeal." Bob put up a good performance but to no avail.

Very sadly, FEP's career as a High Court Judge was tragically short. He suffered a severe stroke in 1953 and had to retire from the Bench. Fortunately, although he had a substantial permanent disability in one arm and one leg, his mental powers were not noticeably affected. He had been appointed to the Bench when there was no retirement age and no pension provision of any sort for the Judiciary and initially his financial future appeared bleak but in the course of time he was able to undertake backroom employment at the Law Courts and the chairmanship of several important committees and of the Governors of his old school, Shrewsbury. His general health was not affected and he lived to the age of 83. The University of Liverpool, where he had taken his Law degree, conferred an Honorary LLD on him in 1956 and he became Treasurer of his Inn – The Middle Temple – in 1964.

Although FEP was, in public, something of an introvert, he had a very lively mind and a very witty turn of phrase, and he was a very entertaining after-dinner speaker when he could be persuaded to perform. The atmosphere of the inter-war years at the Bar and the strong influences of a classical education are illustrated by the ballad composed by Freddy Pritchard and recited at Bar Mess in Liverpool when, as 'Solicitor General of the Northern Circuit' he reported on the activities of the 'stuffs' of the Circuit ie the Juniors not entitled to wear a silk gown.

Judging by the ballad, Freddy Pritchard had a strong love of Macaulay and particularly his *Lays of Ancient Rome* and the resonance between the two would not have gone unnoticed by his audience in the inter-war years but perhaps might not be picked up today!

THE FLAVOUR OF THE INTER-WAR YEARS AND THE BALLAD OF THE LIVERPOOL BAR

(with notes on some of the 'dramatis personae')

This is the ballad composed by Fred Pritchard (later Mr Justice Pritchard) and recited at Bar Mass in Liverpool as a report to the Northern Circuit on the activities of the 'stuffs of the Circuit' – ie the juniors not entitled to wear a silk gown. Lovers of Macaulay will notice the strong resonance between the ballad and Macaulay's *Lays of Ancient Rome*.

THE BALLAD
by Freddy Pritchard

Sir Philip Swift of Liverpool
By his black cap he swore
That the Great Northern Circuit
Should live in peace no more
By his black cap he swore it
And nam'd Commission Day
And bade Bill Graham give it forth
That he was shortly coming north
And with Macnaghten J.

To Cumberland and Lancashire
Bill Graham spread the word
And ev'ryone who lov'd his loins
His loins began to gird
Shame on the coward who shivers
And curses on the MOME
When Rigby Swift of Liverpool
Leaves London and comes home.

But by the yellow Mersey
Was tumult and affright
And Baucher went a nasty green
Whilst Howard Jones turn'd white
And all around the City
The Stuffs stopp'd up the ways
Discussing what might be their fate
Before a few more days.

They held a meeting standing
Outside St George's Hall
Short time was there, you well may guess,
For making plans at all
Out spake OG Morris roundly
Will naught allay your fears?
His bite is nothing to his bark,
I've known the man for years.

Some notes by Charles Elston

Bill Graham – Clerk of Assize for many years. He had a remarkably fruity voice (anyone able to recall Colonel Chinstrap in Tommy Handley's ITMA will have an indication of the sound) – and a nose to match. Neither his wig nor his spectacles were ever quite straight – but he did what was required of him and was popular with the Bar.

AE Baucher had been a solicitor and was older than most of the juniors on the Circuit. In later days he frequently sat – and performed very well – as Deputy Stipendiary Magistrate.

OG Morris was the father of Max Morris, solicitor and partner in Hill Dickinson who was President of the Liverpool Law Society in 1965/6 but died, sadly prematurely, in a car crash. OG left his house in Hoylake during the War to enable the Liverpool and London Protection Association, managed by Hill Dickinson, to move there and he and his wife moved to his home territory near Bangor.

Just then McNeile came flying
All white with haste and fear
"To arms! To arms! You men," he cried,
"Sir Philip Swift is here."
On London Road to Westward
Each member of the Bar
Fixes his gaze and there beholds
The Judge's motor car.

Hugh McNeile (not, of course related to David McNeill J) left his practice at the Bar to take up an administration appointment to become, eventually, Assistant Clerk of Assize.

And swifter, near, and swifter
Doth the red whirlwind come
And now the car is very near
The people are afraid to cheer
But all around us we can hear
The trampling and the hum
Behold, from out the portals
Two trumpeters do bring
Their trumpets. And the world around
Is made to echo with the sound
as musically they propound
that God should save the King.

But the Circuit's face was sad
And the Circuit's speech was low
And darkly look'd they at the Hall
And darkly at the foe.
"His terrifying manner
Has won him dread renown
His ire will be upon us all
Before the sun goes down."

Then out spake Leo Gradwell
That gloomy son of Fate
"To ev'ry man upon this earth
Death cometh soon or late.
And how can man die better
Than facing fearful odds
For the ashes of his fathers
And the temples of his gods."

"Let me go in," he pleaded,
"With all the speed I may
I, with some more to help me
Will hold the Judge in play
In yon Crown Court, no monster,
However fierce he be
As martinet, has ever yet
Abash'd or silenced me."

Leo Gradwell had a distinguished War record being awarded a DSC as Captain of the destroyer escorting convoy PQ17. The Admiralty ordered the convoy to scatter as it believed a German battleship was approaching. Leo gathered as many of the surviving ships together as possible and hid them in the ice floes, after having the ships painted white and then escorted them to safety after the danger had passed. On returning to the Liverpool Bar, he tried to build up an Admiralty practice but that type of work was rapidly diminishing outside London (and was reducing there). He moved to London and became a Metropolitan Magistrate.

Then out spake David Patrick
A Maxwell Fyfe was he
"Lo I will stand at thy right hand
And face the foe with thee."
And out spake David Karmel
An awful blood was he

David Karmel became a QC with Chambers in London but had a busy practice on the Northern Circuit.

"I will abide at thy left side
D'you think he'll notice me?"

Now while these three were tightening
Their bands around their necks
A wave of admiration spread
O'er others of their sex
And stuffs regaining courage
Rush'd brave to their support
And follow'd on their heels and went
Behind them into Court.

Meanwhile the mighty Rigby
Right glorious to behold
His clerk and marshal following
Came in like some great Eastern King
And made my blood run cold.
Full fifty heads were lower'd
Before that great Grandee
Who took his seat amid much dread,
All rob'd in robes of blood-like red,
And fixed his flaming eyes ahead
Where sat the dauntless three.

And then began a battle
The like of which I ween
Has ne'er before on Mersey's shore
Or any shore been seen
Down went the gallant Gradwell
And down went Maxwell Fyfe
And fighting for a felon Karmel yielded up his life.

When at the judge's orders
their bodies were remov'd
he fiercely turn'd on Batt and said
"Convictions must be prov'd
And let it now be known abroad
Throughout all Liverpool,
That, while I'm here, work must be done
With care, and not as though for fun;
And mark my words; for anyone
Who thwarts me as a fool."

Raleigh Batt was Professor of Commercial Law and subsequently of Common Law (both part-time) at Liverpool University from 1919 until 1945 when he was appointed a County Court Judge.

At this the sage Professor
Who hadn't read his brief
Felt rather like a ship must feel
When stranded on a reef,
But with his colours flying

Right gallantly he sank
And Scholefield Allen took his place
In the fore-doom'd rank.

S Scholefield Allen became a QC and Labour MP for Crewe and was not often seen in Liverpool after 1945.

On seeing Scholefield Allen
Sir Philip's noble brow
Frown'd such a frown that in my dreams
I seem to see it now

Before a word was spoken
He issued a decree
That Allen should be taken far
Beyond the lightship at the Bar
Where sharks and monster fishes are
And hurl'd into the sea.

Next enter'd two together
Upon that bloody field
The one was Eric Errington
The other Basil Nield
They stood there full a minute
And openly defied
The monster in the robes of red
Until at length the monster said
With emphasis "I wish you dead"
And then, of course, they died.

Eric Errington also became an MP and QC and received a knighthood.

At last there rose a champion
Who stubbornly defied
Sir Philip Swift until he said
Alas, Alas I'm vanquished
I can't get through this hide.
Stein was that thick skinn'd champion
And still I seem to hear
The rapturous shout that went forth from
The Jews. And even Christendom
Could scarce forbear to cheer.

The statue of Disraeli
Will soon be taken down
And in his stead will raise its head,
Adorn'd in wig and gown,
A new semitic figure
Of whom it shall be told
How Walter vanquish'd Philip
In the brave days of old.

Mr Junior, I move that those Stuffs whom I have mentioned in my speech be congratulated or condoled with as the case may be.

EDWARD WOOLL KC

By William Lister

Edward Wooll was a Norfolk man who was born in Liverpool, on 31st March 1878. He was the eldest son of the Reverend Charles William Wooll, curate of Fairfield Parish Church, Liverpool, a native of Upwell, Norfolk who had married Charlotte Storey of Brunswick House, North Walsham, Norfolk. He then became vicar of Ditton near Widnes in 1884 and lived there until his death in 1910, when he was buried at his birthplace. Edward Wooll was brought up in Ditton and attended Liverpool College, before going on successively to Liverpool University and New College, Oxford, where he gained a first class honours degree in Classical Mods.

He was called to The Bar (Inner Temple) in 1903, and then returned to Liverpool, where he became FE Smith's first pupil at the new chambers that the latter set up at 10 Cook Street and then at his even newer chambers at 25 Lord Street (North Staircase) which comprised 3 rooms and a clerks room.

Harold Jager, who was senior to Wooll, was in the same chambers and he has left a charming portrait of young Wooll's days at the Bar, in his autobiography *Brief Life* (1934). Wooll, he said was FE's best imitator, with the same gift of pungent repartee and a keen and ready wit. In the give and take of chaff in chambers he always more than held his own and not infrequently scored a neat thrust under FE's guard.

He tells a story of a motor journey with Wooll driving FE Smith south from Liverpool to London. Smith's eyesight was not good for the fingerposts, and as they reached Nantwich he enquired where they were. Wooll told him, giving the local Cheshire dialect pronunciation. Smith refused to accept it, and (as he had nothing else to occupy his brilliant mind) adumbrated an accurate pronunciation system based upon the best principles of the English language. It may have been theoretically impressive, but it did not impress Wooll or his sense of humour. At the next enquiry from Smith, his driver pronounced the place name exactly according to Smith's requirement, but in what he insisted was the 'local' dialect, with a result that was quite impenetrable. Both men stuck stubbornly to their principles and bickered all the way down the A5 until they reached Towcester in Northamptonshire when Wooll's pronunciation had moved to the 'mediaeval local' dialect. By this time, Smith had not the slightest idea of where they were and threw in the towel.

'The Grove' at Thornton Hough was Smith's house on the Wirral where he lived well and entertained in style, and kept his beloved horses. Jager says:

"He would often say to (his pupils) Rutledge or Wooll; "I want you to come out to 'The Grove' with me tonight; we must go carefully into that such-and such case." They would go out together; a groom and three horses would meet them at Spital station. Arriving at Thornton Hough, they would potter about the garden; FE and Wooll would practise jumps in the field. I was often one of the party. We would then dine sumptuously, and the rest of the evening would be spent in light and airy persiflage, in chaff, in amusing dissections of various members of the circuit, and in general relaxation. Next morning we would return to chambers, without the important such-and-such case having once been mentioned."

These were heady days for the young Wooll.

When Smith ultimately took Silk and had to vacate his Liverpool chambers Wooll took them over and in 1913 married Nora Goold of Liverpool who bore him 2 sons. The following year, war came and he joined the Cheshire Yeomanry, serving for 2 inactive years in Northumberland before being transferred onto the Staff of the Cavalry Corps in France, where he was mentioned in despatches twice and awarded the OBE. He served there as a Captain until 1919, save for one month's detachment which enabled him to enter Cologne with the 1st Cavalry Division in 1918 after the Armistice and receive the keys of the City from its Mayor, Konrad Adenauer.

At the end of the war, he continued to serve part time with his regiment in the newly formed territorial Army, as a Captain until 1927. He returned to life at the Bar and was immediately much in demand in bigger criminal cases, arbitrations and Local Government Enquiries.

His wife died in 1922 and he threw himself into politics as a High Tory and played a leading part in the activities of the Conservative Party in Liverpool. He fought and lost as a Parliamentary Candidate at St Helens that year and suffered the same fate at Hull the following year.

In 1924 he published his first novel *Man Proposes*, under a pseudonym. It is clear that he was seeking to busy himself to blunt the effects of his wife's death.

In 1928, he transferred his practice to London, with chambers at 1 Hare Court in the Temple (which were Edward Hemmerde's chambers). Having inherited his mother's family property and home at North Walsham in Norfolk he found that his life commuting constantly between Liverpool, Carlisle, London and Norfolk too much of a strain. He remained popular with his Liverpool and Carlisle solicitor clients.

He became Recorder of Carlisle in 1929, thus preserving the link between that City and the Liverpool Bar. Jager commented that he received his appointment from a Socialist Home Secretary, and that it was a tribute to the bluff honesty of Wooll who took no pains to conceal his strong Tory proclivities when he wrote, as was customary, applying for the appointment.

He started to write seriously at this stage – both books and plays. His first venture, a play named *Libel* which was produced in 1934 on the London stage, was the most successful, running for 265 performances at the Playhouse Theatre, and subsequently being produced in 6 other European countries. It was ultimately produced as a film in 1959, directed by Anthony Asquith and starring Dirk Bogarde, Robert Morley, Olivia de Havilland and Wilfred Hyde-White. The Court scenes were extremely dramatic, and the film stands comparison with *Witness for the Prosecution* and *The Winslow Boy* in that sense.

His other 2 plays in 1937 and 1964 call for no comment.

He chose to adopt a pseudonym as the writer of *Libel* – Ward Dorane – an anagram of 'Edward' and 'Nora', which is some indication of how much he treasured his wife's memory.

The play *Libel* was transmuted into a novel in 1935, under Wooll's own name and there were another 3 novels in the next 2 years, none of which (once again) call for any comment. One wonders how well his practice was doing in London, in the face of such literary activity.

At about this period he visited Germany, and had to complete a questionnaire which asked whether he had visited Germany before, and if so, in what capacity. 'Yes' wrote Wooll to the first question, 'As Conqueror' to the second one. It was typical of Wooll's sense of humour: how Hitler's immigration officers viewed the matter is unrecorded.

In 1939, his *Laymans Guide to Libel* was published, but at that moment the world had its mind on other things.

In 1940, at the age of 62, he married his second wife, Vera Moore of Birkenhead who bore him one son and two daughters, and he became a Captain in the Liverpool Home Guard. In 1943 he took silk.

I first encountered him in 1950, when I was a young man, newly articled in Blackpool. He was then 72, about 6' 2" in height, very upright and of whipcord-thin build. His manner was deceptively mild in conference, and he had an Edwardian gentility and unconscious elegance of style and speech. Over the next few years, I would visit him occasionally at St George's Hall, Liverpool for conferences with my principal. His conference room was on the ground floor at the Murder Court end, overlooking St John's Gardens. It was an awful room, cavernous with dark woodwork and ochre walls and with sparse furniture. I have no reason to think that any of the other silks' rooms were any different.

I have an enduring perception that he wore knee-breeches rather than trousers, but I may be wrong. There was certainly a swallowtail-coat, and when he rose the style was that of courtliness. I can never see a heron standing, upright and still, by a river without being reminded of Edward Wooll.

He was not a fashionable silk: by 1950, he was being elbowed aside by the bright, thrusting young men just back from the War. However, he had a life-time's experience and court-craft.

One case he defended for me resulted (for the one and only time in my experience) in a case being laughed out of Court. Two Blackpool councillors had a scuffle in a Conservative Club car park, in the dark and the rain, over black market eggs, and one of them sued for a broken leg. He limped into the witness box with his supporting stick in the wrong hand. I had the feeling that the Judge enjoyed the case even more than Edward Wooll, who exercised his pungent sense of humour in full.

On another occasion, his experienced ring craft brought a much heavier award of damages than his opponent (a very well-known silk, soon to become a High Court judge) had anticipated and advised. As we left Court our opponent came to us in the corridor and said, in unpleasant loud tones, "I hope your client lives long enough to enjoy his damages." Wooll had outgunned him and he resented it.

In 1957, I left Blackpool for practice elsewhere, and I never saw Edward Wooll again. The record books say that he retired as Recorder of Carlisle in 1963 after 34 years of service to that city. He was much-loved in that appointment. 'Wooll' and 'Carlisle' were bracketed together in one's mind. He valued his good fortune, and the members of the Bar who went to Quarter Sessions at Carlisle knew that they would get away with nothing short of a very professional performance. He was FE's pupil, after all. They just had to live up to his standards, which included mercy. I am indebted to Dick Hamilton's book *Foul Bills and Dagger Money* for some of the Wooll anecdotes (as part of the history of the Northern Circuit) and he relates how Wooll, when sitting at Carlisle, had a young barrister before him, holding a watching brief and behaving nervously. He said to him, "You may watch, and you may pray; but now you must sit down." Pure Wooll.

He retired from the Bar two years later in 1965: he had been Leader of the Northern Circuit for a number of years in his time. He went home to Norfolk finally, where he had been spending more and more of his time. He died in late Spring 1970 at North Walsham, aged 92. With his death the curtain came down on the memorable Edwardian era of the Liverpool Bar.

MR JUSTICE BRABIN

By His Honour Richard Pickering

Mr Justice Brabin was known throughout the legal world of the North West simply as 'Danny.' He was also known as one of the ablest advocates which the Northern Circuit has produced. He was born into an old established Liverpool business family on 14 August 1913. The family then lived in Wallasey but as a young boy, Danny was sent to Bishops Court, Freshfield, a prep school before Douai and Trinity Hall, Cambridge. He remained a devout Roman Catholic all his life.

Danny joined the Inner Temple and kept his terms there in parallel with his time at Cambridge. He was called to the Bar on 27 January 1936 but returned to Cambridge to take his Law Degree. A pupillage in London followed with a successful junior who went on to become Mr Justice Pearce.

In 1937 Brabin returned to Liverpool to become pupil to Hartley Shawcross and on 2 February 1938 was elected a member of the Northern Circuit.

Events thereafter moved swiftly. Early in 1939, Melville Kennan left Shawcross's Chambers to set up his own at 34 Castle Street. He was followed by Robertson Crichton and Danny Brabin. The new set was clerked by Kenneth Nugent with Roy Tully as his junior.

Within a few months, war was declared and the members of Chambers separated to play their parts in it.

Danny joined the Royal Artillery and was commissioned in 1940. He was posted abroad first to Iceland, then to North West Europe after the Allied Invasion and in the fighting there he was awarded the Military Cross. He was demobilised in 1945 and returned to resume his practice at 34 Castle Street.

Looked at from the standpoint of today's barristers' chambers, Melville Kennan's were decidedly primitive. Melville sat in a large room that could only be reached by passing through other rooms. Danny had a rather small room that looked only into the central well of the building. Robertson Crichton had the other large room, looking into the dull confines of Back Castle Street. Various juniors and pupils circulated round those three established men. There was a wash basin in the tiny cloakroom, but all other demands of hygiene had to be met at the top of the building, several flights of stairs above. In such circumstances, there may have been more reasons than professional advancement which caused Crichton and Brabin to leave 34 Castle Street in 1947, Kenneth Nugent going with them.

Two further moves occurred in 1949. Brabin married and moved to Chambers in Cook Street, still supported by his very able Clerk, Kenneth Nugent. With that support complementing his own ability, Brabin's career raced forward. He was given a silk gown in 1951 and rapidly became a pre-eminent leader on the Northern Circuit.

That pre-eminence sprang largely from his command of the art of advocacy. Mastery of the brief is to be expected of any barrister but Danny could express that mastery not only with the persuasion of the orator but with something of the power of the actor. In no sense was it the high flown drama of the previous generation of leaders but it was an ability to move from the genial to the menacing or to the positively seductive as the state of the case or the witness or the jury might require. The strongest weapon in his arsenal as an advocate was cross-examination. That ability to move from geniality to menace was at its most effective in dealing with a hostile witness. The questioning would be swift, precise and ruthless.

Among the best known Liverpool cases in which he was briefed as a leader was the Henderson Store Fire Inquiry in which he was instructed on behalf of the Henderson management and staff. The Inquiry took the form of an Inquest on the death of the seven people killed in the fire. The hearing took some three weeks (an enormous time at that period) and was presided over by C J Cunliffe, sitting as Deputy Coroner specifically to hear it shortly before he was appointed as a Judge. A further case with strong Liverpool resonance was the defamation action of Braddock -V- The Bolton Evening News. Brabin and his former pupil master, by now Sir Hartley Shawcross, were engaged in it. When the case was listed at St George's Hall the junior Bar clustered thick about the Court room anticipating a clash of Titans. Sadly, they were disappointed. The two great men did a great deal of walking up and down the corridor together with much shaking of heads and murmured deep discussion and at the end of it all, the case settled. Doubtless very sensibly.

Brabin's ability was not limited to his advocacy. He became Recorder of Bolton in 1953 and presided over those busy Quarter Sessions until his appointment to the High Court Bench. In 1960, he both became Judge of Appeal in the Isle of Man and was elected a Master of the Bench of the Inner Temple. His appointment as a High Court Judge sitting in the Queen's Bench Division came in 1962. For that period, such appointment at the age of 48 must have put him among the most youthful appointees.

Brabin's judicial style inevitably could not quite divorce itself from his style as an advocate. His Court was a place of efficiency, pretty swift movement through the work and general courtesy. On occasions he could not totally resist the temptation to descend into the blood-stained sand of the arena which he had enjoyed so much as Leading Counsel. That did not detract from his reputation as a Judge of ability and great Courtroom presence. In 1965 the Home Secretary turned to Brabin to conduct the inquiry into the horrid history of the murders at 10 Rillington Place and the convictions and hangings which followed. After the years that had passed, not even Brabin's penetrating mind could produce a conclusive result. He thought it probable that Timothy Evans had been hanged for a murder he did not commit but that he had committed a different murder. John Christie who later confessed to strangling six women had, Brabin considered, probably killed the girl for whose death Evans was executed.

Brabin's sense of humour and mischief never left him. Towards the end of his life he was recuperating at Caldy Manor in Caldy and was visited on a Saturday afternoon by two old colleagues, both judges and both from Manchester. Brabin insisted on taking them for a cup of tea with his good friend and former pupil, John Arthur (later Judge Arthur) at John Arthur's nearby magnificent home at 'Oravales'. 'Oravales' is a splendid property surrounded by magnificent lawns and gardens. The three men duly walked to 'Oravales' when they discovered that John Arthur was out and that Brabin knew very well that he would be. When asked about the incident Brabin confessed that the only reason he had taken them to 'Oravales' was to show what he described as 'the two b.....s' from Manchester the magnificent style in which a Liverpool Junior lived!

Brabin is almost certainly best remembered by his colleagues for the way in which he sparkled at Bar Mess. The company, the conversation, the piling of one entertaining anecdote on another acted upon him like champagne. Indeed, as the evening wore on any stranger looking in and seeing Danny laughing, talkative, witty could be forgiven for thinking "That man is full of wine." The reality was that Danny was a life long abstainer. His exuberance sprang from the sheer pleasure that he had in the company round him and the pleasure that his enjoyment generated in them. His too early death on 22 September 1975, aged 62 and after a drawn-out period of failing health, was a very genuine sadness to those who knew him and a notable loss to the profession.

SYDNEY SILVERMAN

By Joe Woolwich

Sydney Silverman with his family at the wedding of his son Paul in 1966.
From left to right: Nancy Silverman, Sydney Silverman, Roger Silverman, Rina Silverman, Paul Silverman, Joe Woolwich (formerly of Woolwich, Lander & Savage and best man on the day) and Julian Silverman.

Samuel Sydney Silverman (known to all as Sydney), the founder of the firm of Silverman Livermore & Co, was born in Liverpool in 1895 to a Roumanian (as then spelt) immigrant father and English mother. Growing up in conditions of deprivation he became a redoubtable fighter for the poor, the underdog and the oppressed.

Sydney's father ran a credit drapery in Liverpool City Centre and Sydney was the second of four children – Ruby, Sydney, Ernest and Alfie (who worked for his father for a time but died young). Sydney won a scholarship to Liverpool Institute and from there to Liverpool University. However, his studies were interrupted by the First World War. He objected to the war and was imprisoned as a conscientious objector for over two years including periods of solitary confinement. Emerging from prison he returned to University, obtaining a BA in 1921. He took up an appointment as lecturer in English Literature at the University of Helsinki from 1921 to 1925. On his return to Liverpool, he re-enrolled at Liverpool University and obtained an LLB (1st Class Honours) in 1927.

He was admitted as a Solicitor and opened his first office at 81 Dale Street, Liverpool, in January 1928. The firm prospered and he moved to 155 Dale Street in 1930. Later, (Sir) Harry Livermore, Charles Prior (once the office boy), Bert Farrand and Eric Goldrein (now a Barrister) became partners.

On his return from Helsinki, Sydney joined the Labour Party. His legal expertise played an important role in Bessie Braddock's successful first attempt to win a Council seat for the Labour Party in the St Anne's Ward in Liverpool. One woman in Gerard Street had acquired the tenancies of many houses on a controlled rent of 75p per week and was sub-letting rooms at between 25p and 53p per week each. Sydney advised Bessie that this was illegal and the result was that Bessie persuaded the tenants to only pay the proper (greatly reduced) amount. As a result, this particular racket was broken and Bessie was helped to launch her successful political career.

He was a close friend and adviser to Bessie and Jack Braddock and was himself elected a Liverpool City Councillor for Labour in 1932. In 1935 he was elected Labour Member of Parliament for Nelson & Colne, a seat which he held until his death in 1968, although it was often a marginal seat. Pressure of parliamentary work meant that while an MP Sydney lived much of his time in London and often returned to his constituency on Friday, stopping in Liverpool to deal with business matters at the firm and with his partners. When Harry Livermore was called up, early in the Second World War, Sydney returned briefly to regular practice in Silverman Livermore.

Sydney was a fighter from his youth to his death, giving himself selflessly to his clients and the causes dear to him. Although his Labour Party contacts undoubtedly played a large part in the success of his firm, there was no doubt as to his exceptional abilities. A brilliant intellect coupled with a forceful personality made him a formidable advocate in the Magistrates Court. He was not always appreciated by the police nor, later on, by the mainly Tory Press. In those days there was no legal aid for civil cases and only a very limited form of assistance in criminal cases in the Higher Courts. He developed a substantial accident practice, one of his cases Ormrod -v- Crosville Motors reaching the House of Lords.

Sydney believed in instructing the best barristers for his clients, irrespective of their politics. He regularly instructed Selwyn Lloyd who, despite originally being a Liberal, became Conservative MP for the Wirral, Foreign Secretary and Chancellor of the Exchequer and, finally, Speaker of the House of Commons before going to the House of Lords. Once, while Sydney was on holiday, Selwyn Lloyd's clerk telephoned Sydney's articled clerk, Joseph Norton (founder of Norton & Co and uncle of the current Attorney General Lord Goldsmith). Most of Selwyn's briefs for the Assizes a few days later had not arrived and Joe Norton had to prepare all the briefs in a rush.

When elected to Parliament, he secured the abolition of the £85 stamp duty on the articles of solicitors' articled clerks, a penal duty if ever there was one. But it was his long and eventually successful campaign to secure the abolition in 1965 of the death penalty for murder which earned him his main place in the history books of Britain. It was a fight which needed all his skill, debating ability and tenacity, coupled with a willingness to carry on despite defeats and the opposition of a sizeable section of the electorate. Sydney was fond of repeating the maxim – 'If at first you fail to succeed, try, try and try again'.

Sydney was not asked to join the Labour Government of 1945, but then his personality was perhaps too individual and he would, in any case, have probably been unwilling to compromise. His brand of left-wing politics was too extreme for the Attlee Government. He was a thorn in the side of every government. If he had a weakness as a politician it was, I feel, his failure to see the dangers of Communism and the tyranny of Stalinism.

Sydney was an ardent Zionist and supporter of the creation of the State of Israel. Religion for him was something of a mental attitude to fellow human beings, rather than one of observance and customs.

Small in size, Sydney was of a generous and sometimes over-trusting nature. Once he allowed a young cellist to occupy their Bauhaus-style house in Hampstead while he and Nancy were away. She converted his large study into an artist's studio, mixing the paints in large pools of colour on the floor. She held a party, including a famous viola player, nicknamed 'the Trout', at which she proceeded to serve a vast quantity of soup containing most of the food in the house. Sydney and Nancy were not amused on their return.

For relaxation when Parliament was in session he would often enjoy Sunday walks to Hampstead Village, sometimes to meet close political friends, such as Michael Foot, and holidays abroad. His home was full of modern furniture and pictures. He loved fast cars, usually Jaguars, which he drove badly partly as a result of poor eyesight. He would sometimes drive the wrong way up one way streets. He once drove my mother and father, in dense fog, down the wrong carriageway of Menlove Avenue. When he realised his mistake, he promptly reversed through the hedges and tramlines then dividing the two carriageways thus crashing through to the proper side of the road.

Sydney married Nancy Rubenstein, a Liverpool cellist, in 1932. They were devoted to each other and Sydney could not have been so successful in his work and politics without her. Sydney could be irascible and occasionally bad-tempered, but fortunately Nancy had a saintly disposition. They had three sons, none of whom entered the law. He inspired affection, devotion and admiration in those close to him and his death in 1968 left a gap in the lives of his friends and family.

BERTRAM BENAS

By Graeme Bryson

Judge Addleshaw, Judge Leigh.
Judge Fraser Harrison, Judge Steel, Judge Trotter.
Judge Burgess, Judge Laski, Bertram Benas, Judge Harold Brown, Robertson Crichton J.

Bertram Benas was called to the Bar at the Middle Temple in 1906 and practiced in chambers in Liverpool as an equity draftsman and conveyancer for over sixty years. He was created a Bencher in 1953 and Reader in the year that he died. He also lectured on conveyancing, and he wrote on those subjects many articles in periodicals and books, including Halsbury's Laws of England. This sort of work does not catch the public eye, and yet his entry was an amazing full column in *Who's Who*, with a CBE in 1954, a long list of Presidencies of learned societies' and much else besides. In his time, he was a distinguished citizen of Liverpool, and worthy of remembrance.

He was of the smallest possible stature. When Liverpool University gave him an Honorary LLM in 1952, the Public Orator compared him to an atom with miraculous superabundant energy radiating from small cubic volume. He seemed to be present, the Public Orator said, at all the societies of his innumerable interests, at the same time.

After he died the B'nai Brith Bertram Benas Unity Lodge gave in 1978, a memorial lecture entitled 'The

Life and Times of a Jewish Victorian' by Professor Tempkin of the State University of New York. I was honoured to give the Bertram B Benas Memorial Lecture in the following year. Indeed I had worked with him in many of his interests for many years, and he was an honoured guest at my wedding in 1938. He used to make an annual expedition to my home in Hightown, and I would take him on a car run into the South Lancashire countryside, while he gave full details of the ancestry of the squirearchy in the various stately homes as we passed them.

And who was this man? His father, Baron Louis Benas (BLB) claimed ancestry to a medieval Polish Jewish King but the line was very convoluted. He was a banker in Liverpool and of good standing and address in Sefton Park. When BLB was pacing the nearby streets awaiting news of the birth of his expected child, he was in Bertram Road when the messenger arrived. So he called his son Bertram Benjamin Baron Benas! Professor Tempkin recounts the sad nature of his childhood. His mother deserted BLB and died soon after, so that Bertram was brought up by a sort of committee of maiden aunts and bachelor uncles. Apparently such a scandal went down badly with the other Jewish families. Also, BLB remained fast to the traditional orthodoxy, while most of the other families (including BLB's wife's family) joined the new Reform. Bertram himself was 'traditional', but the significance of this is beyond me.

After Liverpool College, he got his LLB degree at the new Liverpool University, before studying for the bar and entering Chancery Chambers in Liverpool. Liverpool and Manchester both had Chancery bars, together with the Palatine Court and also access to the Law Courts in London every other Thursday and there was plenty of Chancery work available. As Liverpool High Court Chancery Registrar, I used to travel to London to sit with the nominated High Court Judge. Benas was not a regular attender as his inclination and experience were not that way. But he did write Precedents of Pleading with Lord Justice Scott.

In dress he was the perfect barrister, and was never seen without being in striped trousers and morning suit. And always with an umbrella.

The delays in Chancery work had improved since the days of Charles Dickens, but there were still lots of applications to adjourn to a future date. Benas was the one with this task. He did appear before me from time to time in one application or another but he never seemed at home in this genre, although he was a brilliant lecturer in every other kind of subject.

He became President of the Lancashire and Cheshire Historic Society, of which his father had been an early member. He gave the Centenary Lecture in 1948. Fifty years later, as the then senior member, I was asked to write an article for the 150th celebrations. Before the war, the provincial universities had Parliamentary Representation, and I was Vice Chairman to Benas's Chairmanship of the Liverpool University Conservative Association. And we had several other joint ventures including the Council of Christians and Jews.

The other equivalent local Chancery barrister of his time was Professor Lyon Blease, tall lanky and gangling, and a well known character on the radio of the day. Blease was my tutor at the University, and also a well loved character. He was politically a Liberal, and tried several times, without success, to enter Parliament. I forget for the moment which of them was senior by call as a barrister, but the difference although only a month or so, was very important! They both played their full part in public life.

And what of Benas himself? It was said that he was old at forty, but young at eighty. He retained his vitality of movement and of speech, and we had a close relationship which, as a younger man, I much appreciated. In fact he always seemed pleased to meet his friends, and he was never one to show ill temper. I sat with him at the Liverpool Law Society Annual Dinner in 1968. He was absolutely thrilled to have been appointed to be Reader at Middle Temple for the current term and he was to travel to London the following week to carry out this duty. Sadly he caught a fever in London and died a few days later. I have occasion to visit the Middle Temple from time to time, and I always make a point of reading his name on the wall as a Reader.

There was much of which he was proud including his life governorship of his old school, Liverpool College; also his post nominals CBE BA LLM JP; and he was a very competent player of the organ, particularly the splendid organ at St George's Hall where he was Chairman of the organ society. He would play on my own (electronic) organ, though his short legs made the pedals rather difficult to reach. He liked playing Elgar's *Variations* for my pleasure.

Perhaps one should mention his faithful clerk at 14 Cook Street, Mr Goodman, a man of full height and girth, compared with Benas himself. The Chambers seemed quite Dickensian with briefs and papers everywhere. Barrister's clerks are a very special race and Mr Goodman was one of the best.

And how is this tale to end? Rather sadly, because the type of work done by Benas seemed to become largely irrelevant. The 1925 Property Acts had simplified conveyancing with increasing effect over the years. In his final days, he did some work for the Land Registry in Birkenhead, but little else. He died, still a bachelor, the last of a long line, virtually penniless, and was helped at the end by a Jewish Charity. Although he must have drafted countless wills, he died intestate. His few belongings were sold and went 'bona vacantia' to the Crown via the Duchy. His books and papers seem to have been thrown out for scrap. Professor Tempkin blamed the housekeeper for this. So sad.

But what a memory we have of a really fine and courteous gentleman who graced Liverpool's legal and cultural scene for more than half the century.

MR JUSTICE LYNSKEY

By Graeme Bryson

Northern Circuit Judges, 1950.
Hon. Mr Justice Gorman, Hon. Mr Justice Barry.
Hon. Mr Justice Pritchard. Hon. Mr Justice Willmer, Hon. Mr Justice Ormerod, Hon. Mr Justice Lloyd-Jacob.
Hon. Mr Justice Sellers, Hon. Mr Justice Morris.
Rt. Hon. Lord Justice Singleton, Rt. Hon. Lord Merriman, Hon. Mr Justice Lynskey.

The first thing to settle is the problem of the name Lynskey itself which seems on the face of it to have originated somewhere in mid-Europe, while we know that the Judge's father came from the West of Ireland. According to the Sunday Pictorial on 12th December 1948, Lynskey is an old Irish name with an English corruption, coming from the Gaelic O' Loinscigh, or Linsky, Linskey, Lynchey and Lynch! Very few people know that.

Yes, George's father, George Jeremy Lynskey, was born into a Roman Catholic family in 1861 at Ashgrove, Tuam in the West of Ireland, coming to Liverpool via London University, becoming a solicitor and setting up a practice on his own at 16 (later 30) Lord Street, in the City of Liverpool. He was elected to the City Council for the North Scotland Ward in the Irish National interest, being promoted to Alderman, living at Spring Hill, 26 Thomas Lane, Knotty Ash, later moving to Ashgrove, Seymour Road, Broad Green. He duly married Honora Mary Kearney and fathered six children, George Justin, Edward, Gerard and

Bernard, and two daughters, Mrs Godfrey Byrne and Miss Norah Lynskey. He took his sons George Justin, Edward and Bernard into partnership with him under the title of GJ Lynskey and Sons. Gerard did not qualify, but was managing clerk in the firm. GJ died on 27th October 1921 at the age of sixty. He had led a full life on the Liverpool scene!

And now we turn to the eldest son George Justin, later Mr Justice Lynskey. He became a revered figure in his day, of importance locally and on the national scene, and one of whom his family, school, university, the Law Society, the Inner Temple and Northern Circuit, and many beside had every cause to be proud. As Sir Fred Pritchard wrote in the Dictionary of National Biography (DNB),

"As a Judge, he fully and rapidly justified the golden opinions which the legal profession had formed of him at the Bar. In 1948 he enhanced an already great reputation by his chairmanship of the long judicial inquiry into allegations concerning activities connected with the Board of Trade."

George himself was born at 26 Thomas Lane, Knotty Ash on 5th February 1888, and was educated at St Francis Xavier's College, Liverpool, earning a State Scholarship to Liverpool University where he obtained his LLB degree in 1907 with first class honours, leading to his Master's degree the following year. Two years later he became a Solicitor, also with first class honours and a prizewinner, joining his father's practice, and staying there for ten years. He took time off in 1913 to marry Eileen, the daughter of John Prendiville by whom he had two daughters. He also joined the Palatine Club referred to elsewhere in this book. His talents both with advocacy on his feet, and sitting at his desk in chambers, seemed naturally to lead him to the Bar, and to the Inner Temple, later to become a Bencher.

On being called to the Bar in 1920, George entered chambers at Stephenson Chambers in 30 Lord Street, joining Wilfred Clothier, Glyn Howard Jones, WJ Loughrey, and OG Morris, names which the older amongst us will remember well. His practice flourished and he moved 'across the water' as we say, to live in the Wirral peninsula at 12 Queensway, Wallasey.

During the 1920s his improving status encouraged him to move his home to 33 Sandymount Drive, New Brighton, and his Chambers to 13 Harrington Street to join Eric Errington, Leo Gradwell and others including his pupil, David Maxwell Fyfe.

Sir Fred Pritchard in the DNB went on to say that Lynskey quickly acquired one of the largest practices known at the bar in the present century which enabled him to take silk in 1930 and that his practice continued to grow. Between 1930 and 1939 there were but few cases at the Liverpool and Manchester assizes in which he was not briefed to appear. Lynskey obtained some judicial experience as Judge of the Salford Court of Hundred at an annual fee of £660, sitting part-time only.

The next stage was not quite automatic. In 1944 some judicial vacancies arose, and there was natural speculation as to the likely appointees. Lynskey, locally schooled and from a redbrick university, with a large practice but almost exclusively in Lancashire and very rarely appearing in the Law Courts in London and not generally known there, did not have the background of normal High Court appointments at that time. Also, most of the High Court judges came from specialised backgrounds dealt with exclusively in London. So there was some surprise when Lord Simon, the Lord Chancellor, appointed Lynskey despite this background. His very substantial experience of criminal cases would be very useful on Assize, and so it proved to be that much of his time was spent in this way. I wonder if he was warned this on appointment? Certainly Pritchard (DNB) refers to his 'constant' absence from London trying cases in all parts of the country. He "was trying a case in Manchester last week when he fell ill and died." Horses for courses as they say, and if so, it was a great success, as he proved to be an outstanding Assize judge. In those days, a High Court Judge's salary was £5000pa whereas Lynskey was said to be earning at that time some £20,000pa at the bar!

I sat in the Courts for over thirty years, and knew most of the judges. When they retired, counsel would make the closing valedictories, always saying how courteous the judge had been to counsel and witnesses. In some cases it was absolutely the reverse of the truth. In those far off days, judges seemed super-powerful, and even a frown could petrify a young barrister. The Manchester Guardian reported that Lynskey handled witnesses firmly but with extreme consideration – a lovable man and a truly great judge.

Lynskey had a short period when he hit the national headlines, and made his name well known for years to come. The Home Secretary, Chuter Ede, appointed him to be Chairman of a Board of Trade Inquiry in 1948 to inquire whether there was any justification for allegations that payments or rewards had been given to certain Ministers or civil servants in connection with licences etc or in connection with the withdrawal of any prosecution, and what persons were involved. The Committee sat for 26 days and heard many witnesses. The intended victim was Sydney Stanley, who proved a difficult mouse to catch. On one occasion, Lynskey told him, "I have given you a lot of rope Mr Stanley. Pleases behave yourself." The report was well received, and quickly forgotten.

There was no happy retirement for Lynskey, who died in office. On taking silk, he moved from New Brighton to London with his wife and daughters, Eileen Mary (Mrs Gardiner) and Noreen (Mrs Wightman-Smith). He was a Tommy Handley fan, and he supported Everton at football and Middlesex at cricket, except when they played Lancashire. He remained faithful to his church, and to the Jesuits, and was unwilling to take divorce cases, of which there was a great number after the war. When he died, the Requiem Mass was at Farm Street Jesuit Church in London, the absolution being given by Archbishop Godfrey of Westminster Cathedral. There was also a Requiem Mass in Liverpool at his old school at St Francis Xavier's Church which I attended officially with Judge Nance.

George Jeremy Lynskey became a solicitor about 1885, and fathered three more solicitors. He must have thought that he was founding a dynasty of lawyers, as was the hoped custom at that time in Liverpool. Later generations of the family diversified, as they say, and I understand that none of the family practise the law today. But he certainly produced a winner in his son, Sir George Justin Lynskey.

The Judge's daughter, Mrs N Wightman-Smith has kindly read my paper, and has made three points which I give here verbatim:

(a) He was the first Catholic to be appointed a judge of the High Court since the Catholic Emancipation Act of 1829.

(b) He never had a judgment or sentence overturned in the Court of Appeal; he was very proud of that.

(c) He fought very hard for pensions for judge's widows.

I was myself appointed to Liverpool County Court in 1947 at which time there were still no pensions for widows of judges. They were introduced by the Judicial Pensions Act of 1949 which gave the option of a reduced personal pension in return for a widow's pension. Lynskey died in 1957 so Lady Lynskey was able to benefit from his industry.

I can only assume that it was expected for centuries that Judges would be appointed from the wealthier ranks of society, and that widows' pensions were not considered necessary.

JOSEPH ROBERTS

By Judge David Swift

Joe Roberts (looking sideways with glasses). His son David Roberts is on the far left.

In 1919, a young solicitor returned from The Great War to a land fit for heroes. He had seen service in France first with the Inns of Court Regiment and later with the Royal Horse Artillery. In France, he saw action and was mentioned in dispatches. He left the army a Captain Adjutant and at the age of 24 had high hopes for his future in the law. He found a position as an assistant solicitor with J & W H Sale in Derby but his real wish was to return to his home near Birkenhead. Late in 1919, he achieved that wish.

Joseph Roberts was born in Birkenhead on the 26th May 1892 and spent his youth in Heswall and Parkgate. He was educated at Birkenhead Institute and Birkenhead School, achieving high standards in English, Latin and Greek also distinguishing himself as something of a rugby player. It was his ambition to qualify as a solicitor and he found articles with the firm of Labron Johnson in Liverpool. When he was admitted in June 1913 he had qualified with First Class Honours and won the Clements Inn, Sheffield, Timpron Martin, Daniel Reardon, Atkinson, Rupert Bremner and John Mackrell prizes. Throughout his career he combined his undoubted legal academic abilities with shrewdness and exceptional ability as an advocate.

On returning to Birkenhead in 1919, Joe Roberts entered partnership with Percy Bartlett Hughes and the firm that began with small offices in Duncan Street off Hamilton Square bears their names to this day. Despite the name of the firm, Percy Hughes was always known as 'Bart' and was responsible for the firm's conveyancing during the period before the outbreak of war in 1939. Joe Roberts had little interest in property law and devoted himself to the practice of the common law. During the early years he built up a reputation as an advocate in the magistrates courts and as a skilled litigator in civil and divorce causes. The firm's litigation practice expanded rapidly to include commercial and insurance clients in addition to the many private individuals who made use of Joe Roberts' skills.

In 1928 the Birkenhead Coroner, Cecil Holden, died and Joe Roberts was appointed the Borough Coroner, a post he was to hold until 1st April 1974. Within weeks, he was to encounter the first of very many unusual cases; a case of alleged murder on the high seas. A seaman named Frederick Rickwood died in Birkenhead of a stab wound received in an argument on board the SS Mobiloil en route from Philadelphia to the Mersey. The alleged assailant and his witnesses claimed that the wound had occurred when the ship rolled in heavy seas and a verdict of accidental death was eventually recorded. Many years later, in 1955, a case that became known as 'The Pill Box Murder' was to occupy his mind. Three boys out picking blackberries discovered the naked body of a woman, later identified as Alice Barton, in a wartime pill box alongside the railway in Prenton. Despite the police interviewing 40,000 people, obtaining 1000 statements and securing the assistance of Scotland Yard, no one was ever charged and a verdict of murder by a person or persons unknown was recorded.

Between 1920 and 1936, Joe Roberts developed a large practice over Cheshire and North Wales. At that time, of course, Birkenhead was part of the Wales and Chester Circuit and his knowledge and love of the countryside resulted in many contacts over a wide area. Further recognition of his advocacy skills came with his appointment as Agent for the Director of Public Prosecutions conducting weighty criminal cases before the local magistrates courts. His preparation was meticulous. All briefs for the autumn Assizes were prepared in the long vacation and stacked in rows along the corridor to be delivered in good time for the hearing but not so early as to incur an unnecessary brief fee. In the late 1930s, the firm was expanding. There were two new partners, Douglas Kewish, who later became a Registrar of the High Court, and J P Wilson, who went on to edit Stones Justices Manual. By 1937, the impetus of growth in the litigation practice, particularly insurance and commercial work, necessitated expansion into Liverpool. Much litigation in the city passed through the Liverpool Court of Passage and the Rules of that Court required those who practised in the Court to be Liverpool practitioners. Seeing the advantages of expansion, Joe Roberts was instrumental in the firm acquiring the practice of H G C Day & Co in Castle Street giving Percy Hughes & Roberts a presence in Liverpool and South Lancashire and access to all the Liverpool Courts.

With the outbreak of war in 1939, Joe Roberts and Bart Hughes were left with the task of maintaining what was a thriving and busy legal practice in the absence of other partners. The litigation continued although at a reduced level but the conveyancing dwindled sufficiently for Bart Hughes to help with the County Court work. They were assisted by a loyal staff, a number of whom remained with the firm for very many years; Miss Moston, who started with the firm when the offices opened in Duncan Street, claimed that if the two partners were out her job was to ensure that passing clients remained in the offices until one returned. Joe Roberts' secretaries were Esther Angelman, who married Sir Harry Livermore, another great Merseyside litigator, and Vera Dickie who remained with the firm until 1975.

Despite the difficulties of maintaining the practice in wartime, Joe Roberts threw himself wholeheartedly into other important activities. In 1941, he became involved in raising the local Home Guard which force he

Reception at the Town Hall, Wallasey, for members of the (still largely male) legal profession, 16 December 1960.

commanded until the unit was stood down in 1946. By then he was Lieutenant Colonel and was later awarded an OBE for military service. He also gave his time to the Liverpool Law Society whose Committee he had joined in the 1930s. He served as Hon Secretary for 5 years, then as Vice President and was President from 1943 to 1944. The Annual Report for 1944 demonstrates the amount of work needed first to cope with the effects of the blitz, which destroyed the Law Library, local offices, books and papers alike, and then with the myriad of wartime regulations. In the office of President, there was also a need to take a broader view. Joe Roberts supported the Society's opposition to compulsory Land Registration which eventually came about. He was more successful in advocating a simplification of divorce law and the more convenient trial of divorce cases. His desire that the costs of proceedings brought to clarify legislation should be borne by the State did not get any sympathy from government and, perhaps foreseeing a later age, he complained of "the tendency to legislate by reference to other Acts which often makes it impossible for laymen and very difficult for lawyers to follow or understand".

In 1946, Douglas Kewish and JP Wilson returned from war service. Danny Walsh and Max Reney Smith joined as partners shortly after and the pre war expansion proceeded. By 1966, when Joe Roberts retired from the partnership at Percy Hughes & Roberts to become a consultant there were seven partners, including his son David Roberts, in the three Merseyside offices.

Although it might be thought that Joe Roberts' dedication to the law limited his horizons nothing could be further from the truth. He had many interests outside the practice of law. For many years he served on the Committee of the Cheshire Territorial Association. He played golf and was captain of the Heswall Golf Club in 1932. He enjoyed fishing. His real passion, however, was for farming. In 1935, the family moved into The White House in Heswall where he was able to indulge that hobby. Bruce Humphreys, an articled clerk in the early war years who later became a partner in the firm, recalls that his duties included helping with the haymaking! Joe Roberts established a small herd of dairy shorthorns and kept a number of horses and remained at The White House, continuing to visit the office most days and maintaining an interest in the activities of the firm, until his death in 1975.

DARRELL MACE

By Barrie Marsh

In 1926, a young solicitor (who was born in Bedford but had moved to Liverpool for his first job) had the temerity to ask his employer for a 'rise' in his salary. The young solicitor was already showing considerable talent – particularly as an advocate. Despite this, his employer turned down this request – in fairly peremptory terms.

The solicitor threatened to leave there and then, but the employer was not moved by this. Unabashed, the solicitor left – it would appear that very day. He set up in business in Dale Street on his own account.

The solicitor was DH Mace. The employer was Herbert J Davis. It could be said that neither of them ever looked back.

Another young assistant solicitor at that time at the firm of Herbert J Davis was one, Hector Munro; he subsequently became senior partner and both Hector and his son, Donald, are still remembered with great respect and affection. Munro tried to persuade Mace that he should think again and not be too hasty, but Mace had made his mind up and was not to be deflected; he wanted to have a practice of his own.

Another colleague at the firm at that time was the cashier – a Welshman (born in Aberystwyth) John Morgan Jones. He chased down the street after Mace on the day that he left and pleaded that if Mace was determined to leave he (Morgan Jones) should be allowed to follow him and join the new firm that was about to be launched. Mace told him not to be so silly, that he had no work and no clients and that he could not afford to pay him a wage. With some reluctance, Morgan Jones accepted this advice.

On the very first day of the firm opening for business at 81 Dale Street a 'client' arrived at the office for advice. Mace pressed the client to tell him why he had come to him and ultimately the client admitted that he had gone to another solicitor but that that solicitor had told him to go to Mace. That other solicitor was Jack Behn – the firm subsequently being known as John A Behn & Co and then Behn, Twyford & Reece. Behn always refused to acknowledge to Mace that he had sent him his first client. It says a lot for the character of Jack Behn – and perhaps reminds us of how different the practice of the law was in those days.

'DH' – as he was known – was a great advocate and it was not long before the practice grew. His work was primarily based on the Liverpool City Magistrates Court in Dale Street, but he then began to be more widely known and the work spread to other courts. Although a brilliant advocate, DH was not the greatest exponent in the field of administration and when John Morgan Jones approached him again about a job, DH relented. Morgan Jones was about ten years older than DH; he was a superb administrator and had a very good brain. Mace offered Morgan Jones his 'Articles' and after attending night school and passing all necessary exams Morgan Jones was admitted as a solicitor. He was immediately made a partner. The firm of Mace and Jones was in existence and to this day – about seventy years later – it bears the same name.

DH was pre-eminent as an advocate. For more than thirty years he was the doyen of the Liverpool City Magistrates Court. He also had an exceptional brain. Although he would claim to know absolutely nothing about Conveyancing, if one had a problem in that sphere of the law and consulted him he had an amazing knack of coming up with the correct answer or solution particularly if the problem was of a practical nature. He also had a 'trick' which to this day I have not been able to fathom – when looking for the law in some major tome or work of reference he was nearly always able to open the book at the exact page which was relevant.

I first met DH in 1953. He was then probably at the height of his 'powers'. In those days the Director of Public Prosecutions appointed in each major city an eminent solicitor to act as his agent. The DPP's agent would be instructed to prosecute in the more serious criminal trials and this gave rise to many high profile cases, including some of the more famous murder trials. DH was appointed for the Liverpool area. The appointment as agent for the DPP was a personal appointment – it was the individual and not the firm – and it was much coveted. One aspect of this work, however, did not go down too well with DH and this was that when Counsel was to be used the agent was not allowed to brief Counsel of his choice; the instructions were direct from the DPP to Counsel. This did not always suit DH who had his own very clear views about which barrister was the right one for a particular type of case. It would not be appropriate for me to mention names, but several of them went on to become judges.

The day always commenced with a brief visit to the office – by then in the Pioneer Insurance Buildings at 31 Dale Street – and then an immediate 'adjournment' to the Kardomah cafe or coffee shop in Dale Street where the preparation for the case or cases that day was done. In the Dale Street courts there were three superb advocates in the 1950s – DH himself, Harry Livermore and Monty Reece (then a partner in Behn Twyford & Reece) – a lovely man who died far too young. There was a wonderful camaraderie – and at the same time rivalry – between them. There was also a young advocate on the scene who was beginning to make his presence felt – his name was Rex Makin.

Apart from general advocacy – primarily criminal -there was another area of work where DH's skills and knowledge became pre-eminent. In the 1930s, a whole new tranche of law developed in relation to road traffic and in particular with reference to the carriage of goods 'for hire or reward'. Licences – 'A' or 'B' –

had to be granted before a road haulier could operate and when application was made for a licence this had to be advertised and existing operators – such as 'British Rail' or Pickfords – could object. The applicant had to establish that there was a 'need' for his proposed service; the objectors (who had the existing business) would say that they were already fulfilling any customer needs. There would then be a formal hearing before Traffic Commissioners (in Liverpool they used to sit in the Municipal Buildings) before a decision could be made. DH became the leading expert in this field of the law and his services were in constant demand. The work suited his flair as an advocate and his ability to get to the heart of any particular problem.

Although DH was not really a 'Committee man' his standing within the legal community in Liverpool was such that he was elected to the Committee of the Liverpool Law Society and he became its President in 1949/1950. This was something of which he was extremely proud.

The work of the firm had expanded considerably and it encompassed conveyancing, wills and probate as well as general litigation and matrimonial work. In the 1950s a Royal Commission was set up to look into Divorce Law generally and it was a great honour – both for DH personally and for the firm – when he was appointed as a member of that Commission.

DH would have had problems with the technology of the law as it is today. One of my lasting recollections of him – in the very early days of dictating machines – is of his absolute insistence that the machine was not actually recording what he had dictated into it! I think that the equipment finished up being dropped into the waste paper basket.

Prior to his retirement Mace had gathered a small but first class team around him. Morgan Jones continued to deal with the non-contentious work until he retired in about 1955. By then there were two other partners – Bert Lewis Jones and Brian Fraser Harrison.

ALBERT LEWIS ('BERT') JONES

By Barrie Marsh

In the 1930s, one of Mace's many clients was a small private brewery in Knotty Ash owned and managed by the Jones family – no relation to John Morgan Jones (who with his strict Welsh Presbyterian background did not approve of drink in any form). As was so often the case in those days Jones approached DH about the possibility of his son being articled to him. The son was Albert Lewis Jones, known as Bert, or later – within the firm – as ALJ.

Bert Lewis Jones qualified before World War II, and in his student days he was a fine athlete and a very promising rugby player. In addition, he was very active in the Territorial Army and had reached the rank of Captain in a well known Liverpool artillery regiment (the 59th Medium Regiment RATA) before the outbreak of war. Having served with that Regiment in France in late 1939 and early 1940, he was promoted to Major and shortly afterwards was transferred to North Africa. He served under General Montgomery (as he then was), was involved in desert battle with Rommel and was mentioned in despatches in 1943. On 6th March 1943, when in a jeep reconnoitring a forward position, the vehicle was plastered with mortar bombs and machine gun bullets Bert suffered severe injuries, leading to the amputation of one leg. He was subsequently awarded the Military Cross.

Bert would never speak of the war. My favourite story about one aspect of that time, however, is that his wife and family were attending the small cinema in Pwllheli during the war when the Pathe News came on.

There was Bert Lewis Jones with Montgomery, both being introduced to Winston Churchill. The Jones kids shrieked, 'Daddy'. The cinema audience applauded and the cinema operator played the whole newsreel over again!

After the War Bert was not able to resume his previous athletic activities but despite the problems he threw himself into a whole range of activities. He became a local Councillor for the Neston ward, ran the local Sea Scouts for many years, and was a leading member of the Royal Rock Beagle Hunt. I could never work out why it was that as a fit young man I always finished up about 15 minutes behind Bert when the hounds were in full cry. It was a long time before I found out that the hare tends to run in a circle! Sailing was also a great love and for many years Bert could be found in his Seabird in Cardigan Bay near to his beloved Abersoch. In the earlier days of these activities an old-fashioned stump was used in place of the artificial leg – but there was never a word of complaint.

Bert's sense of humour was revealed during one of his Amateur TT sidecar races in the Isle of Man. The radio commentator was terribly impressed by Bert's bravery in racing competitively in the TT races with only one leg and in describing Bert's driving, expressed his amazement in the commentary that he was riding in that manner and only had one leg! When Bert was told about these comments afterwards, he said words to the effect of "That's nothing, as the chap in the sidecar has no legs at all – it's pretty difficult two chaps racing with only one leg between them".

In the office Bert Lewis Jones dealt mainly with conveyancing and other non-contentious matters. He had one great attribute and that was that, however complicated the problem, he always gave the client immediate and definite advice. The clients loved him for this and he was very seldom wrong – at least so far as I am aware! Having said this I think that even he would have admitted that he was not the greatest academic lawyer that Liverpool has ever known.

Bert became very involved in the affairs of the Liverpool Law Society. He was at various times Hon Secretary and Treasurer for a number of years and he was honoured to become President in the years 1966 to 1967.

Bert Lewis Jones retired at about the age of 60 and went to live in Abersoch. Sadly he died within a couple of years. He was a man of exceptional bravery and extreme kindness – one of the great characters in the legal life of the city.

JOHN A BEHN

By Graeme Bryson

As a boy I lived close to the Police Station in Lark Lane, Liverpool, to which Mrs Florence Maybrick had been taken when arrested. Her arrival there in 1889, and her trial for the murder of her husband by arsenic poisoning was still well remembered. A crowd exceeding 6,000 had waited silently in the summer sun outside St George's Hall, Liverpool for the verdict of the jury which, in this case, was a guilty verdict.

At that time, a murder trial with a guilty verdict carried a compulsory sentence of death by hanging for which purpose the judge wore the dreaded Black Cap. There was a macabre public fascination, particularly if the accused person was a woman as actually happened at the trial of Mrs Maybrick whom the jury had found guilty. Later, there was a reprieve by the Home Secretary, a sentence of life imprisonment being substituted. I seem to recall reading that Mrs Maybrick was at some time released from prison.

The next time that the whole city was to be similarly involved was the great Sack murder trial in the Winter of 1913/14, when the Plateau was similarly thronged. Great applause greeted the result. But what was the Sack murder?

On the 11th December 1913, a bargee had difficulty in opening the canal lock gates near Leeds Street, Liverpool. He pulled a large object from the water which turned out to be a sack. Protruding from the sack were two human legs.

It proved to be the body of Catherine Bradfield, a cheerful 40 year old spinster who managed a sack and canvas shop in Old Hall Street, Liverpool for her brother.

Her body had many wounds; the scalp was cut to the bone.

Suspicion at once fell on the two young apprentices in the shop, George Ball aged 22 and Samuel Elltoft, aged 18. By a remarkable coincidence, the two men had been seen after dark pushing a hand cart from the shop towards the canal and dumping a heavy object.

Elltoft was arrested the next day, and remanded to Walton Prison.

Being an apprentice joiner, he was fortunate in receiving help from his Trade Union. The Union Solicitor John A Behn took up his case.

In the meantime, George Ball disappeared and a £50 reward was offered for his arrest. In fact he had assumed a disguise, wearing a new suit, a flesh coloured shade over one eye, and a pair of spectacles. He pretended to be an Australian and was busy trying to sign on a ship to leave the port, when an informer went to the police and he was arrested on December 20th.

Both men were charged with wilful murder. Elltoft was charged in addition with being an accessory after the fact.

An interesting connection with the Maybrick trial emerged. That trial had been conducted by Mr Justice Stephen. His son Sir Robert Stephen was the Clerk of Assize in the Sack murder trial. The prosecution was conducted by the future Lord Chief Justice Gordon Hewart KC, MP, who opened with a very clear and damning picture of the events leading up to and following the murder.

Ball's defence was that he had been present at the murder which had been carried out by a third man, tall and with a dark moustache. This third man had threatened Ball with a revolver while he, Ball, stood on the staircase.

Ball then said that he had got rid of the body because he would have been immediately suspected, which was in fact the case.

Elltoft gave evidence that he was just going home that night when Ball told him to wait and help him with the handcart to remove some rubbish. He said he was not in the house when the murder was committed and never saw the body at all.

Lindon Riley was instructed by John A Behn to defend Elltoft. This he did to such effect that considerable sympathy towards his client became more and more obvious as the trial went on.

Lindon Riley's powerful speech to the jury ended, "Consider my client's demeanour. Have you ever seen such a spectacle; a boy of 18 fresh from his little triumphs at school and cross examined by the greatest experts of the day." Ball was quickly found guilty; the judge assumed the black cap and passed sentence of death by hanging. Outside, the crowd of 6,000 voices cheered.

Elltoft was found not guilty of murder but guilty of being an accessory after the fact; the jury recommended mercy.

Mr Justice Atkin addressed him, "You have been found guilty of the serious charge of assisting a murderer to conceal his crime. I take into account your youth and the jury's recommendation to mercy. The sentence of the court is that you be kept under penal servitude for 4 years."

This sentence stunned the public. Elltoft's mother was heard to call out, "You brute." There was no cheering from the crowd outside.

By comparison with the death sentence, even 4 years' penal servitude is bearable to a young man of eighteen. The case counted as a great success for John A Behn, until then little known beyond the under-privileged classes of which he himself was a product.

At that time, the solicitors of Liverpool were very much in the English public school tradition. The addition to their ranks of this bustling, pugnacious every day type of man without an aitch in his vocabulary except in the wrong places, was tolerated rather than welcomed.

When he died in 1945, still a bachelor leaving a considerable fortune, he was a resident of fashionable West Kirby where he lived with his two sisters Gertie and Hannah. He had never tried to improve his voice which became in time a great asset. He was a most unlikely lawyer, but he filled a social need in the city long before legal aid made professional representation widely available.

John Arthur Behn came of a line of Danish seamen. He was educated at St John's Church of England school, in the Stanley area of Liverpool. What early jobs he had I do not know but after a time he became a solicitor's clerk in Dale Street, Liverpool.

His great pal of that time was another solicitor's clerk William Proctor, a man with an equally unpretentious background.

It was possible in those days for an ordinary clerk after ten years to be offered articles leading to becoming a solicitor. Both Behn and Proctor followed this course. Proctor proceeded further, transferring to the bar and finishing up as the Senior Liverpool County Court Judge and with a Knighthood, just about the most difficult judge I remember, but that is another story.

Such tuition for examinations as there was, was given by young barristers and solicitors. John A Behn was fortunate in being coached by Rigby Swift, a member of the Northern Circuit and a future High Court Judge.

When John Behn qualified as a solicitor he set up in practice on his own in Dale Street in a building which had earlier been a public house and had only recently been closed as a house of evil repute.

Actually, Dale Street itself was at that time considered to be very much in the Second Division as an address for solicitors. It was the address of most of the Police Court advocates, nearly all men of ferocious voice and a belligerent frame of mind.

My early recollections of John A Behn were that he was more ferocious and belligerent than most of the others put together. In addition to this, his plain speaking made it quite an occasion to be present when he was in court. On one occasion he appeared on behalf of a married lady, who, he said, had been bruised very badly by her husband. Behn addressed the magistrates, "I 'ave 'ere your Worships some photographs of the 'orrible bruises inflicted on my client by 'er 'usband."

With that, the barrister for the husband (now a High Court Judge), objected that the photographs had not been formally proved.

"None of your 'igh Court tricks 'ere," said Behn, "I'll prove them myself," which he did, by going into the witness box.

The story which is most associated with John A Behn is when he was defending a motorist accused of crossing a road junction without giving adequate warning. The motorist had previously informed Behn that he had come to the crossing, sounded his horn twice, looked for traffic and then crossed the road.

When the motorist was giving evidence in Court, he forgot to say that he had sounded his horn. Advocates are not allowed to put answers in a witness's mouth, or to suggest what the answer should be.

"When you got to the crossroads," said Behn, "what did you do before you crossed the road?" The poor man was lost for a reply, Behn however was not lost. He was able to blow his nose reminiscent of the Ingoldsby Legends couplet:

"There too full many an Aldermanic nose, Rolled its loud diapason after dinner."

Behn blew his nose twice, very reminiscent of a loud motor car horn.

"And now," he said, "what did you do before crossing the road?"

"Oh," said the driver, "I blew my horn."

"'Ow many times did you blow your 'orn," said Behn.

"Twice," said the driver, very relieved indeed.

On another occasion the magistrates found his client guilty before he even started to open the defence.

"Your worship," said Behn, "I 'ave to point out that you 'ave not yet 'eard the defence."

"Very well!" said the Chairman of the magistrates, "we will hear the defence now."

"Your worships will most emphatically not," said Behn, "this case will start again with another bench of magistrates!" And it did.

One year John A Behn was asked to adjudicate for the Speaking Prize for the Liverpool Law Students Association. As I won the prize that year, I have always felt a warm feeling of regard for this massive sergeant major type of man with his little old fashioned moustache and his ever present bowler hat which he took off only at the last moment when he entered the court room and which sat dutifully beside him on the solicitors' bench.

Behn claimed to have a stock of questions which put the opposing witness in the wrong whatever he replied. I suppose that they were based on the well known question, "Have you stopped beating your wife?" Whether the answer is yes or no, there is a damaging admission of guilt.

Talking of wives, a young couple came one day to Behn under the impression that he was a Registrar of marriages and asked him to join them in matrimony

"I don't join 'em," he said, "I separate 'em."

In his time, Behn must have defended many thousands of Liverpool's citizens mostly doing his best in hopeless cases, but the odd thing was that once Behn took up a case, he never gave up.

He had been a notable athlete in his younger days. Many prizes had come his way. The gift of dogged determination which is an attribute of all successful athletes was the same characteristic which John A Behn kept all his life. He never gave up a client's cause. If you have to lose, he used to say, go down with your flag still flying bravely.

Most of the police court work was in the hands of a few solicitors all of whom were used to rebuffs, and all of whom developed very thick skins.

One in particular, JH Neville, was in this class. He and Behn invariably rubbed each other up the wrong way. The court would quickly fill if these two were battling it out together.

On one occasion, the fur was flying particularly strongly, Behn taunted Neville beyond all endurance and at last Neville was driven to say, "Mr Behn, what your sort want is more self control."

Behn retorted without the flicker of an eyelid, and it should be noted that Neville was a leading Roman Catholic and very much involved in the religious controversies of the day, "Mr Neville," said Behn, "What your kind want is more birth control!"

It has always been a defect of the English legal system that bringing it up to date has been largely left to private litigants at their own expense. I am very pleased to pay tribute to the solicitors of Liverpool, hard-headed and of independent mind, who have never shirked the responsibility of challenging old fashioned or outmoded decisions.

John A Behn himself was not afraid to go to the House of Lords. In fact there is an old adage: "John A Behn is the wisest of men, when the Lords get mouldy, he briefs Noel Goldie."

On this particular occasion, however, he did not brief Noel Goldie, and the Lords did get mouldy. He acted for a widow Mrs Albert Proctor whose husband had been drowned in the East Float Dock at

Birkenhead in 1920. During a thick fog, white chains were provided as a guide for those on the dock estate, but some other workmen on the previous day had removed a section of the chain and had not replaced it. It was at this point that Albert Proctor was presumed to have fallen in.

Mr Justice Branson tried the action but entered judgement against the widow, finding that, even if the chain had been there, the accident might still have happened. The Court of Appeal reversed this decision by a majority of two to one. The House of Lords by a majority of three to two reversed the decision of the Court of Appeal, so that the widow lost and got no damages for the death of her husband, although four top judges had supported her claim. In that case John A Behn was before his time.

There was still a great tendency for judges to find every obstacle in the way of any plaintiff succeeding against any defendant. No doubt insurance companies think that the pendulum has swung too much the other way, but in any event the case of Proctor v The Mersey Docks and Harbour Board was a shocking example of vacillation by judges at all levels. The law should be certain and clear to all citizens and this is happily now fully-recognised even if it will never be possible fully to achieve. As I mentioned earlier, litigation is often very chancy, the fault sometimes lying with the uncertainty of the law, although it is surprising on how many occasions it happens that witnesses fail to prove as facts, the matters they have come to give evidence about. And it should be remembered that until the facts have been established the case is not even on its feet and the law cannot even be applied.

But this book is about lawyers rather than the law. It is the duty of an advocate to present his client's case to the best advantage. The tussle between solicitors or barristers, particularly in the magistrates' courts, sometimes reaches the stage of downright rudeness. You may wonder that they ever speak to each other again, but you would be surprised to find that they are probably bosom friends. Shakespeare put it very well when he said:

"Do as lawyers do, strive mightily, But eat and drink as friends."

This puts in a nutshell the philosophy of John A Behn.

HARTLEY SHAWCROSS, LORD SHAWCROSS

By Graeme Bryson

Rodney Klevan QC, Hartley Shawcross, Lord Justice Russell. Bar Mess at the Adelphi Hotel, Liverpool to mark Shawcross's 90th birthday. Shawcross attained his 100th year in 2002.

When compared with my student days in the later 1920s and early 1930s, the law these days seems to be terribly complicated. Then one could answer most problems from general principles. In the intervals there have been so many conflicting cases and statutes that it must be very difficult for a really top barrister to present the law adequately and fairly in a complicated case. I wonder that many of them have stayed the course. Lord Shawcross is one who didn't.

Attorney General at the age of 43, and Chairman of the Bar Council a few years later, he seemed to leave plenty of time in hand for an assault upon the even higher legal offices, either politically or judicially. Yet he retired from practice and from his Recordership at Kingston-on Thames at the age of 55. As he said at the time, "The law is a stern mistress, demanding undivided attention."

After some rest, he said he hoped to have an opportunity of gaining greater knowledge of the industrial and commercial activities which, as he said, are so vital to the well being of our country.

Within a week, he had taken up a legal appointment with Shell Petroleum Company and also become a director of the Ford Motor Company. Other top directorates followed, but I hope that he found time to follow what he calls his favourite pursuits of riding and sailing, and of country life in Sussex.

Hartley Shawcross (standing and looking back from the front row of counsel seats) calls for a witness at the Gresford Colliery Disaster Inquiry in 1934.

It may be that he felt that legal preferment might be prejudiced by the verbal impulsiveness which has marred the picture of balance which he otherwise gives.

The language of his attack on the press possibly did him more harm than ever it did the press.

Now, as Lord Shawcross, he is able to survey his past brilliant achievements, even his controversies, with a lordly detachment. He has survived them all and emerged victorious, an elder statesman of the nation and a centenerian.

Hartley's father was an English scholar of some standing and an authority on Samuel Taylor Coleridge whose eldest son was also Hartley. While the most celebrated Hartley family on Merseyside makes jam, doubtless he was named after Hartley Coleridge. I always thought that Hartley Shawcross was a most distinguished name to carry through life.

He achieved the distinction of being Chairman of the Board of Governors of his old school, Dulwich College. He and his younger brother Christopher both left Dulwich to study for the Bar.

Hartley made his first major mark in life when he was placed top in the Honours List at the Bar finals and shortly afterwards, in 1925, he was called to the bar at Grays Inn, thereby following in the footsteps of

Liverpool's two Lord Chancellors, Lord Birkenhead and Lord Kilmuir, who were also at Grays.

In the period between the wars, very few barristers in Liverpool made substantial incomes. I have known barristers return from holiday to take a brief at a guinea or two. Shawcross probably found the offer of a Lectureship in law at Liverpool University very welcome indeed, as he had not been an immediate success in London – but then who was? It was odd that he should obtain this post considering that he had no university degree himself.

The legal faculty at Liverpool University was rather unusual. It was situated on the top floor of a commercial building connecting Cook Street with Harrington Street in the legal centre of the city, and well away from the University itself. With its wonderful library it was a victim of a German Blitz on Liverpool. The lectures nearly all took place at 4.00pm or 5.00pm so that the normal professional life of the staff would not be interfered with. All the professors and lecturers were then barristers in practice in the city. About this time I became a student and found that Hartley Shawcross was my tutor for Roman Law and Private International Law. I hope he will not mind me saying so but we found him to be the dullest of lecturers or perhaps it was the subjects that were dull; I am afraid that very little attention was paid.

The 16 students of my year included two rather tough rugby types, one of whom subsequently played for England and another who afterwards became a staid President of the Liverpool Law Society. They used to idle their time playing above-halfpenny on the desk which brought forth testy comments from Mr Shawcross.

In the same year that I obtained my own law degree, the University gave Hartley Shawcross an honorary degree of Master of Laws while in 1969 he received an honorary doctorate, a distinction which he well deserved, though not in my view for teaching the students of forty years ago.

At the same time that he was a senior lecturer, he was also in practice in Liverpool in the Chambers of Maxwell Fyfe. Maxwell Fyfe by this time was coming up to his most successful Liverpool period and some of his success rubbed off on the other members of the chambers, quite apart from their own connections.

Shawcross was somewhat of a dandy with a voice which seemed to combine an educated south country drawl with a sharp touch to it rather reminiscent of London (perish the thought that I should say Cockney).

It has always surprised me that the Liverpool barristers with the sort of 'stage presence' which has not always gone down to well in bustling Liverpool, seem to have a tremendous success in North Wales. In Shawcross' case, I am not suggesting that he was not a success in Liverpool, but he did have a stage presence and he did do well in North Wales.

It is also surprising in view of his later political views that he had quite a licensing practice, which was considered to be a Conservative perquisite in Liverpool, the tradition being the best part of a hundred years old.

Actually I do not remember that Shawcross betrayed any political views before the war; indeed it is said that he was offered a Conservative seat on the Council. It must have come as a great surprise to many people when he accepted nomination as the Socialist candidate for St Helens to win the seat for Labour in 1945, while his brother Christopher also fought and won neighbouring Widnes in the Labour interest.

I have since been surprised to hear that Shawcross the schoolboy at Dulwich advocated Socialism in the School Debating Society and actively canvassed in the 1918 General Election for the Socialist interest.

He never gave the impression of being overburdened with worries. His cross examinations were almost casual, although he was master of the sardonic phrase at the right moment. Not for him the clenched fists or singing arms of the old type advocate. He was from start to finish, an English gentleman, proud and detached in appearance, but shy in reality.

He had to have great compassion at home. His wife was unwell for long periods; year after year he took her to the fresh mountain air of Switzerland, hoping that she would return restored to full health, which sad to say was never so.

The first case to bring him national prominence was the Inquiry into the dreadful explosion at Gresford Colliery in Denbighshire in 1934, with a total loss of life of 265, the worst colliery disaster since the 1913 disaster at Senghenydd in South Wales.

Colliery disasters are probably the most harrowing tragedies which can be imagined, and there were far too many of them. One got used to the harrowing waiting period; the agonised helpless relatives, particularly the women, at the pit head; the tremendous courage of the colleagues of the doomed men; in fact 3 of the rescue team also died. So destructive was the explosion and fire, that even three years later only three bodies had been recovered.

The loss of 265 men was a loss which called out for vengeance. At the enquiry the mine owners were the natural target for vituperation by all. To represent them was therefore a most delicate task.

This burden was allotted to AT Miller KC and Hartley Shawcross.

Miller had to return to London after a few days so that Shawcross was then on his own. It says a great deal for Shawcross that the employers' position never got out of hand, and it should be remembered that his principal opponent for the Union was Sir Stafford Cripps KC.

It became clear that there had been many irregular practices in the mine but no proper complaint had been made to the management or to the Inspector of Mines, or to the Pit Committee, possibly because it was a mine where only a few of the men belonged to a Trade Union.

To give just one question and answer on this point :

"Q. Did it ever occur to you that the matter was so serious that it ought to be communicated to the Inspector of Mines whom you saw every day?

A. Well, look here, I thought it was, but I'm telling you this. I was taking the same risk as the foreman was taking and I had the same chance and I had to take the same chance as them. If they were afraid to say that, then I was afraid to say it."

When the Report came out it was a bit of a muddle. The Chief Inspector of Mines who was the Chairman, seemed to whitewash the mine owners while his two assessors said that it was the management which was responsible for the safe workings of the mines and that the Chief Inspector of Mines was the last person in the world who should have conducted the Inquiry.

It was however agreed to recommend that all miners should be members of a union which would allow for many beneficial safety precautions under the Coal Mines Acts.

In the meantime Maxwell Fyfe had taken silk and gone to London, leaving Shawcross as the undisputed champion of the Liverpool field. They were to join forces again in the trial of Dr. Ruxton at Manchester assizes, where Shawcross was the Junior. With two leaders, I cannot remember that he examined any of the principal witnesses, but to be there at all was a compliment to his considerable ability.

In Liverpool's many courts, he seemed to appear in almost every type of case, an excellent training for a barrister.

Successful junior barristers are almost driven to apply for silk, with the upheaval (in those days) of having to move to London. There is so much paper work for a junior barrister to attend to that it is a relief to transfer to the very different type of work dealt with by a King's Counsel or Queen's Counsel.

Shawcross took silk in 1939, the same year in which he was honoured by being appointed a Bencher.

What might have become a normal career as a silk was blasted almost immediately by the outbreak of War. He applied to join the services but was prevented by a weakness resulting from an old back injury obtained in a climbing accident.

This must have been very galling because he has always shown patriotism and had earlier been accepted into the Emergency Reserve of Officers. Among other positions during the War, he was Regional Commissioner for the North West.

I do not know what took him to St Helens to fight the 1945 General Election but he emerged victorious to appear at Westminster and to tell the defeated Conservatives just who were the masters now.

His standing amongst his colleagues was such that he at once became Attorney-General and with it Chief Prosecutor for the United Kingdom for the War Crimes Trials at Nuremburg, taking over from his former Liverpool colleague Maxwell Fyfe.

His speeches told in simple but telling language both of our horror at the events and of the noble approach to the trial which was to be a milestone in world history.

This is how he opened his five hour speech as the trial commenced:

"The British Empire has twice been victorious in wars forced upon it within the space of one generation, but it is precisely because we realise that victory is not enough that the British nation is taking part in this trial.

There are those who would perhaps say that these are wretched men who should have been dealt with summarily and swept aside into oblivion, without this elaborate and careful investigation, but not so will the world be made aware that the waging of an aggressive war is not only a dangerous venture but also a criminal one.

From the record of this trial all generations shall know not only what our generation suffered, but also that our suffering was the result of crimes against the laws of peoples which the peoples of the world enforced, and will continue in the future to uphold by international co-operation not based nearly on military alliances but firmly on the rules of law."

Nearly a year later he made the closing speech:

"That the defendants," he said, "participated in and are morally guilty of crimes so frightful that the imagination reels at their very contemplation is not in doubt. Let the words of the defendant Frank be remembered, 'Thousands of years will pass and the guilt of Germany will be remembered.' Total and totalitarian war," Shawcross went on, "waged in defiance of solemn undertakings and in breach of treaties, great cities from Coventry to Stalingrad reduced to rubble. And in their graves, crying out not for vengeance, but that this shall not happen again, ten million who might be living in peace and happiness at this hour, soldiers, sailors, airmen, civilians killed in battle that ought not to have been. In all our countries, when perhaps in the heat of passion or for other motives which impair restraint, some individual is killed, the murder becomes a sensation. Our compassion is roused, nor do we rest until the criminal is punished and the rule of law vindicated.

Shall we do less when not one but 12 million men and women and children are done to death, not in battle, not in passion, but in a cold calculated deliberate attempt to destroy nations and races.

Two thirds of the Jews in Europe exterminated, murder conducted like some mass production industry in the gas chambers and ovens of Auschwitz, Dachau, Treblinka, Buchenwald, Mauthausen, Maidench, Oranienburg."

These were, I think, the most telling speeches of all those delivered at Nuremburg.

Shawcross probably reached the highest point of his professional skill and panache in the Lynskey Tribunal of 1948.

While we had won the war, the fruits of victory seemed a long time in coming. Almost everything seemed to be on rations. Almost everybody seemed prepared to accept a few eggs rather furtively, a half bottle of whisky, or a few yards of cloth at an exorbitant price and with a thrilling sense of guilt.

Sometimes there was a prosecution to show that even the great could not escape retribution. The Lord Lieutenant of Lancashire suffered this fate for making, without licence, a few alterations to carry out his official duties more effectively.

The 'Great Occasion' however was the Government Scandal of 1948 which turned out to be a comic opera occasion with Sidney Stanley as the big buffoon. How this beguiling, garrulous, twice bankrupt, flabby Polish Jew ever got into such high society is a mystery.

But get there he did, and so played off one against another that John Belcher, a Junior Minister at the Board of Trade, was to be entwined at the centre of a bribery scandal which was to result in a Tribunal in which the characters now remembered are Judge Lynskey the former Liverpool barrister and solicitor, Sidney Stanley, John Belcher MP, and Hartley Shawcross.

As Attorney General, Shawcross had the responsibility of bringing the true facts to light which involved both an examination in chief and a cross-examination of the major witnesses. Shawcross was able to pursue the dual role with a quiet, confident ability which was a great credit to British justice. Without the legal trappings of wig and gown, he was still outstanding in the best possible way.

Of course Stanley was the most unusual witness it is possible to imagine, agreeing with almost everything but in such a way that he made it sound as he was the simple injured innocent.

Even Shawcross found it difficult to tie down this large, agreeable, slippery eel, but there was no doubt that it was the same charm which Stanley displayed in court which also had affected the ex-Railway Clerk Belcher, who had entered Parliament with Shawcross in 1945.

In 1948 the Observer, in a special article on Shawcross, concluded with these words:

"The talents of Sir Hartley Shawcross are undoubted. Whether they are balanced by mature political judgment and statecraft it is perhaps too early to judge."

Has the problem been solved? I do not know but his many admirers in the north country will continue to think of him as an excellent product of the Liverpool bar. It was a loss to the law that he did not stay the course in his chosen profession.

DAVID MAXWELL FYFE, VISCOUNT KILMUIR

By Graeme Bryson

David Maxwell Fyfe, then Lord Chancellor, at the Liverpool Law Society annual dinner at the Adelphi Hotel, 31 October 1958. From left to right: Lord Mayor (Harry Livermore), Edmund Davies J, Lord Chancellor Viscount Kilmuir (David Maxwell Fyfe), Glyn Jones J, Thesiger J, E Holland Hughes (President), Stevenson J, and Jimmy Hadfield (Vice-President).

"The nearest thing to death in life is David Patrick Maxwell Fyfe." What a dreadful couplet about Liverpool's most eminent lawyer since the Second World War; Queens Counsel, Member of Parliament, Solicitor General, Attorney General, Secretary for Wales, Home Secretary and Lord Chancellor, in addition to being the Chief Prosecutor at the War Crimes Trials at Nuremburg.

Any one of these distinctions would be enough for most people, but the whole array is quite glittering.

From 1922, when he was called to the bar, until 1954 when he was made Lord Chancellor, David Maxwell Fyfe was part of the Liverpool scene. In so many ways he was the exact opposite of Liverpool's other Lord Chancellor, Lord Birkenhead.

Fyfe was solid, unathletic, slow moving, slow talking, kind at all times, and patently sincere. No Judas taunts were ever cast at him such as Lord Birkenhead had to endure. His progress like everything else he did was slow and measured; he took longer than Lord Birkenhead to become an MP, to become Lord Chancellor. He never gave the impression that his object was the next rung on the ladder of success. He seemed content to do his present job really well. And yet in two rather surprising matters his writings disclose identical attitudes to those of Birkenhead. The first is a burning ambition from an unprivileged start in life. David Maxwell Fyfe put it like this:

"To have become Lord Chancellor of Great Britain with no advantage of wealth, station or influence, is something of which I am proud. There are no heights which a man cannot scale if he so wishes. If he starts without these obvious advantages, then he must toil harder, he must march every inch of the way; what success, comes however early or late, tastes more sweet."

These words are almost Lord Birkenhead's own as in the second surprising similarity between the two. Lord Birkenhead took special pride in calling himself an adventurer. Life is an adventure he said. What is the title of Maxwell Fyfe's autobiography? *Political Adventure*. And what was Maxwell Fyfe's reward for his 20 year services as Minister and Lord Chancellor? He was sacked at 7 hours' notice by Prime Minister Harold Macmillan. It seems strange that the holder of the highest office in the land, the Keeper of the Queen's conscience, the head of the Judiciary and of the legal profession should have such a tenuous hold upon his own position.

During his period in office, he had appointed by recommendation nearly all the judges; judges who are virtually irremovable. But for the Lord Chancellor himself, at breakfast on the 12th July 1963, he was happy in office. By dinner time all was over and as he said himself. "Thus ended at 7 hours' notice the great political adventure on which I had embarked as an undergraduate forty years ago." Liverpool seemed to be a magnet for the Irish and Welsh in particular, but also for the Scots. Maxwell Fyfe was one of the latter, the son of an Aberdeen schoolmaster, a pupil of Watson's, Edinburgh where he achieved no particular distinction. Entrance to Oxford in 1917 required no particular academic distinction, merely a willingness by one's parents to pay the fees and the cost of maintenance. With the Great War then in its deepest stages, Balliol College, like the University itself, had as its students men unfit for war service and a few young men still not of an age to volunteer or to be called up.

With the end of the war Oxford was inundated with returning warriors including Anthony Eden, who had been a Lt. Col. and Leslie Hore Belisha who had been a Major. Maxwell Fyfe led a busy life at Oxford where he became involved with politics, but he was not a top liner like Birkenhead. Not for him the Presidency of the Union, or top honours in examinations; he combined his studies with work for his barrister's examinations and was called to the bar at Gray's Inn in June 1922.

He had been fortunate in meeting or hearing most of the great political figures of the day, and had even been present at Lord Birkenhead's famous 'Judas' Speech.

Like Lord Birkenhead at the same stage of his career, Fyfe was short of money. He was not keen to be an unknown in London where the early years of practice at the bar were unlikely to bring financial rewards. He was fortunate in meeting a great Liverpool character Judge Dowdall who is profiled elsewhere in this volume.

Dowdall suggested that the Liverpool bar would be more likely to yield a quicker financial return and so in December of 1922 he entered chambers with Howard Jones, in 25 Lord Street. Two former solicitors and future judges, George Lynskey and Wilfred Clothier, shared chambers with him, so that he was able to take advantage of their great practical experience. Barristers have some resemblance to taxi drivers; they offer their services for hire and are at the call of the other branch of the legal profession, the solicitors. But in those days, the most usual way of becoming known was to attend the criminal courts in the hope of getting a dock brief at one guinea. This consisted of the accused pointing out any barrister in court and he would naturally try to avoid choosing those with the whiter – and newer – wigs. As it was considered bad form to refuse a dock brief, there was occasionally an undignified exit by the well established barristers if it was known that a dock brief was to be given.

Fyfe was to get his first brief in this manner at Liverpool Assizes when a man accused of entering the Liverpool Warehouse of Cohen & Doll found himself without Counsel to defend him. He pointed to Fyfe who conducted his defence unsuccessfully. The man was found guilty, but to Fyfe's great pride was not sent to prison.

For the next twelve years Fyfe was a junior in Liverpool applying himself assiduously to his work and achieving a reputation for solidity and reliability. It was during this period that I first met him, because he had a great deal of work in connection with the Rent Restriction Act, possibly the most complicated piece of litigation ever devised to deal with the basic rights of simple people. My firm acted for many of the major property owners in Liverpool and my father was an advocate of considerable ability in this field. I remember many a tussle before the County Court Judges, Dowdall, Thomas and Proctor. By the time that my firm entrusted me with advocacy, Fyfe had taken silk and moved to London so that I cannot claim to have crossed swords with him, but I was able to admire the way in which he achieved his successes.

I have often tried to analyse how this success was achieved, but have never really quite understood how it came about.

He was already becoming corpulent; his voice was slow, and rather monotonous, almost dreary. He had a large and rather Teutonic type of head.

He seemed immovable and immune from disaster. Mentally he missed nothing, although facially he seemed to express neither shock nor concern nor pleasure.

This sounds like faint praise, but through it all there emerged his great virtues of sincerity, kindness and ability. One felt that because he had conduct of the case he was on the side of the right. This was in sharp contrast to Lord Birkenhead who always gave the impression that he could have argued just as well for the other side. Three years his junior but very much his contemporary at the Liverpool bar was Hartley Shawcross, as unlikely a socialist barrister as one could imagine, handsome, elegant, well dressed and with a voice to match, Shawcross vied with Fyfe for the more lucrative Liverpool briefs. Each was successful and together they dominated the Liverpool bar.

Fyfe was not engaged in many of the fashionable 'causes célèbres' of his day. Within his first year he had appeared in a murder trial at Manchester Assizes, at a nominal fee in a poor person's defence. His client was convicted although subsequently reprieved from the death penalty. It was an interesting case because Fyfe's client had fired a pistol over the head of a crowd to secure the escape of his colleague who had actually committed the murder. The jury found that they had a common design to help each other and to use all force necessary for this purpose including murder.

As his first year drew to a close, Fyfe had averaged over £3 weekly in fees. It was not sensational but it was a sound beginning. At about this time he was fortunate to be in Carlisle as Junior of the Northern Circuit when there were prosecutions of 64 defendants arising out of riots at Whitehaven.

He was briefed to assist Counsel for the prosecution and received a cheque for £87 the equivalent of 6 months' earnings. No doubt early successes such as this spurred him on with his romance with a Liverpool girl Sylvia Harrison, sister of Rex Harrison, the actor. They only had a 4 day honeymoon in 1925 but they had a lifetime of perfect happiness ahead. It was he said "the sweetest cheque he ever received".

I have heard no amusing anecdotes of Fyfe's cases, no shafts of wit such as are associated with so many fashionable barristers. And yet the atmosphere in his presence was never frigid nor full of gloom; rather was it comforting and friendly. His own realisation of his personality comes out time and again in his autobiography. He seemed to cherish the few kind words said of his various efforts.

But these efforts were more and more appreciated by those with the responsibilities of briefing barristers and his income rose in the early 1930s to a steady £5,000, which was big money for a junior counsel. It encouraged him to apply for silk in 1934, when for one year his income fell back to £3,000, showing how chancy is the decision to become a senior barrister. Others, some from Liverpool, who were successful junior barristers, have utterly failed as silks.

Fyfe found that summer very difficult. A couple of briefs only at Liverpool and Manchester were not enough to keep him occupied where previously he had been a very busy junior. He was very relieved to find that by the autumn he was being sought after again.

In one of his London cases, he was briefed at 350 guineas against Sir Patrick Hastings in a Daily Mail libel case, where he acquitted himself so well that he was briefed again against the other great advocate of the day, Sir Norman Birkett, but as Fyfe himself admits he was defeated horse, foot and guns! I suppose that the Ruxton murder case is the best known of Fyfe's cases, although he was the second silk to Jackson, with Hartley Shawcross as junior. Many will remember this macabre case of the Indian Dr. Ruxton who had lived in Lancaster Square, who murdered his wife and nurse-maid and who cut up their bodies in hundreds of pieces and scattered them over many parts of North England and South Scotland.

I remember particularly how the popular song of the day was rendered as,

"When you grow too old to love,

I'll have you to dismember."

The trial was presided over by that great Lancashire Judge Singleton, while Norman Birkett fought strenuously but unsuccessfully for the defence. Fyfe's examination of Professor Glaister was a model of thoroughness in the technical field of medical jurisprudence.

By now Fyfe was MP (unopposed) for the West Derby Division of Liverpool.

He represented this great division of Liverpool until he was made Lord Chancellor nearly twenty years later. There is no doubt that despite his many important offices at Westminster he retained an intense interest in the welfare of his constituency.

He held strong views however that the work of a Member of Parliament is national in character and that there are dangers in too close an association with the trivialities of constituencies.

War in 1939 found Fyfe at the age of 40, a member of the reserve of officers, but he was assigned, rather dully as he puts it, to the Judge Advocate-General's Department, where he was to stay until the big re-shuffle of the War Cabinet in 1942; then he was appointed Solicitor-General by Winston Churchill, largely on the recommendation of Brendan Bracken.

From this time on, Fyfe was near the centre of the Counsels of State, becoming Attorney General at the end of the War until the Conservatives were surprisingly defeated in the 1945 General Election and went into the political wilderness. The Socialists swept into power bringing with them Fyfe's Liverpool adversary in law and politics, Hartley Shawcross.

In the meantime, plans had been laid for the great trial of the War Criminals at Nuremburg. Fyfe had been the British representative on the first Allied Committee to decide if such trials could be held. There were three schools of thought in relation to the major war criminals, to take no action at all, to 'do a Napoleon', without trial either by execution or imprisonment or finally to give a full and fair trial.

But there was no precedent for a successful trial though there had been a number of failures.

In the discussions to decide the point, Fyfe represented Britain and was elected Chairman by the representatives of the other three countries concerned, United States, Russia and France. Great credit is due to Fyfe for the skilful way in which he handled the production of a mini-charter to govern the conduct and progress of the trials.

And then at the height of the planning, came the 1945 General Election. Fyfe had to divide his time between electioneering in West Derby, Liverpool, and his heavy duties as Attorney General.

While Harold MacMillan and many other Conservative stalwarts were banished from Parliament, Fyfe managed to hold his seat with a comparatively respectable majority of 3,428. He was replaced as Attorney General, and as Chief Prosecutor at the Nuremburg Trials, by Hartley Shawcross.

Fyfe was so involved with the preparation of the trials that Shawcross asked him to become Deputy Chief Prosecutor. In fact Shawcross made only the opening and closing speeches, and did not stay in Nuremburg, so that virtually the whole burden fell on Fyfe during that long, dreary ten month trial.

The evidence-in-chief took four months after which came the cross-examination of Goering. There is no doubt that Goering worsted Jackson the American Chief Prosecutor which set the cross-examinations off on rather a low note.

I have already mentioned how Fyfe was always so appreciative of appreciation. He valued this extract from The Times:

"If Goering could score in debate off Mr Justice Jackson, he had to tread warily in the face of Sir David Maxwell Fyfe, who, gathering up the threads of the diplomatic and military conspiracy, frequently had his opponent defending himself with clenched fists, his face flushed and angry. Five hours or more of remorseless cross-examination by the British Advocate drove home the full impact of the case against the Reich Marshal, who sounded less plausible than at any time during his week in the box".

Fyfe in this cross-examination dealt in great detail with the shooting in cold blood of nearly fifty of our airmen in their attempted escape from Stalag Luft III. Goering had an amazing grasp of facts and was able to produce them in the most telling way, at will. It says volumes for Fyfe that he was able to deal so capably with this redoubtable witness, and to show Goering's full complicity as a War criminal.

Fyfe returned to England a year later to find his party still in opposition. He made his first political speech at Accrington, but as he himself says it was not a great success being too long, laborious and closely reasoned. This is a danger with lawyer politicians, particularly since the old jury lawyers have disappeared. Their training is too technical, their minds and words too pedantic for the popular platforms.

This was Fyfe's last period at the bar and he was much sought after at big fees. It was one of my own duties to tax or assess Counsel's fees at the conclusion of trials, and I well remember being troubled at his fee of 400 guineas in a case involving alleged negligence by a firm of Liverpool Solicitors, in which about £100,000 was claimed. Fortunately, the action was settled, so that I was never called upon to arbitrate in this particular matter. I should say that at the time the normal fee for a Leading Counsel at a Liverpool case on assize was about 25 guineas.

When the Conservatives were returned to power in 1951, Winston Churchill appointed Fyfe Home Secretary and Minister for Welsh Affairs. He was very tickled at his nickname in Wales 'Dai Bananas', after the Fyfe banana boats! I think that Fyfe compared very favourably with any Home Secretary of modern times. All his decisions seemed well balanced and reasonable. Then was to come in 1954, the final and finest chapter in Fyfe's legal saga. He was appointed Lord Chancellor, with the title of Viscount Kilmuir, becoming thereby Head of the Judiciary, Speaker of the House of Lords and a Member of the Cabinet, a unique and illogical trilogy of lawmaker, judge and politician. In this capacity, Kilmuir served three Prime Ministers, Churchill, Eden and MacMillan, while the political fortunes of his party were to ebb and flow and ebb again.

Politically he was at the heart of the great decisions of the times including the Suez crisis. He strongly supported and continued to support Anthony Eden's decision as to Suez and maintained that history would prove him right. Unfortunately Eden's health failed, the country was never united behind the Government, and from the present distance of time, it is hard to see right and wrong.

On the legal side, Kilmuir was responsible for much of the reform of litigation, during his nine years in office. He was also a first class Ambassador of the English legal system, receiving legal deputations from abroad, while he himself travelled to various parts of the world to take part in conferences of lawyers. His speeches still make excellent reading.

The Lord Chancellor was on one of these visits to the United States in 1960 when I had the unfortunate experience of being shot at by a litigant who was dissatisfied with one of my decisions in the Liverpool Bankruptcy Court. Two of my staff were in fact wounded in coming to my aid, before the assailant was overpowered. The Lord Chancellor wrote me a charming and appreciative note, and he later received us all at the House of Lords with our wives, and gave us some tokens of appreciation from Her Majesty. He was very keen to hear of his old friends in Liverpool and made us all feel very welcome indeed.

If I were asked to criticise Lord Kilmuir, I would say that there was very little to criticise, but that his voice, charming in small quantities, became rather overpowering at length; that his speeches while full of sense and cogent reasoning, became rather too much for the ordinary palate.

But I have no wish to criticise him at all. The Liverpool bar and the Northern Circuit are very proud of their two Lord Chancellors in a period of one lifetime. One does not achieve such distinction without a very heavy balance of true worth.

TB (TOM) ROBERTS

By Ted Birch

Thomas Blackburn Roberts (of Cuff Roberts) was born in Pembrokeshire in 1911 of parents dedicated to the care of the deprived and sick through Poor Law Institutions and hospitals, Tom Roberts became a boarder at Liverpool College in 1919. He engaged fully in work and play becoming Head of House and an outstanding member of the school rugby XV being described in the school magazine of the day as 'an untiring leader of the pack'. However, cricket was his first love and he captained the First X1 in his final year.

He became a Governor, a deputy Chairman, and Chairman of Liverpool College in 1979. His contribution to the college was immeasurable. He was also Governor of Huyton College for Girls.

His early interest and competence on the sporting field continued as he played rugby for Liverpool's First XV. He captained Bootle Cricket Club and later West Lancashire Golf Club.

In 1938, he negotiated the best legal agreement of his life and married Joyce Millicent Robinson and had two children, Jill and John.

Tom graduated in Law from Liverpool University in 1932, was admitted a solicitor in 1933 and after assisting the late W C Cuff, eventually joined him in partnership. In 1947 W C Cuff died. In 1948, Tom took Harry Howell into partnership and it proved to be the second best legal agreement of his life as together they established a powerful base of complementary skills which formed the bedrock for the development and growth of Cuff Roberts.

In his legal career, Tom was a notable Secretary of the Liverpool Law Society for six years and in 1965 he became President.

His high reputation as a lawyer and as an honest man doubtless led both to his appointment as President of the Merseyside and Cheshire Rent Assessment Panel and Chairman of the Board of Arbitration which awarded United Kingdom Bank employees a 35 hour week.

He joined the Territorial Army before the 1939/45 war and during the war he served in the Royal Artillery at home and abroad, and with two mentions in despatches, he demobilised with the rank of Major. He subsequently took command of the 533 Light Anti Aircraft Regiment as Lieutenant Colonel until he retired in 1949. He was awarded the Territorial Decoration.

Continuing the family tradition so notably established by his parents, he was Chairman of the East Liverpool University Hospital Management Committee from 1962 to 1973 and then was appointed by the Secretary of State for Social Services the first Chairman of the newly formed Liverpool Area Health Authority (Teaching). This was his principal area of service to the community during the years of 1973/79. One of his greatest interests through these years was the training and education of nurses and nothing claimed his eager attendance more than a Nurses Prize-giving.

He was appointed a Deputy Lieutenant for the County of Merseyside in 1977 and in her Majesty's Jubilee Honours in the same year, a Commander of the Most Excellent Order of the British Empire.

These are the basic facts of the life of Thomas Blackburn Roberts and here I acknowledge the initial research of his old friend, John Kellaway. Impressive as these facts are, they barely do justice to the man himself.

Space will permit only one example of his humour. Having been made a partner in 1967, Tom appointed me Fire Officer. Taking my new found power very seriously, I arranged a fire drill and on the fateful day the whole of Cuff Roberts exited 25 Castle Street and assembled on the pavement – everybody that is except Tom Roberts. I dashed back into the building to find him working at his desk. "Come on Sir," I said "it's a fire drill." to which he replied, "P*** off, I'm busy."

Tom Roberts combined a natural air of authority and leadership with a wonderful sense of humour and a genuine generosity of spirit which made him a man both loved and respected by all who knew him.

MR JUSTICE MCNEILL

By His Honour Richard Pickering and Charles Elston

The unexpected death of Mr Justice McNeill on the 26th February 1990, while presiding over a long and demanding trial, was a sad loss not only to those who knew him but to the profession as a whole. It brought to an end a life which had given much time to work on behalf of the profession and of the public. The trait was inherited. David's father was active in politics, eventually serving as Mayor of Bebington. His mother became Chairwoman of the Cheshire Federation of the Women's Institute.

David Bruce McNeill was born on the 6th June 1922, and was educated at Rydal School and Merton College, Oxford, becoming a Bachelor of Civil Law as well as Master of Arts. Joining the Army, he was commissioned into the Reconnaissance Corps in 1943. He served all the way from North Africa through Sicily and Italy and into Germany.

Called to the Bar by Lincoln's Inn in 1947, David came back to the North West and joined Melville Kennan (father of Mike Kennan, the solicitor) in his Chambers at 34 Castle Street in Liverpool. Those chambers were then in an interesting state. The two bright particular stars of that set, Robertson Crichton and Danny Brabin had left to start their own chambers. They had taken with them the Senior Clerk to 34 Castle Street, the able Kenneth Nugent. The former junior clerk, promoted to look after the chambers, was a man far more noted for his kindly courtesy than his administrative efficiency. The situation was replete

The last reading of the Proclamation at St George's Hall in January 1984.
Judges; Lawton, Nance, Blackett-Ord, McNeill J, Temple QC, Edward Jones, Bingham QC, Pickering, Recorder Justin Price QC

with possibilities for professional triumph or disappointment. David was resolved on triumph.

Melville strengthened the chambers by bringing in Christopher Cunliffe as his number two, Frank Paterson was already establishing himself. Other members of chambers tended to be transient. It was in that milieu that David established himself in the small room in chambers that looked drearily in to the central well of the building, and set about fulfilling his driving ambition.

That vaulting ambition was a major dynamic in David. Those of us who enjoyed his company and valued his great ability were more conscious that he was virtually always on duty in the service of his ambition. Such attitude did not shut him off from concern for his fellows. His political stance was slightly left of centre. At Oxford he had been one of Roy Jenkins' circle. At his marriage to Margaret in 1949, Felicity Attlee, the daughter of the then Labour Prime Minister, was a bridesmaid.

Perhaps it was the envisaged expenses of matrimony as well as ambition that led to him becoming a lecturer in law in 1948 at Liverpool University. But ambition was well served. One of the courses he gave was to the Law Society students, the potential clients of the future. By 1958, the demands of the courtroom, where David's real ambition lay, far outweighed those of the lecture theatre and he abandoned academic work.

David's combination of great ability with remarkable energy had created a very substantial general common law practice. David's returned briefs, products of his success, often irrigated the sparse professional landscape of his juniors in chambers. One learnt to hold such briefs with reservation. It was not unknown for such a junior to be on the very verge of opening the case to the court, when the door would swing open, and David would enter.

David was one of the phalanx of Counsel – nearly all from London – engaged to represent the various parties concerned in the 'Summerland Disaster'. That was the disastrous fire which completely destroyed an almost new leisure centre containing pools, artificial beaches, sun-bathing areas, numerous play areas with equipment for children and distractions for their parents, together with restaurants, bars etc, all protected from the vagaries of the British climate in a building on Douglas promenade, Isle of Man, which was clad with a glass-like material called 'Oroglass'. The fire, in 1973, resulted in the deaths of 50 people and a large number of injuries, many of them resulting from severe burns. The vast majority of those injured and killed were visitors to the IOM. The Manx Government decided that a Public Enquiry was necessary and realising that the resources of the Manx Bar were totally inadequate to deal with such proceedings (the total population of the IOM at the time was well under 50,000) they authorised the briefing of UK Counsel to represent all parties – subject to a Manx advocate being briefed as a junior (in all cases this proved to be in addition to a British Junior thus providing a nice little sinecure for a number of Manx advocates).

All the potential defendants were insured by British insurers – and the insurers who instructed Weightmans had the misfortune to insure 3 of them and provided separate representation for each of them. The Manx authorities, with the approval of the Lord Chancellor, appointed an English Judge, Cantley J formerly of the Manchester Bar and very well-known in Liverpool, to head the Enquiry sitting with 2 Assessors, both expert in fire causation, resistance and protection and fire-fighting. The Judge made it known at the outset that he would only allow one set of Counsel to appear on behalf of all those injured and killed and the solicitors who acted on their behalf instructed David, then a fairly new Silk, as leader with Richard Pickering as his junior. Another Liverpool counsel engaged was RJD ('Ronnie') Livesey, subsequently a QC and Circuit Judge but then briefed by Bill Lister on behalf of Douglas Corporation as Junior to a Leader who was said to be the only English counsel who was also a member of the Manx Bar and therefore eligible to appear without a licence from the Deemster (for which all English counsel had to appear in Court and make formal application before the Tribunal sat). Counsel from London taking part included Robert Alexander QC – now Lord Alexander of Weedon, Andrew Leggatt QC, subsequently a Lord Justice of Appeal, and Michael (now Sir Michael) Ogden, for many years Chairman of the Criminal Injuries Compensation Board.

Cantley J could be distinctly testy but it seemed to Charles Elston of Weightmans that from the start of the Enquiry he went out of his way to be so with David, making it clear very early on that he saw no reason for the injured and dependants of those killed to be represented – or, at least, to be represented actively. From time to time throughout the hearing, which lasted for over 4 months, he interrupted David's questioning of witnesses, quite unnecessarily. All this David accepted with great forbearance, but without altering his conduct of the proceedings in the interests of his clients. Actually the only civil proceedings issued as a result of the disaster were in respect of quantum as all the insurers concerned agreed at an early stage to share the cost of disposal on a full liability basis – and none of the proceedings issued reached trial, all being settled well before that stage.

When the newly-constructed QE2 Law Courts were formally opened by HM The Queen accompanied by the Duke of Edinburgh in May 1984, David was the senior Judge sitting at Liverpool and was also Presiding Judge of the Northern Circuit and was therefore very much involved in the planning of the Opening and played a prominent part in the proceedings on the day. When the Royal party reached the court where the Queen was to perform the formal opening, David sat on one side of her with the Lord Chancellor on the other and the Recorder and a sizeable number of Northern Circuit High Court Judges, plus the Lord Lieutenant (and Charles Elston as High Sheriff at the time) arrayed around. The Address of Welcome was read by the Leader of the Circuit, Benet Hytner QC from Manchester – a rather neat reversal of the position a few years previously when the Queen opened the new Courts at Manchester and the Loyal Address was given by Liverpool's own Edward Wooll QC – in each case a master of words operating in the 'opposition's' home territory. The other High Court Judge sitting with David at this time was 'Pat' Russell (subsequently a Lord Justice) also from Manchester but very well known and liked in Liverpool and a great friend of David. He and David and their wives were a most hospitable and agreeable partnership at the Judges' Lodgings throughout their stay. Both were able to get some relaxation at home at weekends.

David, as the senior Judge, presided at the final sitting at St George's Hall and also (on the same day) at the first normal sitting in the principal court in the QE2 building. The final sitting in St George's Hall was rather subdued, consisting simply of tidying up some unfinished business followed by short but cogent speeches by David and David Gilliland QC, the Senior Counsel present. David and a small retinue then proceeded to the QE2 building where most of the courts were already in session and David went straight to the principal court and after a short introductory speech from him, it was down to business.

The QE2 building was designed with the intention that the Judges' car would be driven straight into the underground car park from where they could proceed by lift to the corridor at the back of the courts having no contact with the public en route. David and Pat Russell strongly objected to reaching court in this way, considering that the Judges ought to be seen by the public, arriving fully robed to carry out their duties, and they insisted – despite protests from the police – on being driven to the front entrance and then processing, preceded by a police officer, their clerks, and the High Sheriff if in attendance, to the lift giving access to the secure part of the building. This practice was continued for a year or two but ultimately the increasing demands of security led to it being abandoned.

Charles Elston was privileged to sit with David on a number of occasions during 1984/5 and from doing so quickly came to realise how carefully he prepared in advance for each day so that he was as completely familiar with the papers for each case in his list as he was with his brief in his days at the Bar. In consequence he was able to conduct a trial quickly but with due regard for the old maxim that 'justice must not only be done but must be seen to be done.' He seemed certain to achieve preferment and it was a cruel blow that he died so suddenly while still in his prime.

Finally, emphasis on David's dedication to his work should not obscure the fact that he had many other interests. He was very happily married to Margaret who was a great support to him at all times and he was devoted to his 4 children. When his children were at preparatory school locally, he was present at every school function he could possibly get to. He was fond of opera and the theatre and was widely read so that he was knowledgeable about a wide range of subjects and an excellent conversationalist, and he also played golf with enthusiasm and enjoyment.

HECTOR MUNRO

By William Lister

Hector Munro, Hubert Perrett and Arthur Mayer as partners in the firm of Herbert J Davis, Berthen & Munro.

Hector Munro was a small, square shouldered man with a perpetual look of intelligence shining brightly from him. He knew that his intellect would always prevail whatever the problem facing him.

He was himself the son of a solicitor (of like name) in practice in Liverpool in the early years of the century, who published a novel in 1911 and who died prematurely in 1916, leaving his wife in penury with four children, so that she was compelled to make a living by taking in lodgers in her small terraced house. His father's bequest to Hector was a love of literature, both British and French. The latter was to become of particular importance in his life.

Hector, who was born in 1900, was educated at Liverpool College. In later years he would say that he always answered the question on a census paper about what education he had received as "None, I went to Liverpool College".

In 1917 he enlisted in the famous infantry regiment, The Artists Rifles (it must have been in their Bantam Battalion) and was shot and seriously injured in the head in France. His life was in serious danger, but he recovered after a year in hospital.

Thereafter he was articled to Arthur Inman, a Liverpool Solicitor who was a legend for untidiness, with papers even tied with string to the electric light cord, if Hector is to be believed. Ultimately his articles were transferred to the respected firm of Oliver Jones, Billson & Co. Upon qualifying he went to live at Toynbee Hall, the University's Settlement in Canning Town, East London, where he acted gratuitously as a Poor Man's Lawyer, whilst working as an Assistant Solicitor with the City commercial practice of Lawrence Messer & Co. His political leanings were towards socialism and he was a member of the Fabian Society.

At this stage of his life, he fell in love with one of his mother's lodgers, a French student teacher, whom he married, and they continued to live at Toynbee Hall, where their son Donald was born. The marriage did not last very long and ended in divorce.

Hector married twice again, but had no other children.

For a short time he practised in the East End of London in partnership with Miss Edith Annie Berthen, who was the second woman in the country to qualify as a solicitor and the first to set up in practice on her own account. In 1927 she was asked by Herbert John Davis, a prominent member of the substantial Liverpool Jewish Community and for a considerable time an Alderman of the City, to join him in partnership. She had been articled to him. She accepted upon the basis that he also accepted Hector (whom he did not know).

Davis had had a number of associates over the years including Darrell Mace as an assistant solicitor, but none of the relationships had prospered. However, the practice of Herbert J Davis Berthen and Munro then came into being, and whilst Miss Berthen departed, Hector remained for the rest of his professional career back in the city of his birth, at Prudential Buildings, 36 Dale Street.

He was very much a lawyers' lawyer. It was a privilege to witness him using the scalpel of his mind on a contract. He was fascinated by the operation of the law, was ready to take on virtually any legal business, whether profitable or not, and was devoted to detail. These qualities were known to and appreciated by his fellow practitioners to the point where many Merseyside solicitors with troubles would make sure that they saw Hector at an early stage. His love of the law transcended the mere practice of it. He savoured the opinions of leading members of the Bar, particularly those of Hartley Shawcross KC. On the international scene, he had high hopes of the League of Nations and he assembled a significant library of books on Comparative Law, centred on France, and particularly the Nuremburg War Crimes trials. The Law did not fill the whole of his mind. His main leisure interests were chess and literature (especially Chaucer, Balzac and Dickens). It was his interest in chess that was to make him famous as a young solicitor.

It has been said that we are all entitled to our 15 minutes of fame and Hector's were spectacular.

It was his interest in chess, both 'over the board' and in extensive correspondence, representing Lancashire at tournaments all over the country, that led to his involvement in the Wallace case. Hector played in the evenings at Liverpool Central Chess Club down the stone steps in Cottle's City Café in Castle Street, after it had closed for the day.

William Herbert Wallace was also a member of the Club, and knew Hector only by sight. On the night of Tuesday 20th January 1931, Wallace's wife Julia was brutally battered to death in their terraced home at 29 Wolverton Street, Anfield, Liverpool. Wallace was charged with the murder a fortnight later and at that stage he instructed Hector to act for him. He was a Prudential door-to-door insurance agent, and by chance Hector was in practice in their building.

It will serve no purpose to revisit the detailed facts of the Wallace case here. Many books have been written on the subject. The object here is to see the case through Hector Munro's eyes as a defending solicitor 70 years ago. Those who would wish to have an account of the case should read *The Killing of Julia*

Wallace by Jonathan Goodman (1976). Hector invited this author to write it, and cooperated with him to provide a readable and exciting, if somewhat partial, account of the whole affair. The case itself is truly fascinating. In the words of Raymond Chandler "The Wallace case is unbeatable, it will always be unbeatable".

The rules of engagement for defenders in criminal cases in 1931 were harsh by current standards. Hector's primary problems were that Wallace had little or no money to pay for his defence, and that Liverpool City Police had rejected any other possible murderer than Wallace, had bent all their efforts on assembling a case against him and no-one else, and were not above suppressing evidence that did not favour their case. It was a low time in the history of Liverpool City Police Force. The basic reason was the Police strike of 1919. There was a Bill then in Parliament that caused the Police Union to call a strike.

The call went largely unheeded, save for London and Liverpool, where more than half the members of the force went on strike and were dismissed. (Hector had enrolled as a special constable out of a sense of public duty and served largely in the London Road area). For a period, Liverpool city centre was wide open to all types of crime and troops patrolled Scotland Road and Byrom St Naval ships were in the Mersey. Crucially 48 of the dismissed strikers had been sergeants and so much leadership material had been lost.

The head of Liverpool CID was a Fenian-hunter from Special Branch, a big hard-drinking man who had just been appointed to the post (having survived the 1919 strike, as many peers had not).

The murder gripped the imagination of Liverpool people. Middle-class murders were few and far between in those days and the prospect of a judicial hanging operated powerfully on peoples' minds.

Hector threw himself into the investigation. Those were days without 'experts' apart from doctors. He did the whole defence investigation himself, haunting the area, speaking to everyone, particularly the witnesses, walking the routes, measuring, timing, taking tram rides that Wallace took on the night of the murder. He got a list of people from whom the police had statements. He lacked time and resources to see them all (the list covered several foolscap pages). He was refused permission to see their statements. He was clear in his mind that the Police were intent on securing Wallace's conviction.

Hector's problems were manifold. That there had been a murder was undeniable. The only suspect in the minds of the Police was Wallace. Investigations into other suspects had not borne fruit. There was no money to fund the defence. There was little time to investigate (bearing in mind other ongoing professional commitments) and to make matters worse at the remand proceedings in the Police Court on Wallace's arrest, the prosecuting solicitor Dick Bishop ('handsome, humorous and a bit of a bully') set out the facts which were calculated to leave no doubt that Wallace was the murderer and in doing so made 18 mis-statements of fact, none of which were in favour of Wallace, and his speech was reported verbatim in all local newspapers. Wallace could make no effective response. From that moment onwards Wallace was the murderer in the minds of the Liverpool public. There was no question at that time of the committal proceedings being unreported. Prejudice was rampant, and Hector was the daily recipient of hate mail. There was also the fact that Wallace was a singularly unattractive man in both manner and appearance.

The only possible source to fund the defence was the Prudential Insurance Company itself. On being approached it offered a sum that was helpful, but far short of the likely fees to Counsel. Then, however, a tentative offer of help came from an unconsidered source, the Prudential Staff Union, of which Wallace was a member. It was decided that in order to resolve the matter there should be a secret mock trial in London, with Union officials from all over the country present, at which the prosecutor's speech from the committal proceedings was read out and then Hector made the defence. After that, Hector was questioned by the officials, who also argued the case among themselves. This lasted two or three hours. Finally a secret ballot was unanimous that Wallace should be helped, and the Executive Council then guaranteed the whole cost of the defence after members had made their own donations, which were (in the event) substantial. As a result, Hector was able to brief an austere but fashionable London silk to defend his client. The trial took place, the prosecution opened high and crumbled to some extent, but the defence was of the view that the jury were not listening to the evidence ('not a buck rabbit among them' according to Bishop). The Judge summed up for an acquittal. The Jury convicted after an hour's consideration, and so Wallace was condemned to be executed. The Judge did not make the normal comment that he agreed with the Jury's verdict. An appeal was lodged. A collection was put in hand to help it, but fared ill among the people of Liverpool. 'He done it, all right' was the typical response.

Wallace appealed on 10 grounds (one of which was the effect of the mis-statements at the Police Court and their effect after newspaper coverage) but only the point that the Jury's verdict was unreasonable was central. No such decision had ever been made by the Court of Criminal Appeal. Jury verdicts were sacrosanct. It was deemed extremely improbable that Lord Chief Justice Hewart, who was to preside and who vigorously championed the Jury system, would be sympathetic. After two days' argument the Judges retired for 45 minutes. Hewart announced the Court's verdict – 300 words took 14 minutes to deliver, 'completely sadistic' according to Wallace's Junior Counsel – before finally saying that the case "was not proved with that certainty which is necessary in order to justify a verdict of guilty".

The timetable had been unbelievably swift by modern standards. The murder was on 20th January, the arrest on 2nd February, committal for trial 4th March, the trial before Mr Justice Wright and a jury at Liverpool Assize began on 22nd April and ended in conviction on the Saturday afternoon 4 days later, after 26 witnesses had been called for the prosecution and 10 for the defence. Wallace was then notified of his date of execution and an appeal to the Court of Criminal appeal was heard over two days on the 18th and 19th May, when the Jury's verdict was quashed.

Wallace's short life thereafter was unhappy. Hector collected libel damages from a variety of newspaper publishers for him for their indiscretions, and Wallace died 2 years after the murder. The informed view at the time was that it was more likely than not that Wallace was the murderer, but that the evidence fell far short of proving that proposition.

The intervening years have brought factors to light which strongly suggest that the murder was committed by an acquaintance of the Wallaces, who was named at the time by Wallace, whom the police only considered briefly. Roger Wilkes' book *Wallace. The Final Verdict* (Triad 1984) sets out that situation well. However, a subsequent book *The Murder of Julia Wallace* by James Murphy (The Bluecoat Press 2001) based upon the prosecution's papers shows that Wallace was the only credible suspect. The controversy continues.

Hector was then able to return to the rough and tumble of a solicitor's life at a lower level for the next 40 years.

Although Hector probably would have regarded himself as primarily a 'common lawyer', his legal availability was very wide and, to use his own expression, he considered himself to be a 'taxi on the rank' ready and willing to take on a wide variety of business, profitable or not (before the days of legal aid). He was a lucid and attractive advocate and practised extensively in the Magistrates' Courts (in those days, tactlessly called the Police Courts). He assiduously attended the District Registrars for his own summonses (this was before the days when Court Clerks were regularly employed to deal with Registrar's summonses) considering that it was courteous and desirable for the Solicitor dealing with a case to attend personally before the judicial authority. His legal enthusiasm extended to a detailed knowledge of the 'White Book' (the guide to Supreme Court Practice) and rare were those who could fault him on a point of procedure. During the 1939-1945 War he went to live in Prestatyn and travelled into Liverpool every day. He was an Air Raid warden in the city and in Prestatyn he was a member of the Home Guard, where he may not have been the most efficient private, but he was undoubtedly the most enthusiastic.

After the war, he devoted substantial time to National Insurance law, becoming a part-time chairman of the Liverpool National Insurance Tribunal to which he devoted great care during the Tribunal hearings and in the formulation of the tribunal's decisions. He developed an encyclopaedic knowledge of National Insurance law, which led him to compile a monumental reference book of over a thousand pages dealing with virtually every detail. Unfortunately, in a very limited market, no publisher would take this on!

In 1960 he was the witness of a near tragedy on one of his appearances before Mr Registrar Bryson. One of his clients was a West Indian clubowner. Eventually, this gentleman was made bankrupt and had to appear at bankruptcy hearing before the Registrar. During the course of this, he produced a revolver, firing at but fortunately missing the Registrar although causing serious injuries to two Court Officials. Hector's military training was immediately to the fore. He made a swift tactical withdrawal to an office down the corridor to a telephone and the Police were summoned. Casualties were thus kept to a minimum! Hector had been shot once before and did not wish to repeat the experience.

His practice, in the days when specialisation was not pursued to any great lengths, covered fields such as divorce (where he was concerned in several cases which, nowadays, might be described as 'fashionable' and in which he briefed Sir John Mortimer's blind father) commercial contracts, arbitration tribunals and tax enquiries. He was not deterred by the arcane depths of Chancery. An Affidavit with nearly one hundred exhibits in a succession case is still remembered. He was even competent, in an emergency, to help hard pressed staff with conveyancing and probate.

An example of Hector's aptitude for detail was the role he undertook as Counsel to an ad hoc Tribunal set up, under the chairmanship of a High Court Judge, to investigate allegations of fraud in the gaming industry in the Isle of Man. He carried out, virtually single handed and, amidst a busy Liverpool practice, over several months, the most elaborate police type investigation, involving the interviewing of numerous witnesses and the taking of elaborate statements, presenting them to the Tribunal hearings.

He retired from active practice in 1970 when his firm amalgamated with Campbell & Co., and became a Consultant. In practice, this meant that he still attended at the office every day, but gave up his room and retired to the boardroom where he became a cuckoo-in-residence. He had the use of the boardroom table where he spread his documents and stacked everything not in immediate use, was constantly wreathed in tobacco smoke, and surrounded by ash which moved like desert sands in any breath of air. Irritation came over him when the room was required for its proper purposes. After all, the lifestyle suited him!

He retired reluctantly. Like nearly all solicitors of his generation he had no pension arrangements and had spent his income without consideration for the future. Most solicitors in the property world had made money by financial deals. Common lawyers did not. Furthermore all solicitors relied on the sale of their practice share of 'Goodwill' at retirement to bring in a capital sum. By the date of Hector's retirement 'Goodwill' had become a dirty word because of the introduction of Capital Gains Tax and had been all but abandoned by the profession. He went with a decent annuity paid by his partners. It was the only alternative to dying of old age at his desk. This was a scenario being played out up and down the country.

His last years were spent with his third wife in Hampstead. He persuaded Neville Coghill that he had misunderstood a material factor in his commentary of Chaucer's *Man of Law's Tale*, and published an article in a literary magazine demonstrating that the plot of *Wuthering Heights* turned entirely on a misunderstanding of the English law of entailment, and that if the law had been properly understood by the author, none of the book would have been worth writing. However, he did feel that his revelation would not result in the book being withdrawn from circulation. He died in 1981.

Solicitors like Hector Munro had a little more time than the practitioners of today, but they commanded the respect of the public and contributed to innate respect for the Law and lawyers in his generation. His integrity was apparent to all.

To the end, he believed Wallace to have been innocent.

MR JUSTICE NIELD

By Charles Elston

Dinner for Sir Basil Nield given by his marshals, Oxford and Cambridge Club, 19 May 1977.

Basil Nield was the younger son of a Liverpool Solicitor, CE Nield, whose firm was Nield & Milligan and who lived at Upton-by-Chester. The elder son Douglas became a solicitor and subsequently a District Registrar who sat at Birkenhead. Basil went to the Bar and from the time when he was called in 1925 until the outbreak of World War 2 in 1939 he was in Chambers in Liverpool. During this time he built up a reasonable practice but he was, perhaps, unfortunate to have entered the arena some three years behind FE Pritchard and simultaneously with Hartley Shawcross, both of whom quickly showed themselves to be high-flyers, and both of whom were at that time rather more spurred on by ambition. On the outbreak of War he was commissioned in the Army and he had a distinguished War record, serving in many more theatres than most. He was on the Staff in East Africa, Palestine, Eritrea, and Persia (now Iran) and then after a spell as Assistant Deputy Judge Advocate-General Middle East he returned to Staff duties in Normandy and the Low Countries, ending up as a Lt.Col. with a Mention in Despatches and an MBE (Mil).

On return to civilian life in 1945, he took silk, and as he had been elected MP for Chester in 1940 he was not very often seen in Court in Liverpool again. Presumably his election to Parliament must have been at a bye election and have been virtually, if not completely, in absentia as he was at the time serving at GHQ Middle East Forces. Possibly he was unopposed as Party Politics were more or less in abeyance during the War. I can recall a few post-War appearances as a Leader at Assize sittings, when he had been allowed to make pairing arrangements – usually with his old colleague and frequent Court adversary, S Scholefield Allen QC, then Labour member for Crewe.

In 1956 Basil Nield was appointed the Recorder and first permanent Judge of the Crown Court at Manchester and four years later he was elevated to the High Court bench where he continued to sit until he reached the retirement age of 75 in 1978. He became the first, indeed the only, Judge to sit at all 61 Assize centres – before the 800-year old Assize system was abolished on the recommendation of Lord Beeching who had previously prompted the truncation of the existing railway system. The result of Basil's journeying throughout the Assize circuits was a book – *Farewell to the Assizes* – which provides very interesting and entertaining reading but is unfortunately now out of print.

Basil Nield was a product of Harrow and Magdalen College, Oxford and it showed. He was in my experience always scrupulously courteous, particularly to ladies and instructing solicitors. In Court he eschewed histrionics but his manner was incisive and he could be a formidable cross-examiner, particularly in criminal cases – there was definitely a hint of the iron hand in his velvet glove. He could be excellent company but, particularly after he had been a Judge for several years (and possibly realised that he was unlikely to go further) he did have moody periods when he was liable to make life difficult for counsel appearing before him. He remained a bachelor but was occasionally accompanied on circuit by his twin sister, Miss Beryl Nield – a prominent figure in Chester where she served both as Sheriff of the City and subsequently as Mayor.

After his retirement, Basil Nield lived mainly at his flat in London, but with frequent visits to his sister's house outside Chester, until increasing infirmity caused him to move to an apartment in Osborne House, Isle of Wight, where he died in 1996 at the age of 93.

SIR SANDERSON TEMPLE QC

by Judge David Lynch

Ernest Sanderson Temple was the son of a solicitor in the family firm Temple & Bargh in Kendal. He was born on 23 May 1921 and died on 7 August 1999 in his 79th year. He was dear to the hearts of all members of the Northern Circuit. His was a long, full life, usefully spent in the service of others.

Sandy Temple (for that is how we knew him and will remember him) was best known as Recorder of Liverpool from 1977 to 1991 when he was at his peak. He often remarked "I said I would do it for five years and I stayed for fourteen". He tackled the workload with enthusiasm and vigour. If a man had to go to prison, then to prison he would go, but Sandy Temple did his best to avoid that course if he possibly could. In this regard he saw himself as a disciple of Charles Henry Hopwood QC, the Recorder of Liverpool from 1886 to 1904 dubbed 'Hopwood the Good' by the Humanitarian League for his compassionate approach to sentencing.

He was a master of the English language. It was a delight to hear him sum up a case using words not in normal everyday use but of an elegance which captivated a Liverpool jury. A good many examples of Sandy's craftsmanship have been preserved in the Circuit's records for those yet to come.

There are many stories of Sandy. At the tribute to Sandy at Liverpool on 10 August 1999, Bill Waldron QC reminded us of two of the best.

Sandy settled a divorce petition which included the following allegation "The Respondent absconded from matrimonial cohabitation and has never returned thereto". There came the inevitable request for Further and Better Particulars of the precise manner of the said absconding. Reply by Sandy Temple, "Initially as a pedestrian and thereafter as a fare paying passenger on a Ribble motor omnibus".

Sandy was Master of the Vale of Lune Hunt for many years. His interest in horses extended to being an umpire in a competition for driving a coach and four. He sat behind the Duke of Edinburgh to assess his driving skill. Unfortunately at a particularly difficult part of the course the Duke lost control and the coach overturned spilling out its occupants. The Duke came to Sandy profuse in his apologies. "Don't worry, Sir," said Sandy, "I imagine your family's good for the damages".

Sandy Temple was educated at Kendal School and went on to Queen's College, Oxford. He was called to the Bar at Gray's Inn in January 1943. Distinguished War Service in the Border Regiment in India and Burma delayed his election to the Northern Circuit and practice in Manchester until 1946. He was awarded the MBE for his war service having held the temporary rank of Lieutenant Colonel when still in his early twenties. Sandy became the pupil of Edmund Rowson (later a silk and the first Recorder of Blackpool) at 26 King Street, Manchester. Sandy's skill with juries in crime and civil and his ability to persuade judges to see his point of view attracted many solicitors and a substantial practice. He went on to 60 King Street as Head of Chambers – in mid 1961 taking on as a pupil Christopher Rose. He took great pleasure watching his former pupil progress to Vice President of the Court of Appeal, Criminal Division.

Sandy took silk in 1969. He was the first Queen's Counsel to stay in Manchester and not move to London. He was particularly proud of that. He was Chairman of Westmorland Quarter Sessions and sat for the last time on 30 December 1971 in Kendal Town Hall where, 21 years later, he was to be admitted as an Honorary Citizen. Manchester's loss was Liverpool's gain when Sandy was appointed as Circuit Judge and came to Liverpool as Recorder. Upon his knighthood in 1988 the Bench and the Bar of Liverpool commissioned a portrait which hangs for six months in the Judges' Lounge in Liverpool and for the remainder of the year in the Robing Room. His memory is further perpetuated by the photograph he presented to the Liverpool Bar of his winning ride in the Bar Point to Point in 1954 on an animal quite different from the zebra/donkey, his transport of later years.

Sandy Temple had an enormous love for the Northern Circuit demonstrated by his regular attendance at mess despite his serious illness. The Circuit was his life and he needed to be with the Circuiteers. He was a 'walking encyclopaedia' of Circuit history. After his retirement he would occasionally telephone me with 'intelligence' of some Circuiteer forgotten by all but Sandy and Sandy and I would set out from his home at Yealand Hall to seek out the Circuiteer and record his reminiscences.

MRS JUSTICE ROSE HEILBRON

By Judge David Lynch

Rose Heilbron was born in Liverpool on the 19th August 1914, the daughter of Max and Nellie Heilbron. Educated at Belvedere School and at Liverpool University, in 1935 she achieved a first class honours degree in law with an LLM two years later.

Her outstanding performance in Bar Finals earned her the prestigious Lord Justice Holker Scholarship. She was called to the Bar at Gray's Inn on the 3rd May 1939. Her many years devoted service to her Inn were recognised when she became a Bencher in 1968 and Treasurer in 1985.

She joined chambers at 43 Castle Street as the pupil of Richard Trotter (later a County Court Judge). She had one pupil, the late Judge John Edward Jones (father of local solicitor Glenys Arden and barrister Michael Jones). Her election to the Northern Circuit on the 2nd February 1940 was proposed by the Recorder of Liverpool, Edward Hemmerde KC.

She soon built up a substantial Criminal and Personal Injury practice because she was a persuasive advocate who gave her all in the preparation of a case and the mastery of detail. Whilst still a junior and without a silk she argued before the House of Lords and against two King's Counsel, one of whom was the Attorney General Sir Hartley Shawcross KC, the case of Adam-v-Naylor (1946. 2AII ER 241)

In 1945, Rose married Dr Nathaniel Burstein and in 1949 their daughter Hilary was born. Hilary followed

Dinner given by the Lord Mayor (Harry Livermore of Silverman Livermore) at Liverpool Town Hall on 4 December 1958 in honour of the legal profession. From top left: Rose Heilbron, Recorder of Burnley; Judge Elwyn Jones; Tom Alker, Town Clerk of Liverpool; Judge Harold Brown; E Holland Hughes, President of Liverpool Law Society; The Lady Mayoress; Judge Laski, Recorder of Liverpool; The Lord Mayor; Judge Fraser Harrison; Professor Seaborne Davies, Pro-Vice Chancellor of the University; Glyn Blackledge, Presiding Judge of the Liverpool Court of Passage; Judge Alistair Hamilton; Jimmy Hadfield, President-Elect Liverpool Law Society; Judge Edward Steel; Darrell Mace; Bertram Benas; Laurence Rutherford; Tom Harley; George England. (At the back some of the company are mirrored)

in her mother's footsteps and took silk in 1987. Rose Heilbron's practice was such that in 1949, after only ten years' Call, she was included in Lord Jowitt's list of Silks.

For the next 25 years she was in constant demand appearing in many important cases at Assize in St George's Hall and on appeal in London.

The criminal case for which she is best remembered is her defence of George Kelly who was convicted in 1950 of the murder of the manager and assistant manager of the Cameo Cinema in Webster Road. The first trial of Kelly and another man took 13 days. At that time it was the longest ever murder case.

The jury disagreed. Kelly was subsequently tried on his own, convicted and hanged. The Court of Criminal Appeal rejected her efforts to have the conviction quashed on the ground that a juror was a convicted felon and was disqualified from sitting. The case has has been referred to the Court of Appeal by the Criminal Cases Review Commission and will be heard in early 2003.

The Law Society Annual Dinner at the Adelphi Hotel in 1979. Gordon Lindsay, John Stebbings (President of The National Law Society), Rose Heilbron J, Barrie Marsh (Liverpool Law Society President), The Very Rev Lawrence Jackson (Provost of Blackburn).

This was just one of the countless murder trials in which she appeared. It was also one of the many firsts she achieved during her career.

Rose Heilbron was the first woman:

(a) to take a first class honours degree at Liverpool University;

(b) with Helena Normanton to take Silk in 1949;

(c) to lead in a murder trial;

(d) to plead a case before the House of Lords;

(e) to be appointed a Recorder. In 1956 she replaced Neville Laski as Recorder of Burnley; she held the appointment until it was abolished by the Courts Act 1971. Thereafter she was the Honorary Recorder until 1974.

(f) to sit as a Commissioner of Assize;

(g) to sit at the Central Criminal Court;

(h) to be elected Leader of a Circuit (Northern Circuit 1973/74) ;

(i) to be a Treasurer of any Inn;

(j) to be appointed a Presiding Judge of a Circuit (Northern Circuit 1979/82).

Liverpool Law Society Annual Dinner at the Adelphi Hotel in 1981. Sir Denis Marshall (Past President of the national Law Society), a colleague of Sir Denis, Phillip Johnson (High Sherriff of Merseyside), Donald Gray (Rector of Liverpool), Sir Kenneth Stoddart (Lord Lieutenant of Merseyside), Peter Howell Williams (President of Liverpool Law Society), David McNeill J, Rose Heilbron J and Tony Ensor (then Vice-President of Liverpool Law Society but now a Circuit Judge).

The first woman High Court Judge was not Rose Heilbron! It was Dame Elizabeth Lane. Rose was the second. She was appointed to the Family Division in August 1974.

She seems to have started a trend as five Northern Circuit women High Court Judges have followed her example – Mrs Justice Bracewell (Family Division 1990); Mrs Justice Ebsworth (the first woman to go directly to the Queen's Bench Division – in 1992); Mrs Justice Smith (QBD 1992); Mrs Justice Steel (QBD 1993); and Mrs Justice Hale (Family Division 1994). Mrs Justice Hale was appointed to the Court of Appeal in October 1999 – the first ever woman from the Northern Circuit to be so honoured. Dame Rose sat with distinction in the Family Division (with a period in Queen's Bench whilst Presiding Judge) until her retirement on the 1st November 1988. Her remarkable achievements were marked by the award of an honorary LLD from the Universities of Liverpool, Manchester and Warwick.

LORD MORRIS OF BORTH -Y- GEST

By Charles Elston

John William Morris' father, Daniel Morris, was a client of my former firm (in the days when it was Weightman Pedder & Weightman before it became Weightman Pedder & Co. en route to becoming just Weightmans) and I can remember when I was articled in the mid 1930s there being a Morris Trust strongbox, the Trust being in favour of Daniel's daughters. I was told that Daniel had been Manager of a Bank, I think the Midland, in Allerton Road, Liverpool. The family came from Portmadoc and Daniel may well have started his banking career in the North and South Wales Bank which had several branches in and around Liverpool before it was absorbed by the then London Joint City and Midland Bank.

John William was born in 1896 and went to the Liverpool Institute and from there to Liverpool University and subsequently to Trinity Hall, Cambridge. Before he graduated at Cambridge, War had broken out and he enlisted in the Royal Welsh Fusiliers and served until the end of hostilities, becoming a Captain and being awarded the MC. On demobilisation, he returned to Cambridge to complete his course and in 1919 he was President of the Cambridge Union. There followed 2 years at Harvard University Law School as Hodges Choate Memorial Fellow before he returned to England and was called to the Bar at the Inner Temple in 1921. At this stage of his career, he appears to have had political ambitions and in 1923 and again in the following year he stood as Liberal candidate for Ilford but being unsuccessful on both occasions he made no further attempt to enter Parliament and instead concentrated on his legal career. However he remained friendly with the Lloyd George family who came from the same part of North Wales and at one time it was rumoured that he harboured romantic ambitions towards the redoubtable Megan. If so, nothing came of this and he remained a lifelong bachelor. Although he had a fine upstanding figure he was softly spoken and his manner was superficially rather diffident. It is said that at the time when his friendship with Megan Lloyd George was attracting attention among their friends one of them asked Megan's mother (the first Mrs Lloyd George who did not live to see her husband ennobled) what she thought of the situation to which she replied, "Oh, I think John Willie would make an admirable daughter-in-law."

Morris joined the Northern Circuit and was in Chambers in Liverpool before he took Silk in 1933, after which he appeared regularly at Liverpool Assizes and he also became Judge of Appeal for the Isle of Man from 1938 to 1945. During the 1939/45 War he served on numerous Government-appointed Committees, including the Home Office Standing Committee on the Defence Regulations 1939-1945, and Committees on War-damaged Licensed Houses 1942/3 and on 'the selling-price of houses' 1945. He also sat as a Commissioner of Assize in 1942 and 1945. Indeed he seems to have been from this stage of his career onwards a favoured choice for service on Government appointed bodies – one of 'the great and the good.' The range extends from Chairmanship of the Reference Tribunal under the Coal-Mining Conciliation Scheme 1955/65 to the Committee on Jury Service 1963/4 and the University Grants Committee 1955/69 with many more in between. He was Pro-Chancellor of the University of Wales from 1955 to 1974.

Morris was appointed a High Court Judge in 1945 and in the following year he came on the Northern Assize and sat in Liverpool. The first Civil case he heard there was one in which my firm acted for the Defendants. The Plaintiff was a seafarer who had sustained injuries by falling down the stone steps of a building in Victoria Street where there was a barber's shop in the basement. This occurred on a Saturday afternoon in summer shortly after the end of licensing hours when the shop was closed and the street was more or less deserted. The plaintiff admitted having just emerged from licensed premises and said that seeing a barber's pole outside a nearby building he decided to get his hair cut – which seemed a dubious proposition to most of those in Court, including, probably, the Judge although he gave no indication to that effect. The evidence as to how dark or otherwise the steps were was conflicting and the Judge decided to inspect the premises in comparable conditions, and having done so he subsequently gave judgment for the Defendants, holding that the steps even with no lights on in the shop posed no hazard to anyone exercising reasonable care. Surprisingly, the Plaintiff appealed and, even more surprisingly as no question of law arose, the appeal was upheld apparently on the grounds that the Judge's assessment was not reliable as he knew there had been an accident when he inspected the premises.

There were few, if any, subsequent occasions when a decision of Morris J was reversed and 6 years later he was appointed to the Court of Appeal, followed 9 years later in 1960 by his appointment as a Lord of Appeal in Ordinary. He sat in that capacity for the ensuing 15 years being generally regarded as an eminently sound member of the House. He received Honorary degrees from the Universities of Wales (1946), British Columbia (1952) Liverpool (1966) and Cambridge (1967). He supported Lord Justice Sellars (another Liverpool law graduate) who performed the opening of the new Faculty of Law Building at Liverpool University in 1965.

Lord Morris gained great distinction in the legal world and in the sphere of public service but he remained at all times unaffected and approachable despite a rather reserved manner. He died on 9th June 1979.

PROFESSOR JOSEPH TURNER

By His Honour Judge William George

Joe Turner in later life at work in Chambers.

Joseph Turner was born the eldest child of a Wigan family in 1911. His father suffered ill health having been maimed by a gas attack in the Great War but he survived to have seven children in all. All the children were introduced to the world as Plymouth Brethren and Joe played the organ in the Chapel. Attending Wigan Grammar School, he was fortunate to be in a year which contained four pupils who all became University Professors. Although he distinguished himself academically, one of his school reports contained the comment 'Woodwork; cannot even glue'.

At Liverpool University, Joe was taught by amongst others Hartley Shawcross who was increasingly busy at the bar – in his final year Joe hardly saw him because Hartley was involved in the long running Gresford Colliery disaster inquiry. Joe, by pestering the Wigan Librarian, obtained access to all the books that Hartley required to be read but told the writer of this note on more than one occasion that he formed the view that Hartley had not read them either. After graduating with first class honours, Joe obtained articles with Arthur Smith and Broadie Griffith, a well established commercial firm in Wigan and then passed his Law Society Final Exams with distinction. Joe married Cora and they moved to St Albans where Joe became a tutor with

Joe Turner as an officer in the RAF in the Middle East in World War II.

a firm of legal crammers for Solicitors' exams. The two lawyers on the staff were Joe and Sebag Shaw (who was eking out a living at the bar). After this, Joe became a member of the staff at the London School of Economics where one of his contemporaries was Seaborne Davies. Also on the staff was Professor Ivor Jennings (the constitutional lawyer) who used to give Joe a lift home to St Albans in a Bugatti along the Great North Road (a somewhat frightening journey by all accounts). After this Joe went to Manchester (where David Blank offered him a partnership) and then on to Liverpool University. At this time, the Faculty of Law was in Cook Street and Joe was living with Cora on the Fylde. The reader may think this a curious fact to mention but Joe's contacts on the Fylde enabled him to preserve eggs in his room at the Law Faculty for distribution to staff and students. All this came to an end when the faculty was destroyed in May 1941 (Joe turned into Cook Street looking for the Law Faculty only to be told by a disappointed member of staff that all his eggs had been destroyed) so Joe joined the RAF and was posted to the Near East. Although he never reconciled himself to having failed the aircrew medical requirements, he did distinguish himself by being mentioned in dispatches and also by the fact that he was never issued with a sidearm He was however issued with a belt and holster and a 'deficiency chit' to keep in the holster for production when threatened.

While in the Middle East Joe became profoundly affected by his visits to the Holy Land – an influence which remained with him to his death as a member of the Church of England. He was also retained to defend personnel in Courts Martial. The prosecutor in one case was the Revd. Garth Moore whom students at Cambridge may remember. Joe's client had been smuggling home in various packets a complete dispatch rider's bike and sidecar rather like Sergeant Radar in *M*A*S*H*. Joe always told the writer that he thought the attempt to smuggle a sidecar was a bit ambitious and indeed this led to discovery of the scheme. Much to the consternation of the prosecutor, however, the defendant was acquitted and it was somewhat uncharitably thought that this was the reason why at the end of 1945 Joe found himself back in London as an Acting Wing Commander assisting with the Courts Martial of personnel returning from the Continent as the armies advanced. Joe was for the first time in his life earning a sensible salary but was put out when told to appear before his commanding officer to be told he was demobbed, given rail warrant to Liverpool with an instruction to report to the Vice Chancellor of the University. After protesting, Joe found himself with the task of restarting the Law Faculty. His initial task was to commandeer a house in Abercromby Square and then to appoint a porter (Danny who remained at the Faculty till the late 60s) and a secretary (Anne) who remained at the Faculty till the mid 70s. Soon students were enrolled and Seaborne Davies became Professor of Common Law and Dean, after losing his Parliamentary seat in the 1945 election. Lyon Blease remained as Queen Victoria Professor of Law (essentially the Chair of Real Property) until retiring in 1949 when Joe succeeded to this chair. In the early 1950s, Joe was also Dean of the Faculty for a year finally retiring from teaching at Liverpool University in about 1955.

Joe was called to the Bar by Gray's Inn in 1946. The evening was somewhat memorable because of war damage: those being called had to queue in the kitchen and Joe burnt himself on an oven. The scar was in fact the only physical evidence he had of his status as a member of the bar because for some reason he was never given a certificate. After pupillage with Edward Ackroyd (a bencher of Lincoln's Inn) Joe joined his Chancery Chambers in Union Court and then in 20 North John Street where he developed a wide-ranging traditional chancery practice including not only the drafting and variation of trusts, advising on conveyancing and taxation matters, company and partnership law but also actions in nuisance and other common law litigation. At the beginning to the early 1970s, the transitional provisions of the 1925 legislation still formed a considerable part of the work as did examination of title in the context of what was then called 'steam conveyancing'. In later years, tax planning advice in particular Capital Transfer Tax (now Inheritance Tax) became increasingly important and Joe launched himself into this with characteristic enthusiasm without losing his gift for dealing with other complex matters sure-footedly although the length of his advices and opinions dealing with perhaps too many nuances and possibilities were sometimes the cause of wonderment. In 1972 Joe became a member of the select band of forty who make up the Institute of Conveyancers.

Over the years Joe also took his fair share of pupils and these included Graham Routledge (later a Canon at St Pauls), Judges Michael O'Donoghue, David Gilliland and William George and silks, David Turner QC (his nephew) and Peter Smith QC. He would have been proud to learn of Peter Smith's elevation to the High Court Bench in April 2002 and his Knighthood.

Up to his retirement from the bar Joe still regularly worked in Chambers from about 7.00am to 6.30pm every day and his only relaxations in later years were music, reading and his house in Goathland where he went most weekends and holidays. In earlier years he regularly attended Rugby League matches particularly at Wigan with, amongst others, John Arthur (Circuit Judge, now retired).

Despite his burgeoning practice Joe always retained an interest in teaching and students. When teaching at Liverpool he held tutorials at his home on Mossley Hill Drive, Sefton Park which became legendary for the food and hospitality provided by Joe and Cora. There are still many lawyers in practice who remember these occasions not only for what they learnt but also for the humour, general conversation and the cementing of friendships in convivial surroundings. In 1962, he took on the onerous task of part time Professor of Property at Manchester University after much persuasion from his old friend Ben Wortley and the Vice Chancellor Sir William Mansfield Cooper. Within a short space of time, the courses in property law, trusts and equity were brought up to date and Joe for a period of 6 years until August 1968 lectured on Tuesday and Friday afternoons. Of course there were complaints that he neglected to mark papers with proper expedition because of pressure of work but the notes taken in lectures were superb and full of humour with germane examples from his practice. In fact, the third year Conveyancing Lectures were attended by students from other faculties including in particular girlfriends of law students. Although Sunday tutorials were no longer possible, an invitation for the third year to come to tea at Joe and Cora's flat in Sefton Park was always well attended despite travelling difficulties.

In November 1977 while sitting as a deputy High Court Judge, Joe had a health warning and decided to retire not only as head of Chambers but also from the Bar. He went first with Cora to his house in Goathland and after her death he came to live near his brothers and other members of his family in Southport. On his death in November 1986, he was buried in Goathland. Joe remained learned and a scholar to the last and immediately prior to his final illness was supervising a thesis concerning the legal and historical background to the residential parks in South Liverpool.

PROFESSOR SEABORNE DAVIES

By Tony Hudson

Students and lecturing staff in 1945-46 at Liverpool University with Seaborne Davies in the centre of the front row. Joan Pickering (later Joan Arthur) is second from the left in the front row and William Geddes is to the left of Seaborne and Lyon Blease to the right, and next on the right is Crossley Vaines. Note the high proportion of women law students which was a feature of the war years. At this time the Law Faculty was housed in the end house on Abercromby Square next to Chatham Street which previously belonged to the family of George Melly. This house is the one with the street-sign in the right-hand corner of the picture.

A great obstacle to writing about Seaborne Davies is that no one who ever knew him could forget him and the legend has been passed on so vividly that many who did not know him feel that they are in command of the plot and the detail of his remarkable story.

Seaborne made his mark in Liverpool as a great teacher of law who took an enormous interest in his students both in the Faculty of Law, where he was a long serving Dean, and in Derby Hall, where he was an almost equally long serving Warden. There can be no doubt that he would want to be remembered above all for this aspect of his varied career and would regard the Faculty of Law Building, at the opening of which by Lord Justice Sellers, he delivered an eloquent speech, as his memorial. His students fully responded at an impressive retirement dinner at the Adelphi.

It needs no stressing, however, that Wales was a dominant influence in his life. He was born 26 June 1904, schooled and retired in Pwllheli. He graduated in Aberystwyth before proceeding to Cambridge, succeeded

Seaborne Davies (centre) in 1950/51 with the Honours Group of Liverpool University. Back row – Michael English (later a Labour MP) is third from left and John Wilkinson and Michael Holloway are on the right. Middle row – Brian Shieldhouse, Helga Taylor, Jeanette Burman, Claire Ginsberg, Inge Bernstein, Sheila Chaplin and Keith Moore. Front row – Ken Wilson, Graham Routledge, Joe Turner, Seaborne Davies, William Geddes, John Newton and Bill Denny.

Lloyd George as Liberal MP for Caernarvon Boroughs, was President of the National Eisteddfod of Wales in 1955, 1973 and 1975, Vice-President of London Welsh RFC, President of local choral and sports societies in Pwllheli and the foundations of his interest in student matters seem to have been firmly laid when he was President of the Student Council of the University of Wales and of the University College of Wales, Aberystwyth. He was High Sheriff of Caernarvonshire in 1967-68 and, having been a magistrate in Liverpool, on retirement from University he continued on the Bench in Caernarvonshire and Gwynedd.

When at Cambridge, he had won the distinction of the Yorke Prize and went on to become a lecturer and Reader in the LSE. During the War, he joined the Nationality Division of the Home Office and his Civil Service experience brought him membership of a number of committees ranging from the Oaksey Committee on Police Conditions to a committee on agricultural education in Wales. The most important of these was the Criminal Law Revision Committee, where he played a part in the preparation of the Theft Act 1968, and Wales was not forgotten here, because he told colleagues in the common room that he tested proposals by their likely impact in Pwllheli market.

All this did not exclude academic distinction. He was President of the Society of Public Teachers of Law in 1960-1961, Pro-Vice-Chancellor and Public Orator of the University of Liverpool and delivered the BBC Wales Annual Lecture in 1967, in which he was careful to include one well known lawyer for every one of the then counties of Wales, and Cooley Lecturer in the University of Michigan. It was from there that he took the idea of the Moot Room in the Faculty Building, a room which he was long reluctant to see used for lecturing. Of his publications, his examination of the early history of patents has proved of lasting worth. In the wider world, however, he will be remembered as an incomparable public speaker, commanding the full range from an uproarious after-dinner speech, taking full advantage of Welsh accent and anecdotes, to the serious demands of his address at the opening of the Law Faculty Building and few, if any, could rise to the challenging standard he set in his day.

Despite his many public and academic appointments, he was the least bureaucratic of administrators. He brought a sardonic anarchism to his treatment of timetables, deadlines and questionnaires which was the despair of University authorities and led one Vice-Chancellor to express his great surprise that anything done by Professor Seaborne Davies should be put forward as a precedent. But what was necessary was

University of Liverpool Legal Society 1957-1958.

PN Jackson, EPJ Chibber, KH Leigh, I Bennett, GM Lee, CB Stephens, P Chan, P Jackson, PD Hoskinson, JN Lindley, GET Brancker, JM Hubbard, BH Crebbin, ME Round, D Hannon, MV Miller.

G Stephenson, ER Haworth, JR Haisley, DR Guratsky, JPR Azurdia, FB Jump, RJ Kesler, PD Brostoff, EO Ogwuegbu, TW Earle, AHA Cook, PG Hyland, MA Gee, D Hill, RJ Green, SM Henderson.

DWK Lobley, MB Dumbill, PC Canter, JA Owen, EB Lipkin, Miss K Mulcahy, Miss M Yates, EM Naylor, MA Globe, AN Fricker, FD Owen, GA Ensor, WH Edwards, K Chadwick, JR Myers, LB Jones, AK Gikunoo, PB Thomas, RB Martin, WL Search.

Miss ML McParlin, Miss MT Garrett, Miss PA Molyneux, Miss MC Goucher, Miss MM Henderson, Miss CJ Slater, DN Max, Mr JD Newton, Prof. D Browne, Prof. DRS Davies, Dr C d'O Farran, Miss CM Wareing, Miss EM Steel, Miss AD Muir-Jones, Miss P Gray.

always done and, when required, he could pull out the right stops. He often told how his request for new curtains for the Abercromby Square Faculty Building, whose limited accommodation and insecure structure severely restricted the growth of the Faculty and its library, brought the new Building into being.

Much of the refreshing vigour of his approach was attributable, as someone once remarked, to the fact that he was an eternal undergraduate and, if truth were told, of all his many appointments he probably valued above all his Honorary Life Membership of the Guild of Undergraduates.

Seaborne's proudest achievement in his own mind was the fact that he was the Liberal MP to succeed David Lloyd George in his Welsh stronghold of Caernarvon Boroughs, on the death of Lloyd George in 1945. To this day it is astonishing to many practitioners in Liverpool that their Professor at University was so close to Lloyd George.

A flavour of Seaborne's rather sardonic humour came when the University, in its wisdom, attempted to improve the dreadful state of car parking at the University in 1972. It was established to be practical for staff to park their cars on the 'roof' of the Senate Building and a letter was circulated to the staff explaining how parking on the 'roof' would assist. Seaborne promptly wrote back with a letter beginning, "I am not ready yet to ascend my heavenly chariot!"

His humour passed with him into retirement. Some years after Seaborne retired, the late Harry Chrimes (one time Chairman of the Council and a pro-Vice Chancellor of the University) enquired of Seaborne why he had chosen to retire to Pwllheli, to which Seaborne replied, "Well, you see, in Pwllheli the transition from this life to the next is almost imperceptible."

LORD JUSTICE SELLERS

by Judge David Lynch

Frederic Aked Sellers was born in Liverpool on 14 February 1893, the son of an owner of coaster vessels. His knowledge of ships proved an invaluable asset at the Bar and on the Bench when he dealt with shipping cases.

He left Liverpool University in 1914 with BA and LLB and went to war. His courage was outstanding. He was awarded the Military Cross for his conduct during the Battle of the Somme in 1916. In 1918, his bravery was again marked by the award of two bars to the Military Cross. He was gassed twice, blinded for three weeks but survived to become a famous son of the Northern Circuit.

He was called to the Bar at Gray's Inn on 14 May 1919 and joined Chambers at 10 Cook Street, Liverpool where he remained until he took Silk in 1935. By this time he had built a considerable practice – mainly in commercial and shipping disputes. He stood unsuccessfully as Liberal candidate in 1929 for Waterloo and in 1945 for Hendon North. Perhaps his most notable case in Silk was Duncan -v- Cammell Laird when he represented the shipbuilders in the House of Lords in claims arising from the tragedy on 1 June 1939 when, during trials, all but three of those on board the submarine 'Thetis' were lost in Liverpool Bay.

He was too old for active service in 1939, so he formed his own company of the Home Guard at his home in Mill Hill in London. They paraded on his lawn and were called 'Sellers' Seventy Soldiers'. He was elected Bencher of his Inn in 1938 and Treasurer in 1952. He was Recorder of Bolton from 1938 until 1946 when he was appointed to the King's Bench Division of the High Court where he sat with distinction for 11 years.

Two of his criminal trials come to mind. One of his first was that of Walter Rowland at Manchester Assizes for the murder of Olive Balchin in 1946. Rowland had been convicted of the murder of his child in 1934 and sentenced to death but the jury recommended him to mercy and he was reprieved. He was released in 1942 to be convicted again for murder four years later. On this occasion there was no recommendation to mercy. In 1950 he tried Donald Hume for the murder of Stanley Setty, a car dealer. It was alleged that Hume, having killed Setty, dismembered the body and dropped the pieces from an aeroplane into the English Channel. There was strong evidence of disposal of the body but the jury could not agree on murder. The Crown did not wish a second trial and the judge sentenced Hume to 12 years imprisonment on his plea of guilty to accessory after the fact. The case is of particular interest because, on his release, and knowing he could not be tried a second time, Hume confessed to the Sunday Pictorial that he had murdered Setty. In 1959, during a bungled bank robbery in Zurich, Hume shot and killed a taxi driver. He was sentenced to life imprisonment and was eventually transferred to Broadmoor Hospital.

Sir Fred served on the Standing Committee on Criminal Law Revision from 1959 to 1969. Expert though he was in criminal law, it was generally thought that he was at his very best in heavy commercial and shipping cases, particularly in the Court of Appeal from 1957 until his retirement in 1968. He never forgot his Liverpool roots and proudly accepted an honorary LLD from Liverpool University in 1956.

He married Grace in 1917 when on home leave from France. They were a devoted couple for more than sixty years. He died on 20 March 1979 in his 87th year. They had four sons and a daughter. One son, Norman (Norrie) followed his father to the Liverpool Bar and was a Circuit Judge in Preston from 1974 to 1990.

At Sir Fred's memorial service at Gray's Inn Chapel on 18 May 1979, his dear friend and colleague, Lord Denning, said "We all called him Fred. It was a mark of our affection for him ... Fred (like Paul) fought a good fight, he finished the course and he kept the faith."

GRAEME (PADDY) BRYSON

By Charles Elston

Paddy Bryson – the picture on the wall behind him is of Judge Fraser Harrison and the damage in the bottom right-hand corner of the picture on the wall is the actual bullet hole when George Wilkie shot at Paddy during his sitting as a Bankruptcy Judge in Liverpool in 1960.

'Paddy' Bryson deserves to feature in this series for his services to the legal profession alone, but those services, considerable as they have been, are almost dwarfed by his other services to the community and to the country and his activities in many other spheres. In the space available it is only possible to touch briefly on a varied and distinguished career – which is by no means over, although Paddy will reach the age of 90 in 2003. In the first place it should be explained why James Graeme Bryson has been known since childhood as 'Paddy'. His parents had already produced two sons and were hoping that their third child would be a girl. When this proved not to be the case, the title of a play being performed at the local theatre – "Paddy the next best thing" – prompted them and subsequently others to give the newcomer the unofficial and almost universally adopted name by which he is best known.

Paddy's father joined the then large and respected Liverpool firm of solicitors TJ Smith and Son in 1919. He is recalled by my generation as a fine lawyer and a distinguished practitioner who was President of the Liverpool Law Society in 1947. After schooling at St Edward's College, Liverpool, Paddy joined the Faculty of Law at the University of Liverpool in 1929 and having graduated LLB with Honours in 1932 he proceeded to the degree of LLM in 1935, in which year he also passed the Law Society's Final with Honours and joined his father's firm. The next ten years were dominated by World War 2 and this period of Paddy's career will be dealt with later. In 1946, he rejoined TJ Smith and Son as a partner, but in the following year he was appointed a District Registrar of the High Court (then comprising King's Bench, Chancery and Divorce Divisions) in Liverpool and Registrar of the Liverpool County Court, his appointment having been prompted (according to one of his own reminiscences) by the wife of Judge Fraser Harrison with whom the Lord Chancellor's representative stayed overnight after interviewing the four applicants for the post. He also became the Admiralty Registrar (by no means a sinecure at that time) and as Registrar of the Chancery Division he sat fortnightly in London for over 30 years. In 1969, he was President of the Association of County Court Registrars. After retiring from full-time duties in the Courts, Paddy sat as a Chairman of the Medical Appeal Tribunal and also as a Deputy Circuit Judge on the Northern and North East Circuits from 1978 to 1984.

Spanning as it did nearly 50 years from 1935 to 1984 Paddy's very active involvement in the legal life of Liverpool overlapped the careers of many – if not most – of the prominent legal figures of the century. In his early days, Rigby Swift was still sitting as a High Court Judge and Sir William Kyffin Taylor (later Lord Maenan) was in his prime presiding over what now seems a relic of a remote Gilbertian era, The Liverpool Court of Passage; Fred Sellars, George Lynskey, Maxwell Fyffe, Hartley Shawcross, Selwyn Lloyd, JW Morris (Lord Morris of Borth-y-Gest), Basil Neild, Fred Pritchard and others were all building up careers at the Bar which were to lead to greater things, and solicitors now remembered by a diminishing few such as John A Behn, S Sydney Silverman (now best known as the member of Parliament who was very largely responsible for the abolition of the death penalty), Sir Harry Livermore, Darrell Mace, and Hector Munro were all well-known to him. In his years as Registrar, those who appeared before him included many who became County Court/Circuit Judges such as Melville Kennan, CJ Cunliffe, Roy Ward, Keith Lawton, Robert Leech, and James Scarlett and not a few who reached the High Court Bench such as George Bean (who died regrettably young), Danny Brabin, Robertson Crichton, David McNeill, and Michael Morland; and, of course, he knew well all those solicitors whose practice involved appearing on Registrar's summonses and taxations among whom Rex Makin and Donald Munro may perhaps be mentioned as prominent examples.

Probably the most memorable incident of Paddy's judicial career occurred in 1960 when he was sitting as a Bankruptcy Judge in Liverpool. A night-club owner, one George Wilkie, who had been made bankrupt was being examined when he produced a loaded revolver and shot at, but fortunately missed, Paddy then shot and severely wounded both the Official Receiver and the Clerk of the Court in the stomach, causing serious injuries and then at close range made three more attempts to shoot Paddy, but fortunately the revolver failed to fire. Paddy and his staff were able to overcome the assailant who was subsequently convicted and imprisoned. For his part in the proceedings Paddy was awarded the Queen's Commendation for Brave Conduct.

Paddy was commissioned in the Territorial Army in 1936, his commission being one of comparatively few signed by King Edward VIII during his brief reign. He served throughout the 1939/45 War, mainly on the protection of submarine and flying-boat bases in the North of Scotland and reached the rank of Lieutenant-Colonel in 1944. On the re-formation of the Territorial Army in 1947 he was invited to re-form his former Regiment which he then commanded until 1952 when he was asked to take over command of 626 Heavy AA Regiment (The Liverpool Irish). According to Paddy, he was asked to take it over because the

General concerned thought that as his name was Paddy he would get on well with the troops – as, indeed he did. He reached the rank of Full Colonel in this appointment and on his retirement in 1955 he was awarded the OBE (Military Division). From 1975 to 1981 he was the very active Honorary Colonel of 33 Signal Regiment.

Paddy was appointed a Deputy Lieutenant of Lancashire in 1954 and when the Metropolitan County of Merseyside was formed in 1974 with Sir Douglas Crawford as the first Lord-Lieutenant he transferred to Merseyside and from 1979 to 1989 he served as Vice-Lieutenant to Sir Douglas's successor Sir Kenneth Stoddart. Arising out of his TA and War service came his long and distinguished involvement with the Royal British Legion (which still continues). He was appointed President of the City of Liverpool Branch as long ago as 1955 and of the Northwest Area from 1970 to 1982. He was Chairman and Vice-President of the Lord Mayor of Liverpool's Poppy Day Appeal from 1950 to 1970 and the RBL honoured him by naming one of their Residential Homes 'Graeme Bryson House' – which he formally opened in 1984. His active involvement in the work of the RBL and other Service organisations continues almost unabated to this day and in 1999 he accepted the Freedom of the City of Liverpool on behalf of the RBL.

Paddy was appointed a Liverpool City Magistrate in 1956 and sat until retirement age, serving on most of the committees including the Advisory Committee for new appointments to which he was appointed in 1961. His service to the Roman Catholic community has also been outstanding and led in 1972 to his appointment as a Knight of the Equestrian Order of the Holy Sepulchre (now advanced to Knight Commander with Star) and in 1993 as Knight Commander of the Order of St Gregory the Great. In the non-denominational field he was in 1990 elected a Knight of the Honourable Society of Knights of the Round Table (founded AD 1720). Paddy sat as a General Commissioner of Taxes from 1968 to 1988 and Chairman of the Merseyside Advisory Committee from 1979 to 1988.

Impressive as the range and extent of Paddy's participation in the various activities already mentioned is, it is in many respects less remarkable than the projects he has embarked on and pursued since reaching the age of 75 when he started a computer course at Southport College and obtained an RSA qualification. He followed this by embarking on an Open University course on computers and professional decision-making which resulted in the award of a BSc degree. Then followed some literary research leading to the publication of his book *Shakespeare in Lancashire* in which he advances the theory that during his so-called 'lost years' Shakespeare was employed as a player at Hoghton Tower and subsequently by the Hesketh family at Rufford Hall – now, of course, known as Rufford Old Hall. For this theory, he makes a strong case without, perhaps, proving it beyond all reasonable doubt. The book achieved wide acclaim and has reached three editions, and it has now been followed by a personal history of the Liverpool Roman Catholic Cathedral (not on public sale) and substantial contributions to this volume. It would be very rash to assume that this will conclude his literary output

All of the foregoing may suggest some sort of inhuman automaton, but nothing could be further from the truth. Paddy is unassuming, always courteous and with no trace of pomposity, and he has no time at all for pomposity in others. He is devoted to his family of two sons and four daughters (and 12 grandchildren) and he was for forty years exceptionally happily married to Jean (Glendinning). Her death in 1978 was a grievous blow to him and the depth of his loss may perhaps go some way towards explaining the extent of activity which has characterised his subsequent career.

BETTY BEHN

By Graeme Bryson

John A Behn never married. The man who was never lost for a word in the courts lived with his two sisters, where, so the story goes, he hardly ever got a word in edgeways. He was to be followed not by a son, but by a niece.

Betty's father, the youngest of four brothers, also qualified as a solicitor, but he suffered from ill-health, and was content to work as an assistant solicitor in the practice until, sadly, he died at the young age of 33.

Meanwhile his daughter Betty Behn, was growing up very nicely and was educated at Liverpool College, Huyton. My recollection is that the old Lord Derby's granddaughters were educated there, which gave it top local social standing. Then came five year articles from 1935, and the Law Society's correspondence course leading to the telegram from London agents that she had passed the Final Examination in 1941. At that time the partners in the firm were John A Behn, George Twyford and Monty Reece.

But in those days, women solicitors and barristers were not considered worthy contenders for the serious business of the law. Apart from Betty, one thinks of solicitors Agnes and Eileen Neville, and barristers Rose Heilbron and Mary Williams, but not many more.

She was taken into the partnership within a year of qualifying, but it was not considered proper for her to engage in knock about duty in the police courts. She was fully occupied with working for Monty Reece, in the civil-injury side of the practice. The next year, Monty Reece was called up for war service, and Betty took over his workload.

But for the War, and the absence of legal menfolk, the acceptance of women might have taken many more years. Rose Heilbron stormed ahead, and never looked back. Betty also gained useful experience to set her up for the years ahead when she was accepted as a worthy protagonist in the field of personal injury compensation law and allied topics, retaining strong links with the Trade Unions.

She developed an expertise in dealing with accident claims and probate work, and she had a formidable reputation as a no-nonsense solicitor. Woe betide any opponent who thought that this female was an easy touch.

The great and formidable John A Behn died in 1945. Betty, George Twyford and Monty Reece remained in partnership until the 1960s when Monty Reece died. George Twyford (a past President of the Liverpool Law Society) died in 1967. Elizabeth Steel (now Her Honour Judge Steel), joined the partnership until 1980. They were replaced by David Ashcroft and Suzanne Graham.

When Betty retired in 1997, tell it not in Gath, she was then 80. One would have expected her to retire to her powerful Mercedes-Benz for further excitement, but she cannot keep away from Dale Street, and she is still to be found, there, drawing wills, and passing on her wide experience.

A 'defendant's solicitor' said to me the other day that he would call on John A Behn's office from time to time and see Betty on perhaps a dozen cases she had an uncanny knack of knowing which cases to settle or to fight.

In the course of her long career, Betty engaged many counsel, mostly successfully, and she retains detailed memories of them, including Sir Noel Goldie, Dame Rose Heilbron, Her Honour Inge Bernstein, His Honour Judge Edward Jones, His Honour Donald Forster, His Honour John Appleton and many more.

I spent an hour with Betty hoping to obtain some exciting tales from her many years in practice. But at the end of every one, she said, "But of course you can't include that!" On one occasion she saw a man laid out on a bench in the waiting room looking for all the world dead. The ambulance was sent for and he was in fact pronounced dead and taken away to the mortuary. The following morning she was in the office when who should appear right as rain but her 'dead' man of the day before! Apparently he had taken a drug like Shakespeare's Friar Laurence's drug to Juliet which gave the form of death for a limited time only.

It was very unusual for Betty to appear in Chambers before me as she had very talented clerks or counsel when appropriate. But she did appear once on a summons to deal with a case where a woman cleaner in a pub left some abrasive fluid unattended in the basement, and her child drank some of it and became very ill. The child by its next friend the father sued the brewery for the negligence of its servant the mother! I must have been rather young at the time and it seemed somewhat unfair. But, of course, the child has its own rights and was exercising them.

In 1929 Sir Hugo Rutherford, as President of the Liverpool Chess Club, presented me with Osborn's Law Dictionary for winning a chess tournament. I have just looked up 'next friend,' and it states that a married woman cannot be a next friend! It's news to me!

There is more to life than writs and litigation. In 1948, Betty married Tom Rotheram who had played in the English Table Tennis Team at the age of 18 and was an acquaintance and contemporary of Fred Perry. Fred was the World Champion in table tennis before changing to the larger tennis racquet. Tom was also an excellent tennis player, being singles champion more than once at the Vagabonds Tennis Club which at that time was the home of excellence for local sportsmen. After nearly thirty years of happy marriage, Tom died in 1975. As for many of us, Betty translates memories into hard work, and in this, she is a fine example.

Nowadays there are lots of women barristers and solicitors in practice, as there are in other professions. Betty Behn's place in Liverpool's legal history is that she was among the very first ladies to qualify and to be accepted. She was one of the leaders paving the way for others to follow.

JUDGE FRANK PATERSON

By Graeme Bryson

The Bar offers its practitioners from Liverpool and elsewhere the opportunity of political progress to the heights of national power. Great rewards are available, and so are the perils of sudden failure and discharge even from the top position. Liverpool has seen its two Lord Chancellors (Lords Birkenhead and Kilmuir) experiencing these diverse outcomes, and in both cases the City lost the long term benefit of their experience.

When Judge Paterson visits Gray's Inn, he notices the escutcheons of past Lord Chancellors Birkenhead and Kilmuir, and he then returns happily to leafy Freshfield, within spitting distance (as they say) of Liverpool.

Frank David Paterson has remained faithful to the City of his birth. His parents were both dedicated Liverpool merchants. His school (Quarry Bank), his University, his practice at the Bar and his Judgeship were all based on Liverpool. And there is much more including his Presidency of the Merseyside Branch of the Magistrates Association. Now in his retirement, he retains his local interest as Chairman of a body to help the Law Faculty of the University of Liverpool to continue to educate the lawyers of the future. The University has awarded him a worthy honorary Doctorate of Laws, but it was a true two-way honour.

Frank arrived on the scene at Mossley Hill on 10th July 1918, a Wednesday, when the first World War had just four months to run. Though unable at that time to express himself to his parents or to the elder children, he did not approve of the contest. Home and school were happy days though he did not claim any special distinctions apart from long distance running, being the first in his school to complete a mile in under five minutes. This did not impress his fellow students when he entered the Law Faculty of the University in 1937. But he did impress them with his debating skills because he was elected President of the Law Faculty Legal Society from 1939 to 1940, the year he graduated as LLB. The following year he was called to the Bar at Gray's Inn.

By this time another war had started, and he registered himself as a Conscientious Objector, a 'fighting pacifist', as a fellow student described him at the Tribunal which accepted the validity of his conscience. He was directed to work on the land, and later to do social work. It must have required great courage to take this stand and to risk unpopularity and opprobrium. And what a long war it was!

Finally, peace returned, and Frank was allowed to proceed with his pupillage to his cousin Harold (later Judge) Brown; but chancery work did not suit him so he changed to Common Law Chambers with Melville (later Judge) Kennan at 34 Castle Street where he remained until 1968, becoming, in due course, head of Chambers. These were, the writer thinks, happy years because the practice, both civil and in crime, grew steadily, allowing his natural interest and ability to develop in advocacy and in the study of the law.

In 1953 he took time off to marry Barbara Mary Gillow of Formby, a union which has happily produced a son, two daughters and twelve grandchildren at the last count.

Silk did not seem just round the corner, but he held terms of office in part time judicial appointments as Assistant Deputy Coroner for Liverpool, President, later Regional Chairman, of the Mental Health Review Tribunal for SW Lancashire and Cheshire, and Chairman of the Ministry of Pensions and National Insurance Tribunal.

In 1968 came his judicial appointment as County Court (later re-titled Circuit) Judge which was to last for nearly twenty five years, sitting mostly in Liverpool and Southport, but also in the Crown Courts at Liverpool, Manchester and Birkenhead, with occasional visits to London where he sat at Wood Green, Knightsbridge, Southwark and Kingston-on-Thames. His new status took him back to the Mental Health Tribunal as presiding Judge, and other duties including Liaison Judge between the Liverpool Crown Court and the Justices of the Peace for the North and South Sefton Petty Sessional Divisions.

For a quarter of a century, this quiet, careful, considerate Judge tried thousands of cases without incurring the wrath of investigative journalism or the Court of Appeal. He was able to return in the evenings to a replication of the happy home he had enjoyed so many years ago in Mossley Hill.

At some point in this story, he became much in demand as an after dinner speaker. These were not off-the-cuff affairs but they were very carefully structured and brilliantly contrived, receiving rapturous applause from one and all. In general he has a ready, and perhaps sharpish wit, so that it does not behove one to trifle with this senior member of the Liverpool legal fraternity. He has a slight walking impediment for which he attaches some blame to the writer of this article who denies all liability.

There is much more, but one should mention his long-term and continuing Presidency of the Liverpool Domestic Mission Society. The Society is one of the oldest charitable bodies in Liverpool. Created in 1836 by the combined efforts of three Liverpool Unitarian Congregations, namely those of Ullet Road Church, the Ancient Chapel of Toxteth, and the Church of Hope Street, it aimed at creating a community settlement in the poorest parts of the City. It is now promoting a community settlement in the Earle Road area of Liverpool in co-operation with what was once the Liverpool University Settlement in Nile Street. Well done Frank!

To conclude, here is a Liverpool Gentleman who has served his city well and continues to do so. He shows no sign of giving up.

MRS JUSTICE ANN EBSWORTH

By Mr Justice Hedley

Ann Ebsworth was one of many who came from another part of the country to practise in Liverpool and then who stayed to give long and distinguished service to her adopted area. She was born into a Services family on the 19th May 1937, her father being a serving officer in the Royal Marines, and she had the sort of itinerant life that attends such families.

Her education led her to read History at London University where she graduated in 1959. Initially politics exercised a fascination for her and, even after embarking on a legal career, she was for some time, until local government reorganisation in 1972, a Member of the old Wallasey Council serving both as Chair of the children's committee and Chair of the housing committee. But it was in the law that her true gifts lay and it was to the law she turned, being called to the Bar by Gray's Inn in 1962.

By that time family life had led her to Merseyside and she joined the (then somewhat unfashionable) Chambers of George England, to whom she was pupilled. In due course, those Chambers moved to 27 Dale Street under AD Papworth and Gerson Newman. She became Head of those Chambers, which have now produced a crop of Judges and Silks, and remained there until her appointment as a Circuit Judge in Liverpool at the young age of 45.

Ann Ebsworth was a formidable advocate particularly in the field of criminal law, though she practiced

Three friends of Ann are pictured here – Henry Lachs, William Morgan QC and William Wickham following their swearing in as Recorders on 15 December 1972.

in family law and was the first barrister in the city to be regularly instructed in that work by the Official Solicitor. She enjoyed the unfailing respect and admiration of both Bench and Bar but never quite built the practice that her skills merited. It was, however, as a judge that her abilities came to full flower and in due course received full recognition.

She had sat briefly as a deputy circuit judge under the old system before being appointed a Crown Court Recorder in 1978 but it was after her appointment to full time office in 1983 that the arrival of a rare talent was announced. She was businesslike and impeccably fair and courteous but foolish the barrister who ventured into her court less than prepared; disapprobation needed only to be conveyed by a look to be fully understood. Though she could appear rather formidable in court, those who knew the private person knew a warm, humorous and generous friend. In 1992 came appointment to the High Court, the first woman to be appointed directly to the Queen's Bench Division. Her main function, she was told, was to handle heavy criminal cases which she did, adding to that the conduct of substantial civil cases with an expertise that may have surprised those who only knew her practice but did not know the person.

Ann was, however, a person of broad interests culturally, politically and across the whole range of human life. She served as a Chairman of Mental Health Tribunals, as a member of the Parole Board as well as for a time taking a lead role in the development of the Judicial Studies Board. She remained single but greatly enjoyed the company of others, seeking it out regularly until forced by serious ill health to retire and lead a quieter life. Hers was an undemonstrative style, one that she commended to others, but one that was especially apt to the judicial role and that she made very much her own. She died on 4 April 2002 after a lengthy and painful illness which she was well aware was terminal and which she accepted with dignity and composure. The respect and affection in which she was held by the profession was demonstrated at a special sitting of the Liverpool Crown Court on 8 April 2002 when the Recorder of Liverpool, the Leader of the Northern Circuit and the President of the Liverpool Law Society paid tribute to her.

THE STEEL SISTERS

By Stuart Christie

Mrs Justice Heather Steel

Heather Steel was born in Warrington, the daughter of Edward (later Judge Steel) and Mary Steel. She was educated at Howell's School, Denbigh and the Law Faculty at the University of Liverpool, taking an active part in the activities at the Students' Union at the University, including appearing in 'Pantopera', the review staged by the students.

She had at an early age announced her individuality by declaring at home that there were too many girls at her school known as Ann or Anne so she was to be known by her second name, Heather.

She was called to the Bar in 1963 and became a member of Gray's Inn, following in her father's footsteps, and joined the Chambers where her father had been a member at 14 Cook Street.

She practised on the Northern Circuit, being Prosecuting Counsel to the Department of Health and Social Security on the Northern Circuit from 1984 to 1986. At the same time she became a Recorder and in 1986 was appointed a Circuit Judge sitting in Preston where she became Senior Circuit Judge. Solicitors in Central Lancashire say that she had a reputation for not falling for sob stories and they would, if they could, keep their defendant clients out of her court.

Heather was a member of the Criminal Committee of the Judicial Studies Board from 1992 to 1995 and worked closely with Mrs Justice Ebsworth in education for the Bar. In 1993, she was elevated to the High Court Bench sitting in the Queen's Bench Division.

Locally, she has been President of the Law Faculty Association at Liverpool University and President of the Merseyside Medico-Legal Society. In London she spent a period sitting at the Old Bailey. She joined the Pattenmakers Livery Company in 1993 becoming a Freeman of the City of London in 1996. She is to be Master of the Pattenmakers Livery Company in 2003.

Heather married David Beattie in 1967 and they have two children, one a surgeon, the other an oil engineer. Following a spell of ill health, she decided to take early retirement from the High Court bench at the end of the Summer Term 2001.

Her Honour Judge Elizabeth Steel

Elizabeth Steel was born in Warrington the elder daughter of Edward Steel, who was the son of Thomas Samuel Steel founder of the firm of Steels, solicitors, in Warrington. Edward himself qualified as a solicitor in 1928 and while at Gibson & Weldon's met Kenneth Roberts who was to be Senior Partner of Walker Smith & Way in Chester and a member of the Law Society's Council for many years. Edward met and married Kenneth's sister Mary and they had two daughters Elizabeth and Heather (Mrs Justice Steel). Kenneth also had two children, Martin, who was to be a partner in Slaughter & May, and Jerraine who was called to the Bar. Edward's brother Tom, himself a well respected solicitor and a member of Steels, also produced a solicitor son, Adrian.

Edward decided that life as a solicitor was not for him and, while the father of a young child, read for the Bar and was ultimately called in 1937 being a member of Gray's Inn. He was a member of the Judge Advocate General's department during the war, both prosecuting and presiding over War Crimes Trials which made an indelible impression on him and then Assistant Recorder of Liverpool. He was elevated to the bench in 1958, originally as a County Court Judge, subsequently a Circuit Judge as well as Chancellor of the dioceses of Liverpool and Manchester.

It might be thought that with a legal background of such depth and quality Elizabeth would make a seamless progress into the Law, but it was not to be. After education at Howell's School, Denbigh, her ambition was to be an actress. It is said that her first appearance before the public was at the Empire Theatre Liverpool at the age of 3 when she was invited on stage by Caryl and Munday having been seen by them dancing in the aisle of the theatre.

Her parents, however, thought otherwise and she became a law student at the Law Faculty at the University of Liverpool in 1955 to be a member of a cohort of students who included, in later life, a Law Lord, a High Court Judge and a number of Circuit Judges, District Judges and Deputy District Judges, as well as a Cathedral Dean.

David Marshall-Evans QC, Denis Clark, Sean Duncan and Heather Steel immediately following swearing in as Recorders in July 1984.

She was articled to Douglas Kewish at HGC Day & Co where she learned that the Long Vacation was spent assembling briefs for the next term, with articled clerks being expected to take an active part, including typing copies of documents. Douglas Kewish became a Registrar and Elizabeth moved to the associated office of Percy Hughes & Roberts to be articled to Joe Roberts a skilled advocate and a meticulous preparer of cases.

Elizabeth was admitted a solicitor in 1960. She was a member of the Young Conservatives rising to become National Vice-Chairman in 1967 and gaining national attention with a speech about unemployment at the National Conference. Edward Heath invited her to serve on a committee chaired by Antony Cripps QC to advise on the law relating to women. The committee, after two years' hard work, produced a report, many of the recommendations of which have been subsequently enacted.

In 1968, Elizabeth became a partner in John A Behn Twyford & Co where she remained until 1980, practising as a Magistrates' Court advocate as well as dealing with civil claims for personal injury cases. In 1980, she became a partner in Cuff Roberts, doing a wide variety of civil work, becoming a Recorder in 1989 (after a stint as a Deputy Registrar) and leaving in 1991 on her elevation to the bench.

During her time as solicitor Elizabeth was a member of the Race Relations Board for eight years as well as a member of the Radio Merseyside Council, the BBC North West Advisory Council and the General Advisory Council of the BBC.

Her interest in the stage has involved her in being a member of the Playmakers at Warrington for many years both as performer and producer and a member of the Board of Directors of the Liverpool Playhouse for some seventeen years, being made a Vice-President when she ceased to be a member of the Board in 1995.

Elizabeth joined the Liverpool Law Society in 1960 as well as the Law Society in London. She became a member of the Liverpool Society's Committee, becoming Vice-President in 1989 and President in 1990, the first woman to hold these offices. It was during her year as Vice-President that the Hillsborough Disaster occurred. The scale of the disaster led to the formation of the Hillsborough Solicitors' Group, Elizabeth was elected onto the Steering Committee and was Chairman of that Committee from its inception in April 1989 until her elevation to the Bench in November 1991.

While Vice-President and President she was involved with the setting up of the Liverpool Mercantile Court. She has also become the first female member of the Committee of the Athenaeum in Liverpool and its first female President in 2002.

On the Circuit Bench, Elizabeth hears criminal, civil and family cases and has sat on civil cases at the Royal Courts of Justice in the Strand as a deputy High Court Judge.

Somewhere in the midst of this activity she has managed to find time to marry and raise two children, one of whom is showing early signs of taking to the law, the other to the theatre!

GRUFFYDD (GRUFF) EVANS, LORD EVANS OF CLAUGHTON

By Gordon Lindsay

This profile touches little on the legal career of Gruff Evans (pronounced Griff) because, although for some 30 years or so we were both practising as lawyers in Merseyside, our paths crossed a great deal more in the world of (mainly local) politics. Before I became thus involved, Gruff was already well known as a Liberal activist, having at an early stage been involved at national level in the Young Liberals of the day, and in the Liverpool University Liberal Society of which he became President. In 1957, at his first attempt (he never lost a local election) he was elected for the Claughton Ward, in which he lived for much of his life, to become the first Liberal for many years to serve on the then Birkenhead County Borough Council.

A few years later, he was joined on the Birkenhead Council by another Liverpool solicitor, Dennis Green. They were often to be seen with Cyril Carr and others at the corner of Cook Street with Castle Street in deep conversation, after a 2/6d lunch at McConnell's between the Law Library and Law Association rooms. As was always the case in Gruff' s company, the conversation was lively and when I became involved in the Liberal Party it was natural for me to join them. Subsequently, we moved to the Beaconsfield at the corner of North John Street and Victoria Street, the political incorrectness of that venue being mitigated by Gladstone's features appearing on the pub sign for some years until the Brewers discovered and rectified their mistake.

Gruff first stood for Parliament in 1964. I had just joined the party, and I remember well his bitter disappointment when the Birkenhead Liberals decided not to contest the election, whereupon he was adopted for Wallasey where he put up a good fight, and again in 1966. At last, in 1970, he had his chance to stand for Birkenhead, and he asked me to be his election agent, but unfortunately that year marked a nadir in the Party's fortunes. Although, despite Gruff's personal standing in Birkenhead, the result was bitterly disappointing for us all, Gruff was big hearted enough to cheer up considerably when only a few weeks later (at the nth attempt) I was first elected to Birkenhead Council, thus starting a period of close political collaboration and friendship between us. In 1973, when upon local Government reorganisation, Wirral Metropolitan Borough and the then Merseyside County Council were created to take on the functions of Birkenhead Council, we both succeeded in being elected to both those Councils. Gruff, having continued as group leader on Wirral Council until 1977 retired from that Council in 1978. Meanwhile, he had become group leader on the County Council, which he retained until he retired having taken up his life peerage to become, with enormous pride, Baron Evans of Claughton.

Meanwhile, he had been serving on most of the governing bodies of the Party, with great distinction. My closest memories of that side of his life were around the annual party conferences, since I served as a member of the organising committee of which he was for some time chairman. His legal training was of the greatest value, for example when dealing with the intricacies of not only the drafting of resolutions, but the analysis of them, by teasing out how they should be broken down to ensure that the right number of separate votes were taken so as to enable decisions to be reached which reflected in sufficient detail the real views of delegates, without unduly lengthening the proceedings. At the same time he would, with a balance of charm and forcefulness, maintain astonishing control of the complex procedures, thus enabling the conferences to proceed with minimum disruption to the programme, and yet a reasonable regard for those with a usually strongly expressed burning desire to discuss what to them was the urgent and pressing matter of the moment.

I have a vivid memory of one year when we were in Margate. Gruff with assistance was contriving to direct matters with one leg in plaster – as a result of playing football with his son David. Margate was not our favourite choice of venue, if only for lack of gastronomic excitement – one evening the best we could do in the best hotel was fish and chips brought in, washed down by Scotch whisky. Gruff would disapprove of me omitting any reference to his liking of that particular tipple; since his sad death my whisky supplies seem to last rather longer. I shall not forget his reaction another time, in Newcastle, when beer arrived in response to his request for 'Scotch'.

Gruff's father, a Welsh builder, sent his son to school first in Bangor in North Wales but, later to Birkenhead School when the family moved to Birkenhead. Gruff enjoyed his association with Birkenhead School and his Law Degree course at Liverpool University, where he formed a lifelong friendship with one of his tutors, Professor Seaborne Davies, himself an ex-Liberal MP (as successor to Lloyd George on his death in 1945). Following National Service the young Gruff became articled to his father's solicitor, Ieuan Davies Howard of Lamb Goldsmith & Howard and spent his entire career with the firm and the merged firm of Bell Lamb & Joynson after the merger in 1988.

Having spent his early years at the office at 42 Castle Street in Liverpool, Gruff moved in the late 1980s to run the Claughton Village office and become Senior Partner in the merged firm following the retirement of Peter Howell Williams in 1990. His work in the early years was principally non-contentious conveyancing and probate but in later years he was a director of Granada Television and he was instrumental in setting up Marcher Sound Radio partly in cooperation with redundant Welsh steel workers.

Out of his three daughters and one son, his son, David Cynlais Evans, was the only one to follow him into the law and is now a partner in Davies Wallis Foyster.

Gruff's Welsh ancestry was a matter of inordinate pride to him, almost to a fault it sometimes seemed to those of us not so lucky. It, of course, came out in his outstanding gifts as a speaker especially after dinner, though few people had any idea of the enormously thorough preparation he would have devoted to what would come across as a wholly spontaneous delivery. All things Welsh gave Gruff enormous pleasure, especially (although he would not have claimed himself to have been a brilliant musician) Max Boyce and other such Welsh minstrels and of course he did much to ensure the strongest Welsh influence on the glee club evenings at the party conference. He loved holidays in Pembrokeshire at St David's, and I remember particularly his prowess at the dodgem cars one long weekend, I think it was to recover after the October 1974 election, when I and my family stayed there with him and another Merseyside solicitor, his longstanding friend and political opponent the late Barry Porter, and their respective families.

No one could deny that Gruff was as large as life in every sense of that expression, but particularly in personality. Sometimes people were surprised at photographs of him as a very svelte young RAF officer, and to learn that in his younger days he had been a keen hockey player at Oxton Cricket Club and also an enthusiastic golfer – it had not always been just the 19th hole which he so enjoyed patronising at the Wirral Ladies Golf Club of a Sunday morning! No one who knew Gruff at all well was surprised when he was offered his life peerage, to become a working member of the Liberal group in the House of Lords, where his deep knowledge and experience especially of local government affairs but also in other fields was greatly valued. It was sad that, all too soon after his elevation, deteriorating health prevented him from playing a greater role in the House.

INDEX